PENGUIN

CHEAT

Titus O'Reily is a writer, presenter, performer and broad-caster known for capturing the trials and tribulations of being an obsessive sports fan. His commentary and sporting round-ups have attracted over 300,000 followers on social media.

As well as his own national comedy tours, O'Reily appears on *The Front Bar*, *The Project* and is a regular on ABC Radio and Nova. He is in demand as a guest speaker at high-profile events like the AFL Grand Final.

Titus has written four books: *A Thoroughly Unhelpful History of Australian Sport* (2017), *A Sporting Chance* (2018), *Please Gamble Irresponsibly* (2019) and *Cheat* (2020).

His unique take on sport has been hailed by some of the most respected figures in sport as 'awful', 'childish' and 'barely comprehensible'. Others say 'hilarious'.

www.titusoreily.com
@TitusOReily

Also by Titus O'Reily

A Thoroughly Unhelpful History of Australian Sport
A Sporting Chance
Please Gamble Irresponsibly

CHEAT

THE NOT-SO SUBTLE ART OF
CONNING YOUR WAY
TO SPORTING GLORY.

TITUS O'REILY

PENGUIN BOOKS

PENGUIN BOOKS

UK | USA | Canada | Ireland | Australia
India | New Zealand | South Africa | China

Penguin Books is part of the Penguin Random House group of companies,
whose addresses can be found at global.penguinrandomhouse.com.

Penguin
Random House
Australia

First published by Michael Joseph, 2020
This edition published by Penguin Books, 2021

Cover design by Adam Laszczuk © Penguin Random House Australia Pty Ltd
Cover illustrations courtesy graphixmania/Shutterstock
Typeset in Sabon by Midland Typesetters, Australia

Printed and bound in Australia by Griffin Press, part of Ovato, an accredited
ISO AS/NZS 14001 Environmental Management Systems printer

A catalogue record for this
book is available from the
National Library of Australia

ISBN 978 1 76089 449 8

penguin.com.au

MIX
Paper from
responsible sources
FSC® C009448

CONTENTS

INTRODUCTION

THE CONDITIONS FOR CHEATING

For life to exist, it's assumed you need water, an energy source like the sun, and carbon, hydrogen, oxygen and nitrogen. This doesn't mean life *will* exist, but the requisite conditions are there.

The conditions for cheating to occur are far simpler. You only need two ingredients: something to compete over and humans. That's it.

The sport doesn't matter, the country is irrelevant, glory or money aren't needed, the gender of the participants makes no difference. Humans and a chance to win – it's that simple.

So it follows that wherever there's sport, there's cheating. Attempting to gain an unfair advantage is as much a part of sport as the heroics, the sweat, the tears, the sacrifices and the triumphs.

There will always be people who will do pretty much anything to win, cooking up schemes that are sinister, comical, ill-conceived

CHEAT

or fiendishly clever. Yet, time and again, we are shocked when the latest cheating scandal breaks.

Lance Armstrong, for example, is held up as a sort of super-villain – an outlier. But as we'll see, in the history of the Tour de France, he is just the continuation of a long tradition. A tradition that goes right back to the second ever Tour, when a large number of the riders caught the train for part of a stage.

It's a worry when you realise Armstrong is not an outlier at all, but rather the norm. Lance Armstrong's cheating isn't even that hard to explain. If you win the Tour de France, there's fame, money and you get to date Sheryl Crow. With rewards like that on offer, it's understandable that someone would decide to game the system.

Plus, if your job involved being constantly surrounded by men who love cycling, you would probably take copious amounts of drugs too. Blokes who love cycling are like vegans: they cannot go five minutes without telling you about it.

I worked with a guy once who every single painful Monday morning insisted on telling me about his Saturday morning ride. He'd tell me in great detail how he'd beaten some personal best time and, much like I imagine Lance Armstrong did, I'd think, *Man, I wish I was on some powerful drugs right now.* As he droned on my dead eyes would have been a clue to my level of interest, but apparently that was too subtle for him.

But humans don't even need powerful incentives to cheat. Being social creatures, we crave the approval of our peers; we want to be seen by others as being good at something. Because of that, cheating is human.* It's in our nature.

This desire for a higher standing in the group means that, at our core, we are all competitive people. Some a little more than others,

---

* People cheat at sport, at business, and even in love. People cheat on their partners, but they also cheat to get partners. Why, even I cheat, my CV says 'I like spending time with friends', which I don't. Well, I think I don't. Truth is, I don't have any.

though. If you've ever had the misfortune of being friends with people who play board games, you understand how someone can take a game way too seriously even when the stakes mean nothing.

People who desperately want to win regardless of the rewards are like silverback gorillas, fighting for dominance in the group. Unfortunately, unlike silverbacks, they're not endangered.

I knew a couple who insisted on playing Trivial Pursuit if you made the mistake of accepting an invitation to their place. It was patently obvious that the husband had gone to the trouble of memorising the entire set of questions and answers.

I remember there was a question, 'Who was Ross Perot's running mate in the 1992 presidential election?' And he said, 'This is just a guess, but was it . . . and I don't know why I think this . . . but is it, by any chance, Vice Admiral James Bond Stockdale?'

Then he'd act shocked he'd got it right. 'It is! Oh my god, I'm as surprised as you are. I must have read it somewhere.'

And I wanted to say, 'Yeah, you read it on the card earlier. Because you're just the worst person ever. You are worse than Stalin.'*

I guess his desire for winning just made him human. We have always cheated, and we'll cheat at anything. Sport is just an area where our competitive nature is brought to the fore, and professional sports are the pinnacle of this. It's a space dominated by alpha types whose whole identity is based on beating others.

This is no new phenomenon. At the AD 67 Olympic Games, no less a person than the Roman Emperor Nero cheated. And he was super subtle about it.

Given the Roman Empire had controlled Greece for a few centuries, Nero had a fair bit of influence. For a start, he had the Olympics delayed by a year, presumably to fit it into his busy schedule of killing his mother and fiddling while Rome burned.

---

* 'Stalin' was another answer this guy always got right.

As the games were limited to Greeks, he also had to bribe his way into being allowed to compete, giving the organisers a lot of money. We all know Olympic officials over the years have shown a fondness for bribes.

Nero wasn't there to make up the numbers, he was there to win, and he was happy to brazenly cheat to do it. In the chariot race, where all competitors' chariots were drawn by four horses, Nero had ten. He literally had more horsepower than anyone else. This turned out to be a rather dangerous move. That many horses were difficult to control and, turning a corner, he crashed out of the race, seriously injuring himself.

But not finishing the race didn't hurt his chances. The Hellenic judges in charge of the games granted him the wreath of victory. Nero rewarded these unpaid officials with one million sesterces.

The tradition of powerful men wanting to be seen as good at sport has continued; Rick Reilly's 2019 book *Commander in Cheat: How Golf Explains Trump* detailed all the ways Donald Trump cheats at golf.

Buying your way into the Olympics hasn't gone away either. At the 2014 Winter Olympics in Sochi, Dominica fielded a team, which is odd for a country based in the Caribbean whose biggest claim to fame is having the world's second-largest hot spring.

This wasn't a *Cool Runnings* type of thing; it wasn't a couple of locals learning to ski in a series of comedic episodes where John Candy stole the scenes.

Their only two competitors were husband and wife: Gary di Silvestri, an American, and Angelica Morrone, an Italian. They didn't live in Dominica, they lived in Montana, whose only similarity to Dominica is that they are both on earth.

Di Silvestri and Morrone had figured out that Dominica represented a loophole that could help them become Olympians. You see, Dominica will let anyone become a citizen. You just need to be a married couple, deposit US$175,000 into the appropriate account at the National Commercial Bank of Dominica and pay the Ministry of Finance another US$3530 in tariffs and fees.

That's a handy tip for all of you.

Gary and Angelica, after buying citizenship, convinced the Dominican government to let them into their Winter Olympic team. This took a bit of doing because, you'd be surprised to learn, a Caribbean island that is still actively being formed by geothermal volcanic activity didn't have a Winter Olympic team.

But Gary and Angelica convinced them that the two of them could form such a team, perhaps on account of the fact that they didn't live in Dominica and were therefore somewhat familiar with the fundamentals of skiing. The couple established the National Ski Association of Dominica, surely one of the most ludicrous organisations ever formed.

Now that they were citizens and part of the country's Winter Olympics governing body, they just needed to actually qualify to compete at the Olympics.

This would have been much harder if, for example, they were representing the United States or Germany. But the way the Olympics work is that smaller countries get more leeway in qualifying, the idea being that the more countries are involved, the better it is for the Olympic movement. Hence Gary and Angelica's interest in Dominica – they would never have made it into an actually competitive country's team.

Gary managed to meet these low qualifying requirements after competing in lower level tournaments in New Zealand and North America. This was despite finishing last in four of six races. Angelica still struggled to meet the criteria, having finished in the bottom three in thirteen of the fourteen races she participated in. This forced her to enter a small competition in Maine for college students, where she finished seventy-fourth out of ninety-five competitors. This performance was apparently enough to get her into the Olympics.

So, at the opening ceremony of the Sochi Olympics, out walked the entire Dominican Winter Olympic team: an Italian and an American. Gary got the honour of being the flag-bearer.

The vast majority of the world's media coverage of the couple had a feel-good novelty factor, when they should have been exposing the dodgy rort for what it really was. There was no doubt that Gary di Silvestri and Angelica Morrone had no right to be there as athletes.

Morrone, at forty-eight, would have been the oldest cross-country skier in Olympic history by seven years – except she failed to even turn up for her race, claiming injury. Out of a field of seventy-six, she was the only competitor who didn't start.

Di Silvestri, forty-seven, at least started his race, lasting a few hundred exhausting metres before pulling out due to 'illness'.

The only two members of the Dominican Winter Olympic team didn't seem to care about winning, or even participating: they were there to party. They were cheating to become Olympians, not to win.

But not all attempts at cheating are so brazen. Some schemes are extremely intricate, with entire teams involved in winning by devious means.

In 2017, the Houston Astros won Major League Baseball's World Series, only for it to be revealed that they stole signs from their opponents, the Los Angeles Dodgers.

Hand signs in baseball are used to covertly tell teammates what the plan is. It might be a coach signalling a base runner to steal a base, but most often it's the catcher behind the plate signalling the pitcher what type of pitch to throw. The sign – for example a fast ball on the inside of the plate – enables the catcher and pitcher to be on the same page.

But if the batter knows what pitch is coming, the chances of them getting a hit improves astronomically. So every baseball team tries to figure out what their opponent's signs mean. Stealing signs is gamesmanship, which is a close neighbour to cheating, but on the right side of the law; figuring out an opponent's signs by watching closely and thinking hard is allowed. Using a camera is not.

In 2017, the Houston Astros had a camera in the stands, which was trained on the Dodgers' catcher, capturing his signals to the pitcher. The camera feed was relayed to the tunnel behind the Astros' dugout at their home field, Minute Maid Park. An Astros player or staff member who had cracked the signs would watch the feed, see what pitch was coming, and then beat on a trash can to signal to the batter what to expect.

The Dodgers' pitchers ended up getting shelled, wondering how the Astros' batters were anticipating their pitches so consistently.

Team cheating usually involves more sophisticated schemes than this, but when things really get dark is when countries decide to cheat. Some of the biggest cheating scandals in sport involve nation sates using their considerable resources to cheat the system and dope athletes, such as East Germany, China and most recently the Russians, who managed to get their entire country banned from the Olympics.

When cheating moves from the individual to the group, and finally to the national level, individual responsibility – a cornerstone of doping enforcement in sport – becomes murkier.

The East Germans began doping nine- to twelve-year-old children in an effort to bring 'glory' to the country. The long-term health impact on these people has been truly horrific, and it's hard to argue that a nine-year-old should have exercised personal responsibility or stood up to an autocratic state. When cheating in sport reaches its pinnacle, it's not just those missing out on medals that get hurt.

Fortunately, cheating is usually more mundane than doping kids. In most cases, it's people doing silly things to gain an unfair advantage, then doing even sillier things to avoid being caught. Take for example the basketballer Donell 'DJ' Cooper Jr.

DJ Cooper is a Chicago-born point guard who just narrowly missed out on being drafted to the NBA, but was still good enough to carve out a professional career in Europe. Which is where we join him, in 2018, when he's playing for Monaco. DJ's latest drug test results had cleared him of taking performance enhancing drugs. But the good news didn't stop there, the testers told him. The test had also revealed that DJ was expecting.

While obviously excited for him, the anti-doping authorities were wondering how this was possible. The answer turned out to be that DJ had used his girlfriend's urine instead of his own, to avoid producing a positive test for something he was taking.

When DJ returns home to his girlfriend he had good news and bad news for her. He'd been suspended from playing for two years, but on the upside: she was pregnant.

It was the most complicated pregnancy reveal in history.

The best bit is that, when DJ Cooper announced he was leaving Monaco, instead of saying it was because he'd been suspended for compromising a drug test, he said it was for 'family reasons'. I guess technically that's true.

DJ Cooper provides a great example of the kind of things not to do when trying to get an edge over an opponent. Not that borrowing your partner's urine is a lesson I thought anyone needed.

In the course of this book you'll come across all types of cheating. A lot of it is very clever, some of it is funny. But never forget that while the cheater usually seems like the more interesting person, each cheat leaves in their wake victims who are infinitely more worthy of praise and who are far better people.

But, as you're about to see, cheating is never boring, and it is never going away.

CHAPTER 1

THE WONDERFUL EQUALITY OF CHEATING

It was November 2000 when a curious package arrived in the German city of Bonn.

Famous for being the birthplace of Beethoven and the capital of former West Germany, Bonn is less famously the headquarters of the Paralympics, which was also the destination of this particular package.

This in itself is not an amazing fact. I imagine packages arrive in Bonn on an incredibly regular basis, including at the Paralympic headquarters. Those at the office probably didn't realise the package's importance when it first arrived either; they were in a celebratory mood, basking in the afterglow of a highly successful Sydney Paralympics campaign the month before. They'd been the best games ever, another big step forward for an organisation that traces its roots back to the aftermath of World War II.

In 1946, neurologist Dr Ludwig Guttmann organised a competition in England for athletes using wheelchairs, in part driven by the number of injured veterans following the war.

Dr Guttmann had ended up in Britain after fleeing Germany shortly before the war. Being Jewish, Dr Guttmann had been looking to get out of Nazi Germany for some time. The Nazi Party had provided him with his means of escape, sending him to Portugal in early 1939 to treat a friend of the Portuguese dictator António de Oliveira Salazar.

Dr Guttmann took advantage of the fact that his travel plans had him returning via Britain. He appealed for sanctuary and the British granted it. Back then, they didn't mind people from the continent coming to live there.

By 1960, just fourteen years after Guttmann's competition, the first official Paralympic Games were held in Rome, with 400 athletes from twenty-three countries competing. It was constant growth from then on, with the 2000 games in Sydney seeing 4000 athletes from 127 countries competing in 551 events, across twenty different sports.

But I digress. When the package that arrived in Bonn was finally opened, its contents were met with confusion. In the package was a Spanish Paralympic uniform, a gold medal from the games and £150, the exact amount each athlete was given while at the games. Why would someone – a gold medallist no less – return their mementos from what was sure a life highlight?[*]

It took a few days, but soon the entire world found out why.

THE MAN WITH THE PLAN

Fernando Martin Vicente was a man of many lengthy titles and significant power in the various bodies that controlled Paralympic sport: he was head of the Spanish Federation for Mentally Handicapped

---

[*] Most surprising for those involved in international sport administration was the fact that someone had handed back money.

Sports (Federación Española de Deportes para Discapacitados Intelectuales – FEDDI), president of the International Sports Federation for Persons with Intellectual Disability, vice-president of the Spanish Paralympic Committee and a member of the International Paralympic Committee (IPC).

He was the father of a child with an impairment, and had founded the National Association of Special Sports all the way back in 1975. Vicente would do anything to advance Paralympic sports. And by that I mean *anything*.

His involvement might not have been purely benevolent. He owned a yacht, eight cars (including a Porsche), five houses and half a dozen large pieces of land. He'd previously been a Madrid city councillor, but Spanish newspaper *El Mundo* claimed his senior roles with the various bodies involved in sports and disabilities had contributed to his £5 million fortune.

Each Paralympics presented both an opportunity and a risk for Vicente. The huge sponsorship deals with multinationals like Telefónica and BBVA were always front of mind for him. If things went well, all the money from the government and sponsors would be vindicated; if they went poorly, the future funding of the many organisations he represented could be in jeopardy. Success had to be assured, and the way to do that was to win gold medals.

In preparing for the 2000 Paralympics, Vicente's eye turned towards a new category. For the first time, Basketball for the Intellectually Disabled would be included in the games.

The rules for the sport weren't changed that much for these competitors. The games were a bit shorter and the lines were moved in, but that was it. In every other way the rules were the same as any other game of basketball. The only major difference was that, to qualify, a player needed to have an IQ below 70.*

---

* To put that score in perspective, just 2 per cent of the American population meet that criteria – although it doesn't prevent them from being President.

Mentally impaired athletes had first been allowed to compete at the Paralympics in the 1996 games. That had been a big step for the IPC – until then, all impairments had been visible.

Missing a limb is hard to fake, trust me, but pretending to have an IQ under 70 is much easier. Therefore, you'd assume the vetting process would have been rigorous. But you'd have assumed incorrectly. In fact, assuming there was a vetting process at all was your first mistake.

The IPC had no official test or review process that governed who met this classification of 'mentally impaired'. The responsibility of making this determination fell to the individual countries, who reviewed all readily available information, including educational documents and doctors' and psychologists' assessments.

Letting the competing countries police themselves works about as well as letting corporations police themselves. That is, it doesn't work at all.

It's not hard to guess the idea that formed in Vicente's mind. What if he found decent amateur basketballers and got them to pretend to be mentally impaired? It was basically the reverse of reality TV, where mentality impaired people try to pretend they're not mentally impaired. If willing accomplices could be found, the necessary approvals could be ticked off by the relevant organising committees and the medical certificates could be faked.

It was an idea as simple as it was morally bankrupt. Innovative thinking like this is not usually found outside of a financial institution. You'd think the hard bit would have been finding people to go along with such a scheme, but depressingly, it wasn't.

This raises an obvious question, which I now put to you: *How much money would it take for you to agree to crush the dreams of intellectually impaired Paralympians?*

It's a question you probably haven't been asked before. But think about it. What would you charge to prevent some actually intellectually impaired people from going to the Paralympics and then cheating the rest of the competition out of a medal?

It's a difficult question. Sure, you might say, of course I'd love to win a medal at the Paralympics by dishonest means, but I'm not sure what the market rate is for doing so.

I understand. You don't want to charge too much and price yourself out of it, but you don't want to undersell yourself and leave money on the table. Either option would leave you looking foolish.

There must be nothing worse than signing on to defraud the Paralympics and then learning the person next to you is getting paid a lot more to do it. That would lead to awkwardness, and possibly even ill will. You have to consider morale on a team full of people feigning intellectual impairment.

Luckily, I can help. The gold-medal-winning team stood to win €150,000, about A$240,250.*

The ten men who signed up for the deception were told that every country did this kind of thing and that, if they won, the funding for Paralympic sport would increase. How could you say no to that sort of logic? You'd basically be admitting you didn't support Paralympic sport.

With the team assembled, they began training, which seems rather unnecessary for the task at hand. Some of the players even participated in warm-up tournaments. They did really well.

CHEAT, BUT DON'T LOOK LIKE YOU'RE CHEATING

The 2000 Sydney Paralympic Games, while not as popular as the Olympics, were still the second-biggest sporting event in the world that year, with big international sponsorship deals from companies like Visa and Nike. They began three weeks after the Summer Olympic Games had concluded.

---

* This was back in 2000. Hopefully that rate for this kind of work has increased to keep up with the cost of living.

For the inaugural Basketball for the Intellectually Disabled tournament, eight countries were involved: Russia, Poland, Portugal, Japan, Brazil, Australia, Greece, and Spain.

Alongside the ten players in the Spanish team participating in the scam, there were two players who did meet the requirement of having an IQ below 70.

It very quickly became clear that having a team of people without intellectual impairments gave you a real advantage when playing against a team of people that did have them. Not that this really needed testing – if I'd asked you beforehand what you thought would happen, you would have probably guessed correctly.

In their first game, against Portugal, the Spanish were up by 30 points at half-time, leading the coach to warn his players, 'Lads, move down a gear or they'll figure out you're not disabled.' Because the players were a great bunch of people, they did just that, winning by only 15 points.

Try as they might, it was hard not to win, and they got lazier trying to hide what was going on. They defeated Brazil by 56 points, Japan by 67 and Poland by 30. This set up a gold medal match against Russia.

It's here we learn an important lesson: if you're cheating at anything, don't win by too much or you'll attract attention.* But as anyone who's ever played basketball with children knows, the temptation to block their shots or dunk on them just becomes too much.

One Australian coach later voiced what many others had suspected: 'There were two or three players from both Spain and Russia who could have competed in our national basketball league. What they did with and without the ball was way above what any of our athletes could have achieved.'

---

* Whenever I cheat, I do it to be just above average. No one gets jealous of you then, or suspicious.

The Russians were hardly strangers to bending the rules in international sport, but Spain's cheats turned out to be superior, winning the gold medal game 87 to 63.

Vicente's plan had worked; Spain had won the gold medal. On top of that, Sydney turned out to be Spain's most successful Paralympics, with the country winning 107 medals and finishing third on the medal table, after Australia and Britain.

Isn't sport wonderful?

YOU LOOK FAMILIAR

Paralympic athletes often point out, quite rightly, that they don't receive the media coverage Olympic athletes do. But the Spanish Paralympic basketball team had no such problems. After their victory, the daily Spanish sports newspaper *Marca* decided to run a big picture of the team. There they were, smiling and celebrating, even though they had just done a truly horrible thing.

But back in Spain, some people reading *Marca* recognised the players, and knew they weren't intellectually impaired. Readers started leaving comments under the online version of the article. I like to imagine someone saw the picture and said, 'Hey, I used to date that guy. He's emotionally impaired, but not intellectually.'

Rumours began swirling that something was not right, and word got back to the team and Vicente in Sydney. But you don't trap a mastermind like Vicente that easily. The players were advised to wear hats and sunglasses so they wouldn't be recognised at the airport on their return.

I've always believed that if your plan involves sunglasses and hats, you're already in trouble.

Despite this, as the players dispersed from the airport in Spain, it seemed that, rumours aside, the plan had worked. Vicente had delivered another highly successful Paralympics, ensuring funding would be there for the next four years.

The world's focus moved on. It seemed they had all got away with it.

Except that, in the days after the team landed back in Spain, one of the players packaged up his uniform, his gold medal and the money he'd received while in Sydney, and mailed them to the Paralympics headquarters in Bonn.

Was it guilt that had finally gotten to one of these men? Well, no. It was a bit more complicated than that.

BACKGROUND CHECKS

Anyone who has run a business knows it's incredibly important to do proper background checks on potential employees. Sure, a good interview and a competent CV are nice, but they can paint an incomplete picture. What you really want to do is a good background check, ring their references, ask around. You want to be thorough.

For example if you wanted to hire someone to, well, let's say you wanted them to pretend to be intellectually impaired so they could cheat at the Paralympics. You'd want to be pretty sure that person could be trusted, wouldn't you? You certainly wouldn't want to find out later that they were an undercover journalist. That would cause you all sorts of problems.

It turns out that Vicente should have done his homework when he chose Carlos Ribagorda to be one of the ten players on the team faking an impairment. It's a sad world when you can't trust someone you've paid to defraud the Paralympics.

An investigative journalist, Ribagorda had been invited to train with the team five months out from the Sydney games, and immediately saw the opportunity for a scoop. He was especially surprised when he was trying out for the team. The only things he had to do were six push-ups and have his blood pressure taken. There was no IQ test.

The lack of an IQ test is surprising, but the six push-ups is even weirder. Why six? Even I can probably manage six, and I take a moment to regain my breath when I stand up.

'There were five months of training with not a single disabled person in sight. The two genuinely disabled players came from outside Madrid,' Ribagorda revealed later.

As he trained for the Paralympics, Ribagorda began to wonder what was motivating the men around him. They couldn't all be doing it for a journalistic scoop. Although imagine what an even more amazing story that would have been, if the team was made up solely of journalists trying to write an exposé.

Aside from the money, Ribagorda said, 'I think people saw it as a free trip to Australia. There was even some pride at wearing the Spanish team strip.'

This seems completely ludicrous to me. Imagine feeling pride in wearing a national uniform while committing an outrageous scam. It speaks to the power of the human mind to rationalise any behaviour, a theme that will crop up again and again when it comes to cheating.

During his time undercover, Ribagorda had kept in touch by email with his editor at *Capital*, a Spanish finance magazine. Once the gold medal was secured, he was ready to write his tell-all story.

The staff at the magazine were under no illusions as to the scale of the story. Carlos Salas, then the editor of *Capital*, said, 'We prepared the headline "Fraud at the Paralympics" as well as the front cover of the magazine the day after [Ribagorda] told me what was going to happen.'

The article would outline not only the cheating at the Sydney Paralympics but also the Spanish team cheating at the preceding world championships in Brazil and the Iberian Cup in Portugal.

Ribagorda laid out how the Spain's FEDDI had deliberately recruited athletes who were not intellectually impaired to 'win medals and gain more sponsorship'. He also criticised the lack of checks by the IPC and claimed some athletes in other categories such as track and field, table tennis and swimming were also neither intellectually nor physical impaired. 'Of the 200 Spanish athletes at Sydney, at least fifteen had no type of physical or mental handicap – they didn't even pass medical or psychological examinations,' Ribagorda wrote. The article suggested this type of cheating was hardly limited to the Spanish team.

Scathingly, Ribagorda wrote, 'I couldn't believe it when I was told that the whole Paralympics movement was a farce.' Editor Carlos Salas would later say that printing the story was 'one of the most unpleasant exclusives I have ever published in my life'.

A POORLY AIMED PUNISHMENT

As with any scandal, the shock of it going public was quickly followed by attempts at shifting the blame. Vicente began by protesting his innocence, saying, 'It is very sad. There was no bad intent.' He claimed he had no involvement in checking the medical records of the players.

But the pressure was too intense and, basically, no one believed him. Forced to resign, he still protested his innocence: 'If someone wants to cheat, it's difficult to detect. It's easy to pretend you have little intelligence, but the opposite is difficult.'

Anyone who has watched politicians recently would agree that feigning intelligence is *very* hard, if not impossible.

With Vicente gone, the IPC moved to protect their reputation. After all, they had not put in place any checks on individual countries verification processes. It's one thing for individuals and even countries' to cheat, but to have no processes in place to guard against cheating is damning. The IPC really had no idea who had cheated and who hadn't.

Rule number one of crisis management is to limit the crisis to involve as few people as possible, and that's what the IPC did, stating, 'It was only just this sport. It was just the Spanish team.' However, this wasn't the accepted view of anyone outside of the IPC.

The IPC's next decision suggested they didn't believe what they were saying either. In December 2000, they banned all intellectually impaired athletes from the Paralympics. This ensured that innocent athletes took the biggest hit.

'A lot of athletes around the world are devastated by that,' said Nick Parr, chief executive of the English Sports Association for People with Learning Difficulties. 'This goes beyond disappointment. They have trouble understanding. There are English athletes who think that, as they are being punished, they must have done something wrong.'

Australian swimmer and six-time Paralympic gold medalist Siobhan Paton said, 'I can't understand why athletes such as myself must pay for the sins of a few Spanish basketballers who tried to cheat. We have done nothing wrong.'

But the IPC wouldn't be moved. They had been embarrassed on the world stage and they weren't confident that there were systems in place to prevent it happening again. They decided to throw it all into the too-hard basket. After all, the IPC had been slow to include intellectually impaired athletes in the first place; remember, they were first allowed to compete only in 1996. Their participation in the Paralympics had been very short-lived.

Robyn Smith, the chief executive of the Australian branch of the IPC, certainly viewed the ban this way. 'If you have two or three cheats, you throw them out. You don't ban the entire country or all athletes from that sport. We feel there are many groups within the IPC that have a problem with athletes with an intellectual disability . . . So when the chance to get rid of our athletes came up in Sydney with the Spanish, many were rubbing their hands saying, "You beauty. Get rid of them all."'

Time and again this is the problem: the impact on those not involved in the cheating is often significant and ongoing. An entire sport can be tarred with the same brush. The IPC decision meant that the people who cheated received much less of a penalty than the innocent athletes, which is certainly a novel way to try to curb cheating.*

While the Spanish players were stripped of their ill-gotten gold medals, innocent intellectually impaired athletes received what was effectively a life ban. Many of them never got to compete at the Paralympics because it wasn't until 2012 that the intellectually impaired were let back in.

It would take even longer – thirteen years – for Vicente and the fraudulent players to face court. Vicente was found guilty of fraud and fined €5400 (A$7729) and made to return €142,355 (A$203,752) in government subsidies FEDDI had previously received.

The charges against all the cheating players were dropped once Vicente plead guilty, despite earlier protesting his innocence. Given their crime left innocent athletes in the wilderness for twelve years for something they didn't do, this seems incredibly lenient for both Vicente and the players.

EVERYBODY CHEATS

When people hear about the antics of the Spanish Paralympic basketball team, a common response is to wonder how anyone could stoop so low. It's a fair question. This case is viewed as bottom-of-the-barrel cheating because the victims are intellectually impaired. But cheating is cheating: something is always stolen from the innocent, regardless of who they are.

---

* Punishing those not even involved in a crime is an interesting approach. I'm not aware of any judicial system that is based on this model. The closest is when a teacher keeps the whole class back because one person did something.

A big part of the reason the Spanish cheaters could do something so audacious is because people fundamentally misunderstand the Paralympics – even the people running them. Paralympians are seen by most people as 'pure', different from other sportspeople and deserving of our admiration just for getting out there and having a go. Many have referred to the Paralympics as 'inspiration porn', the type of thing that appears on Instagram and aims to be profound but usually misses the point completely.

Make no mistake: the Paralympics are pure competition. The people competing are ruthless athletes who are there to win, often at any cost. We are not talking about the Special Olympics, where the focus is on inclusivity and participation.

This misunderstanding of the Paralympics goes some way to explain why the IPC didn't even put in place proper checks. They were in part driven by a paternalistic view that all the athletes involved were inspiring, wonderful people, who would be immune from cheating.

But being a sportsperson with an impairment makes you no more or less a person. Just as it makes you no less likely to be a victim of cheating, it also makes you no less likely to cheat. Despite the desire to lift these athletes onto an inspirational pedestal, people with a disability are boringly human.

While the Spanish team got all the attention at the Sydney Paralympics, there were eleven doping cases. As well as the doping, there's an ongoing furore in Paralympics over the classification system for physically impaired athletes. Every physically impaired athlete is classified into different events based on the type and severity of their impairment. This is to ensure anyone's impairment has a minimal impact on the outcome.

The opportunity to cheat exists because impairments can vary wildly: you might have some vision or restricted vision, you could have limited movement of a limb or no movement at all. The idea is that the classifications make each contest fair, and like all attempts to make sport fair, there are athletes who work hard to tip the scales in their favour and make things a little less fair.

Some para-athletes have been known to fake their level of impairment in order to receive a lower classification and compete against athletes who really do have that severity of impairment. A 2017 investigation by *The Guardian* reported that para-athletes in numerous sports were accused of preparing for classification exams by taping limbs for long periods to reduce flexibility, or among those with cerebral palsy taking ice-cold showers to further weaken muscle tone.

It turns out some people are happier to win a gold medal at a lower classification than to compete for glory at their true level. As with all sport, winning is the key bit.

In swimming, classification cheating is seen as so widespread as to call the whole sport into question. In 2019, Irish para-swimmer Ailbhe Kelly retired at age twenty, citing frustrations with the system, and in 2020, British swimmer and former world champion Amy Marren left Paralympic swimming, posting on social media that 'there is a long way to go before it becomes a level playing field'.

And while all you need for cheating to occur are humans and a competition to win, financial incentives and fame do increase the frequency of cheating. The Paralympics are now big business, with 4.1 billion viewers tuning into the Paralympics in 2016 – double the number from 2004.

The Paralympics prove that as long as the conditions for cheating are met, cheating will occur. It might feel worse when the victims are intellectually impaired, but all the experience of the Spanish team taught us is that no one can be trusted: humans will cheat in any circumstances, no matter who the victim is.

Athletes without impairments will cheat athletes with impairments out of victories, and athletes with impairments will cheat athletes with impairments out of victories too. People are people. They can be wonderful, or they can be cheats.

CHAPTER 2

AN INDIVIDUAL PURSUIT

Now that we've established that cheating is widespread and no sport is immune, let's move on to all the wild and wonderful ways in which individual athletes cheat.

We really should acknowledge the inventiveness of the world's best sporting cheats. Creatively, they're right up there with the world's great artists – they see things differently. Their imagination is not constrained by pesky moral boundaries. Natural ability doesn't constrain them, it's something for them to overcome.

Cheating comes in so many wonderful forms. There's opportunistic rule bending, petty rule breaking, premeditated plans of great ingenuity, tampering with equipment, spying, doping and my favourite: idiotic harebrained schemes.

The 1904 Olympic marathon in St Louis is perhaps one of the best examples of all the different ways people can cheat. It was a fun, glorious mess of a sporting event.

MEET ME IN ST LOUIS

Some things just go together. Bacon and eggs, mac and cheese, politicians and lying, and perhaps the best combination of all, the Olympic Games and cheating. An Olympics without cheating is like a wedding without any family infighting – theoretically possible, but yet to occur.

From the moment the modern Olympics began in Athens in 1896, cheating was part of the fabric of the games – much as poor logistics and junkets for the organisers would be in later years.

By the third Olympics, cheating had become bizarre, with the marathon – the marquee event – offering a glimpse into the future of the movement.

The 1904 Olympics in St Louis, Missouri, were a disaster in every way possible, the 'shaved-head Britney Spears smashing a car with an umbrella' of the Olympic Games. In fact, the cheating was probably the most normal thing going on.

Things got off to a bad start for St Louis when they were not selected to host the 1904 Olympics. After Athens had hosted the first modern Olympics in 1896 and Paris held them in 1900, the International Olympic Committee (IOC) decided to award the first non-European games to Chicago.

But the summer of 1904 coincided with St Louis holding the World's Fair, a large expo designed to show off the cultural and industrial achievements of the participating countries. St Louis planned to display new technological wonders such as electric plugs, the X-ray machine, and perhaps most important to my life, the ice-cream cone.

A big part of the St Louis World's Fair was the celebration of the centennial of the 'Louisiana Purchase', the largest real-estate deal in history. In 1804, the United States, under the presidency of Thomas Jefferson, had purchased 2.14 million square kilometres (530 million acres) for $15 million from France, then led by Napoleon Bonaparte.

At the time, 'Louisiana' was not the current American state of Louisiana, it was a much larger swathe of land, an area larger than France, Spain, Portugal, Italy, Germany, Holland, Switzerland and the British Isles combined. The land acquired in the Louisiana Purchase was so big it was eventually divided into all or parts of fifteen future American states.*

As was the way of the time, the French weren't exactly selling something they owned; they controlled very little of the land. What they were selling the embryonic United States was the right to negotiate with the Native American tribes that occupied the land. That was nice of them!

As you can imagine, the United States did those negotiations with great care and sensitivity.

St Louis had been part of the deal and, a century on, the purchase was certainly something to celebrate from the United States' point of view. It had nearly doubled the physical size of the country, and at $15 million, or about 4 cents an acre, it was arguably the canniest real-estate deal of all time.

When the people running the Louisiana Purchase Exposition World's Fair, as it was known, discovered the Olympics were to be held in Chicago, they were furious. They threatened to destroy the nascent Olympic movement by running a competing athletic extravaganza as part of the World's Fair. The IOC, not as powerful as they are now, quickly folded under the pressure and agreed to move the games to St Louis.

The IOC saw St Louis as a third-rate American city, so they weren't exactly happy about it. After being forced to make the move, Olympics founder Baron Pierre de Coubertin threw some shade on St Louis, explaining that he didn't attend the games because he 'had

---

* All of Arkansas, Missouri, Iowa, Oklahoma, Kansas, and Nebraska; big parts of North Dakota and South Dakota; parts of Montana, Wyoming, Colorado, Minnesota, Louisiana, New Mexico, Texas and even small bits of what are now the Canadian provinces of Alberta and Saskatchewan.

a sort of presentiment that the Olympiad would match the medioc-rity of the town'. Ouch.

The baron's view on the mediocrity of St Louis must have been shared by the rest of the world – the majority of countries refused to come.

DON'T MEET ME IN ST LOUIS THEN

In 1904, getting to the United States from Europe and the rest of the world was expensive and slow. It required long ocean voyages and, on top of that, getting to an in-land American city like St Louis meant a 1000-mile train trip. Adding to the complexity, the Olympics were to run for the duration of the World's Fair, five months in total, making the whole thing a logistical nightmare.

This resulted in only twelve countries bothering to attend; of the 630 athletes participating, 523 were from the United States. As you can imagine, the Americans did very well in the medal tally, winning 239 medals. Second place was Germany, breathing down the Americans' necks with twelve medals.

The lack of true international competition meant the standard was low. So low that no one was surprised when American gymnast George Eyser won six medals, including three gold, even though he had a wooden leg.

Despite the lack of international interest, the simultaneous World's Fair and Olympics went ahead with great enthusiasm from the United States. There were all sorts of weird and wonderful sights, including the world's largest organ, Abe Lincoln's boyhood cabin, and new foods like cotton candy and peanut butter. It was all standard stuff for a fair in the modern world, except for one exhibit: the human zoo.

Yes, a human zoo. It featured 'living exhibits' – 3000 indigenous people from around the globe, housed in displays based on their 'natural habitat'. For example, there was a Philippine village spread out over 47 acres, populated with Filipinos, designed to show off America's latest territorial acquisition, gained after the war with Spain.

Other smaller villages were also on display for 'Pygmies'* from Central Africa, indigenous Mexican groups, Syrians, Turks, various Native American tribes, Patagonians and the Ainu people of Japan. Visitors at the fair could wander through these exhibits and watch each group as they simulated a normal day back home.

It was a teeny tiny bit racist. Luckily the United States has learnt from its past and got rid of racism altogether these days.

HERE'S AN IDEA

With the Olympics running alongside these exhibits, James E Sullivan, the man who had persuaded the IOC to move the Olympics to St Louis, had another idea. What if for the Olympics, the various groups of 'savages' at the fair competed against each other in a variety of sports?

Sullivan's plan was to hold a 'Special Olympics'** lasting two days. The various groups would participate in both the Olympic sports and in events he assumed indigenous people would be good at: stone throwing, mud fights, blowgun shooting.

Sullivan was keen to demonstrate the inferiority of these 'uncivilised tribes' compared to the white athletes competing in the actual Olympics, so he enlisted the help of Dr WJ McGee, president of the newly established American Anthropological Association and head of the Department of Anthropology at the World's Fair.

McGee brought his own views on how the indigenous groups would perform. He thought Native Americans had 'marvellous endurance' as long-distance runners, Black South Africans had

---

* Correct! That term is considered insulting, and is hated by the numerous tribes and ethnic groups it's been applied to in the past.
** This is the term he used. Not to be confused with the current Special Olympics, the sports organisation for children and adults with intellectual and physical impairments.

boundless stamina, Filipinos were remarkable climbers and divers, and the native men of Patagonia were agile and muscular. His hope was to gather data from the two days to prove this.

While McGee's views might read as marginally more enlightened than Sullivan's, unfortunately his main aim was to use this data to create a 'scientific' racial hierarchy. Hearing of this plan, Olympics founder Pierre de Coubertin was outraged. 'As for that outrageous charade, it will of course lose its appeal when black men, red men and yellow men learn to run, jump and throw, and leave the white men behind them.' He would be proven fairly correct on this point.*

Unsurprisingly, Sullivan and McGee's dream of proving the white man's physical superiority didn't quite go to plan. To begin with, the crowd was almost non-existent, as the last-minute planning of the event meant the Department of Exploitation** (as the marketing and PR department was then called) didn't have time to promote it properly.

Not that they didn't give it a red-hot go, stating the competitions were intended to test 'startling rumours and statements that were made in relation to the speed, stamina and strength of several savage tribes'.

Other problems that plagued the event included the fact that the various indigenous athletes had not been trained in any of the sports, didn't take them seriously and, in many cases, had no interest in participating. The Ainu people of Japan were happy to climb trees for

---

* De Coubertin was himself no stranger to outdated thinking. Of women's sporting competitions, he said he thought them 'impractical, uninteresting, ungainly, and, I do not hesitate to add, improper. Woman's glory rightfully came through the number and quality of children she produced, and that where sports were concerned, her greatest accomplishment was to encourage her sons to excel rather than to seek records for herself.' His comments are weirdly close to my (strangely unsuccessful) Tinder profile.

** They named things accurately back then.

fairgoers, but only because they were getting paid for it. Far from being 'simple natives', they knew exactly what was going on.

In other cases, the sports were so foreign that the indigenous groups didn't even know what to make of them. Sullivan responded quickly by dropping water polo from the program, for example.

Eventually, through coercion and paying competitors, the Special Olympics went ahead on 12 and 13 August 1904.

Things did not go well.

One event – throwing a 56-pound weight – only had three competitors, who all decided it was a silly exercise and refused to participate in the second round.

The 100-yard sprint also proved a nightmare. Every group spoke a different language so explaining the rules was nigh impossible. The Mbuti competitors from the Congo region of Africa became more interested in the starting gun than the actual race.

The race was a mess. Some competitors ran backwards, others in figure eights. Breaking the tape at the finish line wasn't well understood either and some runners stopped short or ran underneath the tape. Some ran to the tape and then waited for the rest of the field to catch up, and then they all went under the tape together.

It's hard to know how much of this was a lack of understanding of the rules and how much was due to the participants knowing this was insulting and deciding to make a mockery of the whole thing. After all, history has shown that there isn't a group of people on earth who can't learn a sport if the mood takes them.

The second day was meant to be events the 'natives' had more affinity with. The program featured a tree-climbing contest, archery, fighting demonstrations, a Mohawk versus Seneca lacrosse match, tug of war and mud throwing. But it went just as badly as the first day.

In the tug of war, the Arapaho competitors, historically from the plains of Colorado and Wyoming, arrived in traditional dress, took one look at the mud they'd be dragged through and rather sensibly decided to give the whole thing a miss.

Sullivan and McGee had high hopes for the javelin and the shot-put, believing these were events the indigenous athletes would be predisposed to. Yet only three of the twenty-four competitors in the javelin got to the 25-foot mark, with the final report on the Special Olympics remarking the javelin throwing was 'another disappointment'.

Sullivan and McGee expected the Patagonian men, from the sparsely populated region of the southernmost part of South America, to do very well in the shot-put due to their large size. But they were so bad that Sullivan said of the best attempt, 'It was so ridiculously poor that it astonished all who witnessed it.'*

The final report summed up Sullivan and McGee's thoughts, stating the indigenous athletes 'proved themselves inferior athletes, greatly overrated'. Later events would prove this conclusion to be entirely untrue, and the Special Olympics instead displayed only the racist assumptions of the organisers.

However, the St Louis Olympics showed they could treat all athletes poorly, regardless of their skin tone. No more so than in the marathon. While Sullivan and McGee believed the indigenous athletes behaved poorly, this was nothing compared to what the white Americans would deliver.

PLANS FOR THE MARATHON

There are few athletic contests that are designed to break a person mentally and physically like the marathon.

No, I haven't done one myself per se, but a lack of taxis one night meant I was forced to walk several kilometres home from the pub and the memory of it haunts me to this day.

The marathon had been conceived for the first summer games

* I've had this phrase said to me twice in my private life.

in 1896, when the French linguist Michel Bréa proposed an event that would retrace the footsteps of Pheidippides, the messenger who sprinted 25 miles to Athens after the Battle of Marathon in 490 BC. He brought word of victory over the invading Persian army, but unfortunately after delivering his message dropped dead from exhaustion.*

Inventing a sporting contest based on an event where the only person who had done it died seems like a bold move to me, but the IOC loved the idea and ticked it off for both Athens and Paris.

The 1904 marathon in St Louis, however, made the IOC regret their enthusiasm for this ultimate test of endurance. In St Louis, planning for the marathon had been so shambolic that the event almost killed numerous competitors.

It was to be run over 24.85 miles** and, unlike modern marathons, the streets were not shut down for the runners. Instead the roads were full of people going about their daily lives, the majority oblivious to the marathon taking place amongst them. The competitors were forced to dodge delivery wagons, trains, street cars, kids and all you'd expect in a busy turn-of-the century American city. In many places cracked stones littered the streets, making the path uneven and dangerous to run on, meaning competitors had to carefully tiptoe their way through.

These days a marathon usually begins in the morning, to take advantage of the cooler temperatures, but the organisers of the St Louis Olympics lacked anything in the neighbourhood of common sense. They decided to start the race at 3 p.m., to really take advantage of the high temperatures and humidity St Louis turns on in the summer.

---

* Pheidippides seemed very dedicated to getting his message through. These days, he'd probably be one of these people sending a lot of unsolicited private messages. His dying words were, 'Joy to you, we've won. Joy to you.' I bet him dying at their feet put a real dampener on the celebrations.
** The modern marathon is run over 26 miles and 385 yards, or 42.2 kilometres.

The hot weather meant the roads, most of which were unpaved, were covered in several inches of dust, making breathing difficult. If that wasn't enough, the runners were expected to deal with seven hills, varying from 100 feet to 300 feet high, many with incredibly long and steep ascents.

The course itself was described by one World's Fair official as 'the most difficult a human being was ever asked to run over'. This was probably true, although Pheidippides may have disagreed.

This all guaranteed nightmarish conditions for the race, but there was an extra kicker for the competitors: water would only be available at two places along the course. First at a water tower 6 miles into the race and then at a roadside well 12 miles in. Amazingly, this wasn't poor planning but a conscious decision by the organisers to minimise fluid intake for the competitors, to test the impact of 'purposeful dehydration'.

The genius who had this idea? None other than James Sullivan, originator of the 'Special Olympics'. He was an ideas man, Sullivan. They weren't good ideas, but he made up for that with pure quantity.*

The announcement of only two water stations didn't seem to get any complaints from the competitors, which shows you what a different time it was. Now people carry enough water to cross the Sahara even if they're just leaving the house to go to a café.

As the day of the marathon dawned, the runners faced an incredibly difficult course over uneven ground, with the public still using all the roads, at the hottest time of the day, with almost no water. Luckily it was the Olympics, so those competitors were guaranteed

---

* Sullivan went on to establish the Amateur Athletic Union (AAU). They present an annual award in his name to 'the most outstanding amateur athlete in the United States'. Previous winners include golfer Bobby Jones, basketballer and former US senator Bill Bradley, basketballer Bill Walton, decathlete Caitlyn Jenner, swimmer Mark Spitz, runner Carl Lewis, diver Greg Louganis, runner Florence Griffith-Joyner, footballer Peyton Manning and swimmer Michael Phelps.

to be a highly professional bunch, well conditioned for what they were about to face.

AN AMATEURISH GROUP OF AMATEURS

Given getting international athletes to St Louis had been difficult, the field for the marathon was overwhelmingly dominated by competitors from the United States. And calling them 'highly professional' is a bit of a stretch.

A few – Sam Mellor, Al Newton, John Lordon, Michael Spring and Thomas Hicks – had participated in marathons before, either at the first two Olympics or in the Boston Marathon. New Yorker Fred Lorz had placed fifth in that year's Boston Marathon and fourth the year before. He was a bricklayer by trade, so he only trained at night, making running at the peak of a hot, humid St Louis day an interesting challenge.

Apart from these Americans, there were men who had done some level of running before, but nowhere near a marathon. Two Greeks took part, continuing that nation's proud history in the event. The only problem was neither of them had participated in a marathon before.

More importantly historically, the first two black Africans to ever compete in an Olympics were in this race. Two Tswana men,* Len Taunyane and Jan Mashiane, were in St Louis because three months earlier they had responded to an advertisement in Johannesburg's *Rand Daily Mail*: 'Boer War Exhibition. A chance for the unemployed! £4 per month and deductions.'

The Boer War Exhibition was part of the World's Fair and was performed twice daily, with 600 performers taking part. The show recreated two key battles, Colenso and Paardeberg, with numerous explosions, horses, sword fighting and even a musical number.

---

* The Tswana people are from south-western Botswana and the North West province of South Africa.

The purpose-built pavilion had a river built into it and could seat 15,000 a show, at the cost of 50 cents a ticket.

Taunyane and Mashiani had done quite a bit of work to get into character for their shows: they had participated in the actual Boer War, which had only finished two years before.*

Both men had been dispatch runners during the war, so when asked to participate in Sullivan's Special Olympics, they did so, given it was nice to run without the threat of being shot at. Apparently both men impressed with their running on the day, because they were asked to run in the Olympic marathon as well. This was mainly due to the fact that the numbers needed a boost – barely any competitors had shown up.

In fact, so desperate were the organisers for some international representation, they also accepted the entry of the wonderfully named Félix de la Caridad Carvajal y Soto.** He was a postman from Cuba who had walked the length of his country to show off his endurance and to raise money for his trip to the Olympics.

It showed a rare obsessiveness about the Olympics, but unfortunately Carvajal was obsessive about other things too – when he arrived in New Orleans, he promptly lost all the money he'd raised in a game of dice. This resulted in him having to hitchhike to St Louis, a mere 650 miles away, only to arrive with no money for accommodation. Luckily Carvajal was by all accounts one of the most jovial, friendly people you'd ever meet, and he managed to befriend the US men's weightlifting team, who allowed him to stay with them.

Still, hitchhiking 650 miles and living with a bunch of muscular strangers is not the marathon preparation regime most professional runners would recommend.

---

* This is the type of commitment to a role that makes even Daniel Day-Lewis look like he's just winging it.
** Despite having all these names, he was known as Andarín Carvajal.

With Taunyane, Mashiani and Carvajal now enlisted to boost the size of the field, everything was ready for the big race. What could possibly go wrong?

THE MARATHON BEGINS

Tuesday 30 August 1904 saw thirty-two men assemble for the start of the marathon. They were greeted by a humid afternoon, well on its way to the soaring 32°C it would reach during the race.

The tone for the race was set when the five-foot-tall Carvajal arrived at the starting line wearing a white long-sleeved shirt, full length pants, a beret and a pair of Oxford leather shoes. Carvajal's affinity with large, muscular American men continued when a United States discus thrower took pity on him and helped him cut his pants into shorts with a pair of scissors. Other participants were not much better prepared; Taunyane and Mashiani had no shoes at all.

At 3.03 p.m., David R Francis, president of the Louisiana Purchase Exposition Company, fired the starting pistol to get the race started, and the runners began by completing five laps of the stadium before heading out onto the course through St Louis and its surrounds. Most of the runners would wish they'd never left.

As if to underline that not a lot of thought had gone into the logistics, a big group of vehicles set off in front of the runners, carrying officials, doctors and journalists. This was not a great plan, as the vehicles kicked up so much dust that many of the competitors had trouble breathing. There is no more majestic site than a bunch of marathon runners having to stop to cough the dust out of their lungs.

Not far into the race, William Garcia from California collapsed in the middle of the road, unconscious from inhaling the dust. It had coated his oesophagus and ripped his stomach lining, causing him to haemorrhage. He had to be rushed to the hospital.

Garcia came very close to being the first death at an Olympics, with doctors stating if he'd gone untreated for another hour he would have died.*

While Garcia was lying gracefully unconscious in the middle of the road, other participants were also starting to struggle with the combination of dust, heat and no water. The United States' John Lordon, who'd actually won the Boston Marathon the year before, suffered a bout of vomiting ten miles in and gave up. That year's Boston winner, Michael Spring, didn't do much better, soon collapsing from exhaustion on one of the punishing hill climbs.

The bricklayer who had performed well in Boston, Fred Lorz, also ran into trouble. At the 9-mile mark he collapsed from dehydration and hopped into a support car, waving at spectators and fellow runners as he passed.

The punishing course hadn't finished thinning out the herd. Sam Mellor was next, experiencing severe cramping while leading the race. It turns out not having any water when you're running in extreme heat isn't great – I'm not sure an experiment was really needed. Soon Mellor could only walk, before eventually retiring.

Others were having less predictable trouble. The Tswana runner Taunyane had encountered a unique problem in a marathon: he had been attacked by a wild dog, and it had chased him a mile off course. This was a strategic setback.

The friendly Cuban, Andarín Carvajal, was having a better time than most. He wasn't in distress, but he wasn't near the lead either, due to him pausing regularly to chat to spectators. At one point he stopped a car when he saw the occupants were eating peaches.

---

* The first death at the Olympics did come from the marathon, but it was at the 1912 Olympics in Stockholm. Portugal's flag bearer, Francisco Lázaro, collapsed at the 19-mile mark (30 kilometres) with a body temperature of 41°C. It turned out that to protect himself from the sun, Lázaro had covered himself with suet – beef fat – and it had prevented him from being able to sweat properly. Eerily, Lázaro had said before the race, 'Either I win or I die.' At least he died being right, but probably not in the way he'd hoped.

As part of his unorthodox preparation for the event, he hadn't eaten for forty hours before the race and was now starving. He asked the occupants of the car for a peach, but they refused, so he snatched two and ate them as he ran.

A bit further along, in his fruit-obsessed state, he stopped at an orchard to eat some apples. Unfortunately they weren't ripe, and he began to experience stomach cramps, so he lay down and had a sleep.

Yet Carvajal's was not the worst strategy of the race. By this stage, the British-born American Thomas Hicks was in the lead, but he too was in real trouble. About 10 miles into the race he was displaying all the signs of extreme exhaustion. His support team turned to what would soon become the Olympics' most consistent tradition, doping.

AND THE WINNER IS . . .

Before Hicks' support team could begin doping their runner into another dimension, a new contender for the gold medal had emerged. Or re-emerged.

After Fred Lorz had retired at the 9-mile mark, the car he'd hopped into overheated at the 19-mile mark. Getting out of the car, Lorz discovered that a 10-mile car ride had done wonders for his condition. He decided that he would continue on foot for the last 5 miles.

Lorz soon passed the struggling Hicks. A man attached to Hicks' camp had seen Lorz in the car earlier and now yelled at him to stop, but Lorz continued on into the stadium, where the crowd, unaware of Lorz's mid-race motoring adventure, began roaring and cheering because they thought that an American was about to win. He crossed the line in under three hours and looked in remarkably good shape for someone who had completed a marathon in some of the toughest conditions ever.

US president Theodore Roosevelt's daughter was overseeing the celebrations and placed the winner's wreath on Lorz's head.

TOO GOOD TO BE TRUE

For someone who had just won the 1980 Boston Marathon, Rosie Ruiz looked remarkably fresh. Even though she was neither sweating nor breathing heavily, she had just run the course in 2:31:56, the third-fastest time ever recorded by a woman in a marathon.

Almost immediately, suspicions were raised. To begin with, none of the other runners could remember seeing her during the race.

The story became even more unlikely when it was revealed that Ruiz had taken up running only eighteen months earlier. Records showed she had competed in the New York Marathon, finishing twenty-third with a time of 2:56:33. While impressive, that made a time of 2:31:56 even more unlikely. People don't shave off twenty-five minutes just like that.

As doubts swirled, Ruiz explained, 'I got up with a lot of energy this morning.' Now, this doesn't sound like enough of an explanation, but I can't be sure – I've never woken up with any energy, let alone lots of it.

People began to examine the photos and film from the race, and Ruiz wasn't in any of them, except during the last 860 meters. Spectators also came forward to say that they had watched Ruiz jump out of the crowd less than a kilometre from the finish line.

Soon her New York performance came under scrutiny too, with witnesses saying they had sat with her during the race and had a chat while she was catching the subway in her running gear and race bib.

It took eight days, but finally the organisers in Boston stripped Ruiz of her title. However, she refused to admit any wrongdoing and kept her winners medal.

Ruiz passed away in 2019, having never admitted to anything. But a friend of hers said she had confessed to him she'd cheated on purpose, but had won by accident. 'She jumped out of the crowd, not knowing that the first woman hadn't gone by yet. Believe me, she was as shocked as anyone when she came in first.'

It turned out Ruiz had just wanted to do well in order to impress her colleagues, many of whom were keen runners. It's a potent reminder that it's never worth trying to impress your colleagues.

Just as she was about to hang the gold medal around his neck, several members of the crowd began to point out the car journey. One witness reported that 'someone called an indignant halt to the proceedings with the charge that Lorz was an impostor'.

The cheers quickly turned to boos. Lorz used an age-old excuse for when you've been caught doing the wrong thing: he said it was just a joke.

It was a blatant bit of cheating, but it had almost worked.

WHAT'S YOUR POISON?

While Lorz was temporarily being crowned the winner, the real leader – Thomas Hicks – was in real trouble. He was being urged on by his team, trainer Hugh McGrath and doctor Charles Lucas. Having seen Lorz pass him, and not knowing about his automobile assist, Hicks assumed he was no chance to win. For a man battling extreme fatigue, this was a demoralising thought.

Seven miles from the finish line, Hicks told his team he wanted to lie down. With Hicks about to collapse, Dr Lucas stepped in to provide some assistance. He administered him 1/16 grain of sulphate of strychnine, swallowed down with some raw egg whites.

Yes, you read that right. Strychnine, the poison.

Now, I'm personally of the belief that giving someone poison should call into question your credentials as 'support crew'. But apart from being widely used as rat poison and an effective murder mystery device in literature, strychnine, in very small doses, does act as a stimulant of the central nervous system.* It enables neurons to fire even when the body's neurotransmitter levels are very low due to fatigue.**

---

*   Please don't take strychnine. I shouldn't have to write that. Also, don't give it to someone. Just leave it alone.
** This is a beneficial thing in athletics, aside from the whole 'risking death' bit. Also, at the time, strychnine in small doses had some prominent fans. The novelist HG Wells once observed that 'strychnine was a great tonic that took the flabbiness out of a man'.

Hicks' support team also had a flagon of brandy to help him along but, being true professionals, they decided to see how the strychnine went before giving him some.

The administering of strychnine to Hicks was the first documented case of doping in the Olympics – documented because performance-enhancing substances were not illegal in the Olympics at the time. In fact, if anything, the difference between a professional and an amateur back then was the professionals had access to this latest 'sports science'.

So how well did the strychnine work for Hicks? Well, it worked in the sense that he kept shuffling along, not really running but at least moving in a vaguely forward direction.

Not long after, Hicks received news Lorz had been disqualified, meaning he was officially back in the lead. This seemed to perk him up for a bit, but at about the 20-mile mark he was ashen and limp. His support team did what anyone would do: they administered more strychnine and egg whites. They also gave him a sponge bath in warm water in the middle of the road.

This kept him going, but with 2 miles to go he started hallucinating, telling his support team that the finish line was still 20 miles away and that he wanted to stop. He also asked for some food, so the good Dr Lucas gave him some of the brandy.* Hicks was offered tea as well but refused it. He was an athlete, after all.

Fuelled by strychnine, raw egg whites and brandy, the breakfast of champions, Hicks plodded on, walking up the last two hills and sort of stumble-jogging down them.

His doctor observed later: 'Over the last two miles of the road, Hicks was running mechanically, like a well-oiled piece of machinery. His eyes were dull, lusterless; the ashen colour of his face and

---

* I'm informed brandy is not considered a food.

skin had deepened; his arms appeared as weights well tied down; he could scarcely lift his legs, while his knees were almost stiff.'

So things were going well.

When Hicks finally entered the stadium, over half an hour after Lorz, the crowd was watching a man on the verge of death. He was barely moving his feet, jerking spasmodically, and had turned a terrible shade of grey. He basically looked like an extra from *The Walking Dead*. His trainers were forced to step in and carry him, with Hicks' feet shuffling along in a tragic parody of someone running, barely touching the ground. It was an athletic *Weekend at Bernie's*. A total farce.

Despite being carried across the finish line, Hicks was declared the winner. Not that he was aware of it – he'd fallen unconscious. Attempts to put the gold medal around his neck were put on hold.

Four doctors worked on keeping him alive. It was touch and go. For the second time that day, the St Louis marathon had almost claimed the title for first death at an Olympics. It took a full hour of these doctors administering aid to prevent Hicks achieving this record. It was only after this treatment that Hicks was able to leave the stadium. He had lost about 4 kilograms.

Hicks said of the race, 'Never in my life have I run such a tough course. The terrific hills simply tear a man to pieces.'

This was partly true, but taking poison had come incredibly close to killing him. Any more strychnine and he probably would have died.

But Hicks not only survived, he went on to run several more marathons, and lived until the age of seventy-six.

AT LEAST NO ONE DIED

Of the thirty-two men who started the race, only fourteen actually finished it, the worst ratio in the history of the Olympic marathon.

Hicks had crossed the finish line at 3:28:53, the slowest Olympic marathon ever. Six minutes later, Albert Corey crossed the line, followed by Arthur Newton with a time of 3:47:33.

This gave the United States gold, silver and bronze, although, like the rest of the farce, this wasn't actually that impressive. Hicks had been born in England, and Corey was French, he just didn't have the right paperwork so he had been listed as being from the United States.

While Hicks had almost died on the finish line, the Cuban Andarín Carvajal had awoken from his nap in the orchard feeling rejuvenated and had continued on, amazingly coming in fourth place. Considering he had stopped to talk all along the way and had a sleep, this is a stunning effort.

The two men from Tswana also performed well overall. Taunyane ended up ninth and Mashiani came in twelfth, despite the challenging incident with the wild dog.

What a mess. The race almost ended with a winner who had travelled by car, and the actual winner had been so doped up he almost died.

It would be easy to see this level of cheating as particular to the time, but you'll come to see that this is timeless behaviour when it comes to the Olympics. The only difference now is the athletes have to hide their cheating.

After the race, Lorz was banned for life for his car trip and attempting to pass himself off as the winner. However, less than a year later, he apologised and managed to convince officials that he never really meant to claim victory. The ban was lifted and he went on to win the 1905 Boston Marathon. This time he did it on foot.

There were also protests over Hicks' use of strychnine and the fact he was carried over the finishing line by his trainers, but James Sullivan refused to listen. After all, strychnine wasn't a banned substance at the time, and you get the feeling Sullivan just wanted the whole thing to be over.

The IOC itself was aghast at the whole spectacle, especially the near deaths, and gave serious consideration to banning the event from future Olympics. But they reconsidered and, despite protests, the marathon was run again at the London Olympics in 1908. It was here that the modern distance of 26 miles and 385 yards was first used, the rumour being that the Princess of Wales wanted her children to be able to watch the beginning of the race from the Windsor Castle nursery, so the distance was set to make that possible.

As for the use of strychnine, at the 1992 Olympics in Barcelona, Chinese volleyball player Wu Dan was found to have taken the drug. Wu said it must have been in a herbal medicine she had taken. Yes, it must have been.

CHAPTER 3

GAMESMANSHIP

The top professional athletes and coaches live in a world where only one thing matters: winning.

Sure, they talk about things like sportsmanship, but that's like banks having slogans along the lines of 'we care about our customers'. They don't really mean it; they just know it sounds good.*

When all you think about is winning – believing it's the only thing you'll be judged on – it's a slippery slope. You will do bizarre things. Things you'd never do in the cold light of day.

Even if there's only a miniscule chance something will shift the balance in your favour, you will try it. After all, sometimes sporting results come down to millimetres or hundredths of a second.

That said, an obsession with winning doesn't always lead to cheating. Often, the lengths that athletes and coaches go to are completely legal, and sometimes they're also completely pointless. But this attitude of leaving no stone unturned in the quest for victory is

---

* Or like saying, 'Your friends sound really fun, I'd love to meet them,' when you're on a first date.

an indication of the mindset of the cheat. They understand that the smallest advantage can be decisive.

SPREADING JOY TO ALL FOUR CORNERS

While most athletes don't cheat, a large number are susceptible to doing strange things to help them win under the pressure of competition. For some, it's about wearing the same underwear for years, or growing in-season beards; for others it might be not letting anyone else touch their equipment, or sleeping with their bats. Whatever they're superstitious about, a surprising number of sportspeople have insane beliefs around what affects their ability to win.

Take for example Barry Fry, manager of English football club Birmingham City in the mid-nineties.

Birmingham City moved into their stadium, St Andrew's, all the way back on Boxing Day 1908. Apparently the new stadium came with a 100-year curse – an optional extra you don't really want.

The rumour was that a group of Romani people had been evicted from the area to make way for the stadium and so put a curse on the land as a parting gift. Over the years it seemed the ground really was ill-starred, with terrible on-field performances punctuated fairly regularly by unfortunate events.

In 1908, the very first year they played at the new stadium, the club was relegated to the second division.

During World War II, two German bombs hit the ground, causing significant damage. As a result the stadium was closed by the police, the only ground in the whole country to be shut during the war.

The good news was the closure was lifted soon after, only for the main grandstand to burn down in 1942. This time the cause wasn't German munitions but the National Fire Service, an organisation designed to *stop* things from burning down.

A small fire had broken out in a brazier and a member of the National Fire Service grabbed a bucket, believing the contents to be water, and threw it over the fire. For some reason the bucket was full of petrol. Most of the main stand burned down, meaning the National Fire Service had effectively finished off what the Nazis started.

The financial hit to the club meant it took a decade for the stand to be rebuilt.

In the eighties, the club's continuing misfortune on the pitch led manager Ron Saunders to hang crucifixes from the floodlights in an attempt to negate the curse. Surprisingly, this had no effect.

By December 1993, when Barry Fry was appointed, the club's fortunes seemed to be changing – the team won two of its first three games with him as manager. But three months later, with no further wins, even Fry was starting to believe in the curse. He decided to turn to the Romani community for advice on how to lift it.

'We called in a bloke to lift the curse and he told me that the only way to fix it was to go and have a pee in all four corners of the ground,' Fry said. 'I am not normally superstitious but after three months I was willing to try anything, so I went and took a leak on all four corner flags. It took me a while – it's not that easy. Lo and behold, we went on to win seven of our next ten games, drawing twice and losing just once, so it must have worked.'

It certainly wouldn't be easy; a fair intake of fluids would be required, and explaining it to anyone who caught you in the act would be an awkward exchange.

I'm almost certain the Romani bloke was just having a laugh to see if Fry would do it, and probably still regularly tells the story of how he convinced the Birmingham manager to urinate on all four corner flags at the stadium.

This is where the lust for victory can take you – suddenly you're urinating on your own pitch because you think it will help you win.

At least in Fry's case this bit of superstition was harmless. Human urine is actually an effective fertiliser, so the groundskeeper was probably left wondering why the grass was growing so much higher around the corner flags.

Not all superstitions are harmless, though.

In 2008, in Zimbabwe, players from a second-division team, the delightfully named Midland Portland Cement, were instructed by their coaches to swim in the Zambezi River to 'cleanse them of bad spirits'.

The only problem was that the Zambezi River has a strong current and is teeming with crocodiles and hippopotamuses.* Probably breaching numerous workplace safety laws, sixteen players went in. Only fifteen came out.

THE SHADOWLANDS

The pressure to win doesn't turn everyone superstitious, but that kind of thinking is all part of wanting to tilt the playing field in your favour.

This can lead people into the shadowy netherworld of 'gamesmanship', where the limits of the rules are pushed to gain advantage without necessarily breaking them. Often this is to gain a psychological edge over opponents, but it strays into the physical too. Gamesmanship can occasionally drift over the line into cheating, but more often than not it's completely legal, if morally questionable.

Of the legal methods, there are plenty. For example, groundskeepers around the world have long practised the dark art of preparing surfaces that suit their team. In every football code, your groundskeeper can simply water the field a lot more to slow down a faster team's running and take the pace out of the game, or they can leave the grass a bit longer to slow down rolling balls.

In baseball, they water the base paths and turn them into muddy swamps to slow down teams that steal a lot of bases. Or they make

---

* Hippopotamuses are the world's deadliest land mammal, killing an estimated 500 people per year in Africa.

the height of the mound in the visitors' bullpen (where the opposing pitchers warm up) different to the one on the field, so the pitchers have to adjust when they start playing for real.

In cricket, groundskeepers prepare a pitch to suit their bowlers, either for fast bowling or spin bowling. In Australia they are rock hard to suit their preference for fast bowling, whereas in India they make them suit spin bowling, often resembling a dust bowl more than a cricket pitch.

But changing the nature of the playing surface isn't the only way home teams can tip things in their favour.

At the 1980 Moscow Olympics the javelin event was being held at the Central Lenin Stadium in Moscow. You'll be shocked to learn the Russians did something a bit dodgy.

When it was a Russian athlete's turn to throw, the ground staff would open some giant gates that were normally kept shut when events were underway. By opening the gates, a wind would enter the stadium behind the throwers, giving the Soviet athletes a significant advantage. The gates would be quickly closed again for any other countries.

It worked, too. A Russian, Dainis Kūla, won gold. He received some additional help from the local officials, who ruled legal a throw that had landed flat instead of with the point sticking into the ground.

Opening the gates to let a breeze in is considered old-fashioned these days. From 1982 until 2013, Major League Baseball's Minnesota Twins played in an indoor stadium, the Hubert H Humphrey Metrodome. A superintendent at the stadium, Dick Ericson, has admitted that he used to help the Twins during close games by tweaking the ventilation system while they were batting to help the ball travel further.

'If they were down two runs and you're still hoping for them to have the advantage, you'd want to be blowing all the air out and up as much as you can. I don't feel guilty . . . It's your home-field advantage. Every stadium has got one.'

Who knew cheating by air conditioning was a thing?

What's amazing about a lot of these schemes is that the outcomes could often be miniscule.

Take for example a fun trick basketball teams do. If you're playing a team that has a fast, high-scoring offence, you simply put up brand-new nets. New nets are tighter, so after you score the ball doesn't drop through straight away, the net slows it down and the other team has to wait before they can attack. This takes time off the clock and gives your team more time to get back on defence.

Realistically, this would only make an incredibly small difference, but that doesn't stop the practice being widespread. The Boston Celtics were renowned for using basketball nets that were made out of some sort of wool and almost held the ball after each basket, slowing games down significantly.

Of course, it also means teams attempt to counter the practice. The Loyola Marymount Lions were the highest scoring team in United States College basketball in 1989/90. Playing on the road, the night before a game they would practice in their opponent's stadium and inevitably found that every arena had brand-new, tight nets. Their coach Paul Westhead later revealed, 'We would have one of our guys stand on a chair and just stretch each net out for about twenty minutes. It became our routine.'

This is the level of obsession that is brought to bear on winning.

And it's not all on-the-field stuff, or related to climate control. Everything off the field has been tried too. From making sure there's no hot water in the visitors' changing rooms, limiting an opponent's access to the ground or court before the game, or making your opponents have a long walk from where their team bus can park to the locker room – it's all been tried and tested.

Even away from the playing arena, tricks can and will be played. Take for example the former coach of the Australian national soccer* team, Guus Hiddink.

Hiddink is a hugely successful manager, having coached Real Madrid and Chelsea, as well as South Korea, Russia, the Netherlands and Australia. He's not only seen every trick in the book, he has a plan to counter each of them.

When Australia was attempting to qualify for the 2006 World Cup, they had drawn Uruguay in a play-off game. They had to play each other home and away, with the aggregate winner qualifying.

The first game was in Montevideo, where Australia had suffered in a previous campaign. The Uruguayan fans marshalled outside the Australian team's hotel and attempted to keep the players awake the night before the game by chanting, singing, beating drums and setting off firecrackers.

Hiddink, however, had been around. He knew these sorts of antics occurred when playing overseas. So he set the Australians up to stay in Buenos Aires, in neighbouring Argentina, and simply flew them to Montevideo at the last minute.

Australia lost the first game 1–0, but this was a close enough result that the Australians could qualify if they won the return leg in Sydney.

Again, Hiddink showed his experience. Not only did the Australians fly back to Sydney by private plane, he booked blocks of seats on commercial flights back to Sydney to make it hard for Uruguay's team to travel together and forcing them to have multiple stopovers.

Whether the disrupted flight plans of the Uruguayans had any impact on the final game is unknown, but it was the Australians

* I've used the term 'soccer' throughout this book just because it's easier, as 'football' means different things in different countries. I know this will annoy soccer fans, but I've learned it's impossible not to annoy soccer fans, so I haven't worried about it. I'd also like to quickly add that I do love soccer, it's a beautiful sport, please don't hurt me.

who held their nerve during extra time and penalties to qualify for the 2006 World Cup.

Booking international flights that you're not even going to use shows that sportspeople can get really creative when it comes to denying their opponent any advantage while keeping it technically legal. But gamesmanship resides in the shadowy grey area between legal and illegal. It's very easy to stray over the line but not think of what you're doing as cheating.

Take for example Olden Polynice,* an NBA centre who had a fifteen-year career playing for the Seattle SuperSonics, the Los Angeles Clippers, the Detroit Pistons, the Sacramento Kings and the Utah Jazz.

Polynice wasn't the most talented player, but this just made him more determined to get every advantage possible. He said he always made sure to never let an opponent get any mental edge and he was coached to be that way. In revealing some of the tricks of the trade, he shows how players with that mindset can unwittingly creep into outright breaking the rules.

In basketball, after a play is whistled dead, say for a timeout, often the player holding the ball will take a quick practice shot. But not when Polynice is around. 'Sometimes he does that because he's having a bad shooting night and he's taking that shot to find his groove. [SuperSonics coach] Bernie Bickerstaff told us to jump up and knock that shot away. Don't give that guy the chance to get his confidence back.'

This is of course a little childish, but completely legal.

However, Polynice would also niggle opponents when he was on the bench. If a player was inbounding the ball near him, he'd pull their shorts to distract them. Sure, that's only a minor infraction, but that's exactly how you cross the line – with something

---

* Polynice was selected eighth overall in the 1987 NBA Draft by the Chicago Bulls, but was immediately traded to Seattle. In return, the Chicago Bulls got a player by the name of Scottie Pippen, who you may have heard of. It could be argued Chicago got the better of this trade.

small. Once you start stepping over that line, things seem more and more permissible.

PLAY MOST FOUL

In sport, the gateway drug for more serious cheating is playing for fouls.

It exists in every sport. When you watch the NBA, you'll see players flopping at the slightest touch. The NFL is the same – players try to draw a pass-interference penalty by dramatically throwing their arms up and falling over. In Australian Rules players throw their head back to get a free kick for a high tackle like they're in the Zapruder film.

Tricking the referee or umpire into giving you a free is an artform. And one sport stands head and shoulders above all others: soccer players take dives that would make Nicolas Cage accuse them of overacting.

As I write this, I can feel soccer fans getting ready to track me down in a dark alley, but the fact is, diving in soccer is a bigger deal than in other sports for two major reasons.

The first is that the reward is so high. In soccer, when you get taken down illegally in the penalty area, you get a penalty kick. Depending on the league, that gives you around a 75 per cent chance of scoring a goal. Goals are incredibly hard to come by in soccer – the rough average of goals scored in a game is between two and three – so conning your way into a big chance to score one has a huge upside. If you can win a penalty, and get one goal, it can have an enormous impact on the game.

Few other sports have such a significant reward for a foul or penalty. If you get fouled in the act of shooting in basketball, you usually get a chance at two points – at best you can get four. In a sport where teams regularly score over 100 points, this is hardly as significant as a goal in soccer.

This low ratio of foul-to-game-impact can be found in Australian Rules too, where if you get a free kick at best you get a shot at goal. While that might give you six points, it won't have the same impact as a goal in soccer.

This isn't to say these sports and others don't have problems with athletes playing for frees, but the effect is so much smaller.

The second reason soccer has a problem with diving is a cultural one. Playing for frees is considered part of the game, and as a result the various authorities that control world soccer have historically not cracked down on it.

The players haven't, either. Players who flop don't become pariahs. In fact, many of the greatest players do it regularly, which hardly sends a message to the next generation that diving is wrong.

Seeing a player collapse like they've been shot is common on the soccer pitch, as is feigning an injury to take time off the clock or break the other team's momentum. A player reacting like they've been hit by a car will often be stretchered off, only to magically recover the moment they cross the sideline, at which point they become desperate to be allowed back on the pitch.

The incidents of famous dives in soccer – often on the highest stage, the World Cup – are too numerous to mention. But let's have a look at some of my favourites.

The 2018 World Cup saw Brazil's Neymar take a truly spectacular slow-motion dive against Costa Rica. He'd been touched with an amount of force I would rate as slightly weaker than a baby's breath.

Not that this was Neymar's first bit of play acting; he is one of the best players in the world, which is very impressive given he appears to suffer from extreme vertigo, falling over constantly. He also seems to be incredibly brittle; every time he falls over, he rolls around in pain so extreme that it looks like a bad street theatre performer pretending they're on fire.*

Brazil has a fair bit of form here, with their striker Fred winning a penalty during Brazil's opening 2014 World Cup game against Croatia, diving in the box due to a defender being in the local government area.

Sometimes diving isn't done for a penalty but to get an opponent red-carded. French defender Lucas Hernandez admitted he was deliberately throwing himself to the ground in an attempt to get Aussie defender Mathew Leckie sent off when the two countries met in the 2018 World Cup.

Often these bits of play-acting are unintentionally hilarious. Perhaps the funniest of these moments was at the 2002 World Cup, when the Brazilian player Rivaldo was about to take a corner. He demanded the ball from Turkish player Hakan Ünsal, who, in a rather churlish act, kicked the ball straight into his thigh. Clutching his face, Rivaldo reacted like a person struck by a barrage of artillery. But, critically, the referee fell for it and sent Ünsal off.

It's a common stereotype that South American players are the worst when it comes to staging, but European players are hardly paragons of virtue. In the 1990 World Cup, West Germany's Rudi Völler dived to win the decisive goal against Argentina, Portugal's Cristiano Ronaldo turned the 2010 World Cup into a study in artistic diving, and Germany's Jürgen Klinsmann dived so beautifully you almost forgave him – he even celebrated goals with a joke dive.

All this overacting is slowly being challenged thanks to the significant technological progress in recent years. The rise of the video assistant referee, which was codified in FIFA's laws in 2018, enables penalties and fouls to be reviewed in slow motion and from multiple angles, during the game.

---

* Yes, you're right. Putting 'bad' before 'street theatre performer' is a tautology.

But the other change is that every fan now has a video camera in their hand, meaning every bit of action on the pitch is captured not only in high definition from multiple broadcast cameras but from thousands of other angles too.

Then there's social media. Every dive is now shared and commented on. Neymar, for example, has been publicly ridiculed for his play-acting, even having to publicly defend himself. His dive at the 2018 World Cup became a meme, the ultimate punishment (or honour, depending on the situation) the modern world can bestow.

No longer can players escape the opprobrium that comes from being a diver, but technology didn't always operate quite so quickly.

A FLARE FOR THE DRAMATIC

Consider one of the most outrageous attempts of faking an injury to ever occur. In 1989, qualifying for the 1990 World Cup had become incredibly close in South America's Group Three, coming down to Brazil and Chile.

The first of two games between Brazil and Chile had been in Santiago and was heated even before the opening whistle. Brazilian player Romário had said publicly of Chilean coach Orlando Aravena, 'I am going to shut Aravena's mouth.' However, he wasn't able to fulfil his vow, because he was red-carded three minutes into the match for his part in a brawl. Aravena was himself sent off later in the game, as was Chilean midfielder Raúl Ormeño.

The result was a 1–1 draw, with the Chilean newspaper *Futbol Total* reporting: 'It was not a game, it was a war.'

On 3 September 1989, the final game of the group stage was Brazil against Chile, to be played in Rio de Janeiro. Whoever won would go through to the World Cup. It was a daunting task for Chile, playing in front 141,000 hostile fans at the legendary Maracanã.*

It this tense playoff, the Chilean goalkeeper Roberto Rojas came to the fore. His prowess between the goal posts had earned him the nickname 'The Condor', for his ability to fly across the net.

Rojas's skill was on show in the first half, as he repeatedly made key saves to keep Chile in the game. But he also earned the wrath of the crowd for consistent time wasting. After each save he'd hold on to the ball for a very long time to slow down the fast-paced Brazilians.

Despite this, the Brazilian attacking wave kept crashing on the Chilean defence, and at the start of the second half, Brazil's Careca put the home side ahead.

The Brazilians had all the momentum. But in the sixty-seventh minute all hell broke loose in the stadium. A Brazilian fan, Rosenery Mello, threw a flare onto the pitch from behind the Chilean goal, and, as every eye in the stadium turned to the smoke swirling around, they saw Roberto Rojas, lying prone on the ground.

With the smoke from the flare providing a dramatic backdrop, Rojas's still form was surrounded by players and support staff. He eventually emerged, his face streaming with blood.

The Chilean players all retreated to the locker room for the next three hours, claiming their safety couldn't be guaranteed. Argentine referee Juan Carlos Loustau attempted to convince them to go back and finish the game, but to no avail.

Instead, Chile prepared an official protest, and it seemed it was likely to be successful. Brazil's World Cup hopes seemed to have literally gone up in smoke. Rosenery Mello, who had thrown the flare,

---

* The Maracanã Stadium is not to be confused with Los del Río's 1994 hit song 'Macarena', which is actually about a girl named Macarena who cheats on her boyfriend with two friends while he's drafted into the army.

CHEAT

became the most hated person in Brazil. She was quickly arrested by police, which was probably the best thing for her safety.*

Unlike now, in 1989 there weren't thousands of mobile phones to capture the incident, and the TV cameras that were following the action had missed the moment the flare hit Rojas.

However, one photographer working at the game had captured the incident, Argentine Ricardo Alfieri. He had seen the flare being thrown and noted that it had landed nowhere near Rojas.

'I went upstairs and told my story, what really happened, but to see the reality we had to develop the photos. They couldn't be developed just anywhere, only in professional studios. They asked me if I could develop them and I just wanted to go back to Buenos Aires. I could see I was in a mess that was not of my own making. They got permission to develop them in a publishing house, we went there and there was the photo of the flare.' The photo wasn't available until the next day. 'Up to that point when the photo was developed, Chile were going to the World Cup, Brazil were going to be eliminated.'

Over the next few days, the photo of the flare landing harmlessly near Rojas was published across newspapers. Further medical examinations also showed that Rojas's injury didn't have any signs of burning.

Which still left the question of why Rojas was bleeding profusely. Rojas eventually confessed to deliberately cutting himself with a razor blade that he had smuggled onto the pitch in his goalkeeper's glove.** He said he'd planned from the start that, if Chile were behind, he'd do something like that to try and get the result overturned – the flare just gave him the perfect cover.

* Nothing safer than being in the custody of the Brazilian police.
** Cutting yourself with a razor to draw blood is a common trick in professional wrestling. In one match in 2007, 'Abdullah the Butcher' cut himself and Devon Nicholson aka 'Hannibal' for just such an effect. Often this is done with the consent of both wrestlers, although in this case it wasn't. Even worse, it gave Nicholson hepatitis C. He sued and a court awarded him $2.3 million in damages and legal costs. The lesson here is to only use razor blades for shaving and not cutting your forehead for dramatic effect.

In response, Brazil was awarded a 2–0 victory, a result that saw them go through to the World Cup. Chile were banned from the qualifiers for the next World Cup.

Rojas received a lifetime ban. Sergio Stoppel, president of the Chilean Football Federation, the coach, Orlando Aravena, and several players were also sanctioned; FIFA believed they had prior knowledge, or covered things up after the fact.

Questions of who knew what and when remain murky even today. Rojas always claimed he acted alone but defender Fernando Astengo, who was also was suspended, said in 2013, 'It was in the changing room when I realised that it was all false. There were a few of them who staged what happened in the Maracanã. I believe that, apart from Roberto, there were six others, players included.'

As for Rosenery Mello, the woman who had thrown the flare, she went from being a villain to quite the celebrity in Brazil. She was given the nickname 'La Fogueteira', meaning a person who builds and sells pyrotechnic products. A few months after these events she was paid a few thousand dollars to appear in *Playboy*. It's always nice to have a happy ending to such a dramatic story.

SLEIGHT OF HAND

When it comes to crossing the line from bending the rules into cheating, the next step up from pretending to be fouled is doing something illegal and simply hoping the referee doesn't see it.

Take for example the final of the 2002 Heineken Cup*, Europe's top-tier Rugby Union competition for clubs. Irish team Munster took on English club Leicester Tigers. Now, I'm not a student of history, so I'm unaware if the Irish and English had any bad blood before 2002.

---

* The Heineken Cup is for clubs from countries whose national teams compete in the Six Nations, which are England, France, Ireland, Italy, Scotland and Wales.

Very late in the game, Leicester were leading 15–9, but Munster had a scrum close to the Leicester line. This was a great attacking situation: Munster had the feed into the scrum, which usually gives you the ball, and a scrum means the opposition's forwards are all tied up, allowing your backs to go one-on-one with theirs.

At this late stage, a try followed by a conversion would see Munster win the game by a point.

As the crowd roared, Munster's Peter Stringer fed the ball into the scrum. But, with the referee's sight obscured by the scrum, Leicester forward Neil Back quickly used his hand to push the ball back to his side of the scrum – an illegal act. His cheating unexpectedly gave the ball to the Tigers. They kicked the ball down the field into touch and moments later the game was over. Leicester were the champions of Europe.

Back was a veteran. He'd captained both his club and country, and he knew exactly what he'd done.

Munster fans were obviously outraged, but many others praised Back for his 'quick thinking'. And therein lies the problem with gamesmanship. Even when it's blatant cheating, it's seen by many as 'clever'. The papers the following morning described Back's actions as 'smart', 'streetwise' and 'crafty'.

Immediately after the game, Back said, 'In the heat of the moment all sorts of things happen. But we rode our luck today and deserved to triumph.'

I guess you really do make your own luck sometimes.

Later on, Back reflected on his cheating. 'This game is all about little edges – particularly in finals – and doing what you can to win. That was a very crucial scrum. Our defence held up well and I did what I had to do to ensure a win,' he said.

Dean Richards, Leicester's director of rugby, was asked if he thought that Back's action amounted to cheating. He said: 'At the end of the day Neil Back is a winner. If anything, Munster could take a look at some of the penalties they won in the scrum, when the decision should have gone the other way.'

This excuse – that everyone does it and therefore it's alright – is the universal motto of sportspeople caught cheating. Remember, though, that it's also the refrain of children: 'But Mum, everyone else was throwing rocks at Billy too!'

If your best defence is that other people also cheat, you don't actually have a defence, you only have a rather obvious statement.

The great secret of successful cheating – winning something through dishonest means – is that it's a bitter fruit, leaving a horrible aftertaste.

Not long after winning the trophy, Back revealed how heavily his actions weighed on him. 'In a way, I wish I hadn't done it. I have to be honest about it. I don't like people thinking I'm a cheat. I don't want that slur. I'm not a cheat. I had a lot of mail over that incident, mostly negative. There were letters saying I was a cheat, some of them from Leicester fans, which was a bit hurtful.

'If people wanted to make me feel bad about what happened, they have. That's disappointing and I know it upset my wife, Alison. If I thought there was any possible way of redressing it, I would consider it. I regret it because I don't like to think that, because of that one incident, there are people who think I'm a cheat.'

Despite Back's regrets, there's no evidence that the world of sport learns from anyone's mistakes.

CHAPTER 4

SENSIBLE AND OPPORTUNISTIC CHEATING

In all human endeavours, not as many of our actions are in our control as we'd like to think. Set the incentives and disincentives a certain way and it's amazing how people will change their behaviour.

We've seen in soccer that cheating is inherent in the game. Because the payoff for diving is so big, and traditionally the downside is so small, it makes players more likely to do it – it's hard to resist the temptation.

Other sports are no different. Sometimes the way a sport or a tournament is structured provides almost irresistible incentives to cheat. In fact, in some cases you'd be silly not to cheat.

When it comes to this type of cheating, I'm sure your thoughts, like mine, go straight to the hotbed of intrigue and underhanded tactics that is lawn bowls.

BAD BOYS

Lawn bowls is a fiery enough sport to begin with, but the 2009 Asia Pacific Championship in Kuala Lumpur featured Gary Lawson, known as the 'bad boy of New Zealand bowls'. It was always going to be a tense affair. I bet you all remember watching it.

Now it probably doesn't take much to be known as the 'bad boy' in bowls. Perhaps Gary once put something in the recycling bin that should have gone in the normal bin. But as well as being the lawn bowls equivalent of Dennis Rodman, Lawson was also a record fourteen-time New Zealand champion. Due to his skill, in 2009 Lawson was the captain of the New Zealand fours side. The team had already qualified for the quarter finals, but first they had to play one more group match, against Thailand.

This is where the incentive to *not* win comes in to play. It quickly became clear that if they lost that game against Thailand, New Zealand would avoid Australia in the knockout stage, essentially giving themselves an easier draw.

This is hardly a unique case. Losing to increase your chances of winning later on is a regular occurrence in sport. It also happens when teams 'tank' for better draft picks, finishing lower on the ladder to get access to the best talent.

In that final group game, New Zealand had four dropped shots, handing Thailand the win, 17–15. The bad boy of New Zealand bowls had struck again.

However, another consequence of this result was that Canada missed out on progressing to the knockout rounds, and they made an official complaint. The New Zealand officials investigated and found that not only was their own team guilty of throwing the game, it had done it before, against Ireland in the world championships.

Lawson received a six-month suspension. While suspended, Lawson got into a drunken verbal exchange with a taxi driver, with the driver alleging he made racial slurs and said he would kill him.

Lawson was charged with assault but the judge ruled he did not have a case to answer.

Still, it shows why lawn bowls has such a dangerous image, and why so many people feel concerned about letting their children play bowls, preferring they take up boxing.

FISTS OF STONE

Would you believe that even boxing has had incidents of cheating? I know, it surprised me too.

One particularly nasty method is to add plaster to the bandages fighters wrap their hands in. When the fighter starts to sweat in the ring, the plaster starts to harden, so getting punched by them is basically like getting hit by concrete. Even with gloves on, it's a significant advantage.

This is why I don't box – that and my good looks.

THE LAW OF UNINTENDED CONSEQUENCES

Other sports have also fallen prey to designing tournaments that turn out to make losing worthwhile. The blood sport that is badminton encountered this problem on no less a grand stage than the 2012 Olympics in London.

The Badminton World Federation (BWF)* had decided that, instead of a pure knockout competition, they would have a round robin tournament from which players and doubles teams qualified for knockout stages.

It was the first time the Olympic badminton tournament would feature a group stage, previously it had been straight to knockouts. But the BWF wanted more matches for television and more opportunities to feature the lesser badminton nations.

---

* You always have to be careful with acronyms. The World Taekwondo Federation was named in 1973 but found that, with the rise of the internet, their acronym 'WTF' started to take on, in their words, 'negative connotations'. In 2018 they changed their name to just World Taekwondo.

The BWF should have learned from lawn bowls. As had happened at the 2009 Asia Pacific bowls championships, badminton doubles teams started to find themselves in positions where losing would help them avoid certain teams in the knockout phase.

Unlike bowls, though, it wasn't just one team that decided to take advantage of this.

It all came to a head in the women's doubles tournament on 31 August 2012 – a date that will live in infamy.

Two teams playing early in the day – the Chinese team of Yu Yang and Wang Xiaoli and their South Korean opponents Jung Kyung-eun and Kim Ha-na – both worked out that it would be better if they lost. Each of them would still advance to the next round, but they would avoid another Chinese pairing who were ranked second in the tournament.

In a sold-out Wembley Arena, in front of 6000 fans, these two top-ranked badminton pairings both attempted to lose the game. It was gloriously farcical. What should have been an elite match turned into something resembling a group of people trying out badminton for the first time, on the beach, for a laugh. While drunk.

These professional players could barely serve over the net, and when they did, the shuttlecock went miles out of the court. There were endless double faults. Everyone in the arena suddenly twigged to what was happening and started booing. Even worse, IOC President Jacques Rogge was in the audience.

The referee, Thorsten Berg, had to step in and warn the players over their conduct. It didn't help. The longest rally in the entire game was four strokes. At one stage the tournament director came out onto the court to remind the players of their responsibilities.

Eventually, despite their worst efforts, the Korean pair won 21–14, 21–11. The Chinese team had successfully avoided their compatriots.

Except the result meant it suddenly made sense for another South Korean team and an Indonesian duo that were facing each other later that night to also both try to lose. The crowd felt a sense of déjà vu. Gail Emms, who had won a badminton silver medal for Britain in 2004, was commentating and she felt sorry for the crowd who'd paid to be there: 'They basically got a show where my two-and-a-half-year-old could have won one of those matches. The girls were serving so far out. It was so embarrassing.'

The BWF kicked all four teams out of the tournament for breaching two parts of the players' code: 'Not using one's best efforts to win a match and conducting oneself in a manner that is clearly abusive or detrimental to the sport.'

But the reality is that the BWF had a big hand in all this. If you create these kind of incentives, you get the silly results you deserve.

THE SILLIEST GAME EVER

While lawn bowls and badminton have produced some odd outcomes, nothing compares to what the organisers of the 1994 Caribbean Cup accidently manufactured. This soccer tournament ran from 1989 until 2017, for teams in the Caribbean Football Union. It was basically tax havens playing off against each other.

The organisers in 1994, like the BWF, had good intentions – they wanted to improve the tournament. But, as we know, the road to hell is paved with good intentions. The people running the Caribbean Cup wanted to ensure that all matches would have a winner, an honourable aim in a sport often cursed with draws.

To achieve this, they decided to implement a variation of the golden goal rule: the first goal scored in extra time not only won the match, it would count as double. This would motivate teams to go for it because it would give them an advantage if at the end of the group stages things came down to goal difference. This turned out to be a truly terrible idea, but a hilarious one.

In their last group game, Barbados faced off against Grenada. The stage was Barbados National Stadium, with a capacity of 15,000.

Due to the standings in the group, Barbados had to beat Grenada by two goals to make it through to the knockout stages. Winning by one goal would not be enough, due to their goal difference, and Grenada would go through instead. Simple enough.

The home crowd was therefore pretty excited when Barbados took a 2–0 lead during the game, and with the end of the match nearing, everything seemed to be working out well.

Until, with just seven minutes left, Grenada scored, making it 2–1.

The situation exploded. Not literally, but mathematically. Despite the fact Barbados were still leading, they needed to win by two goals. It looked like they were going out.

Unless they scored a goal – any goal.

Because of the new rule, if the score was tied at the end of regular time, it would go to extra time and Barbados could then score a golden goal that would count as two, taking them through. If they couldn't score themselves, conceding a goal – or scoring an own goal – was suddenly a great outcome for the Barbadians.

It led to a frenzied few minutes where Barbados tried to score at both ends of the pitch. You had Barbados attacking both goals and Grenada desperately defending both. It was certainly one of the strangest moments in sport, except it was about to get stranger.

Barbados finally managed to score – an own goal, but it helped. The scores were now tied and the match would be going to extra time in three more minutes, where a golden goal would see Barbados through.

Unless, in the remaining three minutes of regular time, Grenada scored. At either end. Even a 3–2 loss would see Grenada go through on goal difference.

So now you had Grenada attacking both goals and Barbados defending both. It was the sports version of the movie *Inception*.

But Grenada didn't manage to score by the end of regular time and, in extra time, Barbados scored. Their plan had worked.

Perhaps Grenada's manager James Clarkson summed it all up best: 'I feel cheated. The person who came up with these rules must be a candidate for a madhouse. The game should never be played with so many players running around the field confused. Our players did not even know which direction to attack: our goal or their goal. I have never seen this happen before. In football, you are supposed to score against the opponents to win, not for them.'

The rule was rescinded after the tournament.

CARPE DIEM

Not all cheating involves a clever, or not-so-clever, premeditated plan. Sometimes cheating is as simple as someone taking advantage when they spot an opportunity.

At the 1936 Olympics in Berlin the double sculls was a major rowing event, so big that Adolf Hitler had shown up to watch the favourites, German rowers Willi Kaidel and Joachim Pirsch.

During the qualifying heats, the British pair of Jack Beresford and Dick Southwood noticed that the Germans seemed to be getting off to flying starts. Studying them, they noticed that they would in fact take off early, before the official start of the race.

The German pair had noticed that when the starter lifted his megaphone to say 'ready, set, go', he couldn't see the field because of the size of his megaphone. So Kaidel and Pirsch would begin rowing the moment the starter raised the megaphone to his lips, getting several strokes in before the rest of the field. It was clever, and I guess when the Führer is sitting in the stands expecting you to win glory for the Third Reich, you look for any way to not lose.

The British pair were outraged, of course, so in the finals, racing against the Germans, they did the exact same thing. They won.

I'm not sure how Adolf reacted to the Germans losing, but he always struck me as a reasonable guy.

THE FOG OF WAR

The fog hung heavily around the Louisiana Downs racetrack on 11 January 1990. So heavily, in fact, that anyone watching from the grandstand could barely see the horses as they raced around the track.

The punters could vaguely make out their investments starting off, but then they disappeared into the fog, emerging to cross the finish line minutes later like spectral cavalry from another world.

In the eleventh race, the fog still obscuring vision beyond a few meters, the 23-to-1 outsider Landing Officer was eased into the gates by his jockey Sylvester Carmouche Jr. At the jump, Carmouche cursed – he'd hopelessly mistimed the start and was well behind. It would take some doing to stay with the field, given Landing Officer was a long shot to begin with.

Within seconds, all the horses had disappeared into the blanket of fog. For several minutes, the punters waited to see who would emerge in the lead. To everyone's surprise, it was Landing Officer.

This was especially surprising to anyone with knowledge of Louisiana racing. Landing Officer, a five-year-old, had raced in fifty-three races and only won five of them. Not only had Carmouche piloted Landing Officer into the lead, they were now leading by 24 lengths, an extraordinary feat. Landing Officer finished only 1.2 seconds off the track record. Given the wet conditions and the low visibility, this was an unbelievable result.

So unbelievable that no one actually believed it.

It soon became clear that, shortly after the horses had slipped out of view, Carmouche had slowed his horse, which was running last, and waited for the field to come around again.

Carmouche's first problem was that in judging when to take off again, with visibility almost non-existent, he'd had to rely on sound, and fog does weird things to sound. He'd therefore misjudged where the field was and took off too early. His victory was so large as to immediately raise suspicion.

His second problem was that, despite the fog making it very hard to see, the eight other jockeys would have noticed someone passing them. A man on a large horse is hard to hide, even in heavy fog.

Protests were immediately lodged. How could Landing Officer enter the fog last but emerge from it first, with no one having seen him pass? The video tape was reviewed by stewards. While it was not particularly helpful, it did seem that at the few points where you could make out the field, there were only eight horses, not nine.

The final problem for Carmouche was the inspection immediately after the race. James E Broussard, a veterinarian who worked for the Louisiana Racing Commission, noticed that Landing Officer not only wasn't breathing hard or sweating, the wraps on his legs and his entire body were clean – difficult to achieve when running a mile on a wet track.

By contrast Something Strong, the second-placed horse, was covered in both sweat and mud splatters, and was breathing heavily.

The Louisiana Racing Commission quickly overturned the race results, awarding the win to Something Strong. Carmouche eventually received a ten-year ban, of which he served eight. He was found guilty of attempted theft and sentenced to thirty days in jail, as well as being fined $250 plus court costs.

Throughout it all, Carmouche protested his innocence: 'It ain't right. I know I ain't did it. I never did anything wrong in my life. I rode the race, and I win.'

CHAPTER 5

MORALLY CHALLENGED

It's time for a reminder that the majority of athletes don't succumb to the temptations of gaining an unfair advantage. They strive to win by being at the top of their game.

Entry-level cheating tends to happen when people who are, let's say morally challenged, meet opportunity or decide to exploit bad incentives. Often it's someone who behaves badly away from sport and just continues on that way on the field.

Sometimes, though, it's someone who has no sense of sportsmanship. For some, morals are foolish things that simply get in the way of winning. Basically, they are people who would normally go into crime or politics but happened to have some sporting ability.

LACES OUT

The NBA player JR Smith has had what many would call an 'erratic' career, despite winning an NBA championship with the LeBron James–led Cleveland Cavaliers in 2016.

He's played for the New Orleans Hornets, the Denver Nuggets, the Zhejiang Golden Bulls in China, the New York Knicks and the Cleveland Cavaliers. He is known as a talented but at times lazy player, often missing training or not giving it his all.

He's also had a troubled time off the court, mainly in relation to his driving. In 2007, he and then Denver Nuggets teammate Carmelo Anthony were involved in a car accident. Neither was injured. In 2009, however, Smith was driving when he went through a stop sign and collided with another car. He and one of his two passengers, Andre Bell, flew out of the vehicle in the crash – neither had been wearing seatbelts. Bell later died from his head injuries.

A grand jury declined to indict Smith for vehicular manslaughter, but he pleaded guilty to reckless driving and was sentenced to ninety days in jail, with sixty of those days suspended.

For their part, the NBA suspended Smith for seven games.

Smith's driving record showed that, previously, he'd been suspended from driving five times in the space of eight months. And yet, even after all this, in 2012 Smith was arrested after failing to show up in court for a charge of operating a motor scooter with no valid licence.

What Smith's driving record shows us is that his judgement was never good. So when I tell you he used to cheat on the court, you'd hardly be surprised.

What is surprising is how odd his cheating was.

While he was playing for the New York Knicks in 2014, a free throw was being taken by the Dallas Mavericks star Dirk Nowitzki. Smith was lined up along the key, next to Mavericks forward Shawn Marion. As they waited for Nowitzki to take the shot, JR bent down as if to check his shoes, only to untie Marion's laces.

On the spectrum of cheating, it's about as silly as you can get. Marion caught Smith doing it and looked at him in disbelief. After the game, the NBA warned Smith to never do it again.

That really should have been the end of it, but this being Smith, he took to Twitter and tweeted that he did it every game. This was no idle boast: footage of Smith doing it numerous other times has emerged since.

Any sensible person would have laughed the whole thing off and never repeated it, but Smith was not a sensible person. Three days after having a go at Marion's shoelaces, in the Knicks' very next game, Smith attempted unsuccessfully to untie the shoe of Detroit Pistons forward Greg Monroe during another free throw.

Despite the minor nature of the cheating, these incidents highlight a characteristic that might be a factor in who decides to cheat: a not-very-clever person.

The NBA didn't see the humour in the second incident. Smith had blatantly ignored their warning and he was promptly fined $50,000 for 'recurring instances of unsportsmanlike conduct'.

Where the warning had failed, the fine worked. Smith later said, 'I do care about the fines because it's loss of money, but other than that, I like to have fun. I would do [the shoelace thing] again if there wasn't a fine.'

If you're wondering where $50,000 stands in terms of NBA penalties, let's look at some of Smith's other fines. In 2012 he was fined $25,000 for posting a photo of his girlfriend Tahiry Jose's naked bottom as she lay in front of the TV. Smith quipped it was making it difficult see the basketball on the TV.* Then, during the NBA playoffs in 2013, Smith was fined $5000 for 'flopping', which is essentially the same as diving in soccer: staging for a free.

This means the NBA ranked these misdemeanours, from least to worst:

1. Intentionally playing for a free.
2. Posting a picture of your girlfriend's bottom on Twitter.
3. Untying someone's shoelaces.

---

* Later on, Tahiry revealed that the photo was taken after her and Smith's first date, even though it was tweeted out months later. Who says romance is dead?

OVERLY AFFECTIONATE

As heinous a crime as serial untying of shoelaces is, National Hockey League (NHL) player Brad Marchand has JR Smith licked in the idiocy stakes.

The Canadian, who plays for the Boston Bruins, is known as a serial pest in the NHL, and has a slew of fines and suspensions for dirty play, including elbowing opponents in the head. But it's Marchand's penchant for licking opponents that has earned him the most notoriety.

Like all these things, it started off slowly. In 2015, Marchand kissed his teammate Jarome Iginla after Iginla scored the winning overtime goal.

This in itself isn't illegal. You can kiss a teammate if they're alright with it, and Marchand repeated the act almost a year later, after he scored a winning goal off an assist from Max Talbot. Marchand attempted to kiss Talbot but a visor prevented him from doing so.

After the game Marchand explained, 'I just said to him, "I could kiss you right now." His visor was in the way. I'll try anything once.' Except he'd now tried it twice.

In February 2016, the Dallas Stars' Patrick Eaves and Marchand squared off as if a fight was about to break out. Instead, Marchand leaned in for a kiss – Eaves pushed him away.

Next up was the Toronto Maple Leafs' Leo Komarov, who Marchand took a fancy to. As the two grabbed each other in a tussle, Marchand kissed Komarov on the cheek. Komarov said of the incident, 'I told him I have a wife and a baby so I can't do it right now.' When asked if it bothered him, Komarov smiled and said, 'No, I kind of liked it.'

In April 2018, things escalated again. Kissing no longer satisfied Marchand. Playing Toronto again, Komarov and Marchand exchanged several punches, then Marchand licked Komarov's face.

'I thought he wanted to cuddle. I just wanted to get close to him,' said Marchand. 'He keeps trying to get close to me. I don't know if he's got a thing for me or what. He's cute.'

It was reported that the NHL ordered Marchand to stop licking people, but this turned out to be untrue. The NHL even went to the trouble of putting out a statement denying they had asked Marchand not to lick people. I bet the communications person who had to write that statement never thought they would have to issue a media release denying his employer had told someone not to lick people.

Just a week after the league had made it clear they hadn't told Marchand to stop licking people, Marchand licked Tampa Bay's Ryan Callahan.

After Marchand got Callahan with a low hit, Callahan retaliated with several punches, and Marchand, of course, licked his face. Marchand said of the incident, 'Well, he punched me four times in the face, so, you know, he just kept getting close. Nothing big.'

The next day the NHL announced that now they *would* tell Marchand to stop licking opponents on the face. NHL deputy commissioner Bill Daly said, 'Yes, we will be communicating with the club. We don't expect it to happen again.'

Unlike JR Smith, Marchand decided to stop, at least for now.

This is what happens in the pressure cooker that is sport: administrators have to take time out of running the league to tell a player to stop licking opponents' faces. You can't plan for this sort of stuff.

DENTAL RECORDS

After kissing and licking, there is an obvious next step: biting. It's not great that it took until the current millennium for some people to learn about consent. Some still haven't learned, and this is certainly the case when it comes to biting in sport, something that happens with alarming regularity.

Probably the most famous instance was when Mike Tyson bit off part of Evander Holyfield's ear in 1997. What is often lost in the story is Tyson actually bit both of Holyfield's ears – after the first incident, the bout was allowed to continue, and it was only after further biting that the match was stopped.

Tyson was suspended for a year and a half and fined $3 million, but he is not the only athlete to have bitten opponents.

Back in the seventies, Cincinnati Reds pitcher Pedro Borbón bit so many opponents he became known as 'the Dominican Dracula'. Borbón was known for his love of fighting, and whenever a fight broke out you could bet he was biting someone.

In 1974, a game against the Pittsburgh Pirates broke out into a bench-clearing brawl. It was chaos, with punches being swung everywhere. In the middle of it all was Borbón, pulling Pittsburgh's Daryl Patterson's hair while biting him on the neck, like a scene from *True Blood*.

Patterson had to get a tetanus shot after the game, which is probably sensible if someone who regularly bites people does it to you. This being the seventies, Borbón didn't receive any punishment.

Biting penalties in sport were still lax in the eighties, when during Game 4 of the 1986 Stanley Cup Finals, Claude Lemieux of the Montreal Canadiens bit Calgary Flames forward Jim Peplinski's finger so hard he hit bone.

Lemieux did not receive any punishment. Peplinski quipped after the game, 'I didn't know they allowed cannibalism in the NHL.'

It looked like Claude Lemieux had gotten away with almost biting someone's finger off, but he would get his comeuppance.

By 1996, Lemieux was already the most hated player in the league for his dirty play. But in that year's playoffs, when he was playing for the Colorado Avalanche against the Detroit Red Wings, he checked Kris Draper from behind, sending him face first into the boards. It was an incredibly cheap shot. Draper suffered a concussion, a broken jaw, a broken nose and a broken cheekbone.

The NHL has a different view than most sports when it comes to punishing people, letting a lot of it be sorted out on the ice by the players. They believe that if the players know they're likely to get thumped if they do something stupid, it lowers the likelihood of incidents.

I'd say the evidence might not show that. It might be that hockey people just love fighting.

After Lemieux's hit, Draper had to undergo extensive reconstructive facial surgery and had his jaw wired shut for weeks. A few days after surgery, Draper's teammate Darren McCarty came to visit him. McCarty was on the Red Wings team for his fists – he was the team's enforcer. Every NHL team has someone who can fight and will protect his teammates.

Later on, McCarty revealed all he said to Draper during his visit was, 'Don't worry. I'll take care of it.' Which he did, 301 days later, when the Colorado Avalanche played the Red Wings again, at Joe Lewis Arena in Detroit.

In the first period, Colorado's Peter Forsberg got into a fight with Detroit's Igor Larionov. The play stopped and the other players watched on, a few wrestling with each other.

Both McCarty and Lemieux were on the ice, but McCarty was grappling with the Avalanche's Adam Foote so couldn't get to Lemieux. But then his teammate Brendan Shanahan entered the fray, freeing McCarty to go after Lemieux.

McCarty spotted Lemieux and skated towards him. Before Lemieux had noticed the Red Wings' enforcer was coming for him, McCarty clocked him.

Lemieux fell to the ground and McCarty followed, continuing to land blows, while Lemieux did what's known as 'turtling':

curling up on your knees with your head on the ground and covered by your hands, like a turtle going into its shell.

It was probably best he did or McCartney could have killed him.

The rest of the ice exploded into fights, with even the two goalies going at one another. When order was restored, Lemieux was taken off the ice, straight to the locker room, blood streaming down his face and looking very wobbly. McCarty, meanwhile, skated to the penalty box to deafening cheers from the Red Wings crowd.

This being hockey, McCarty served his penalty and then returned to the game, going on to score the winner 39 seconds into overtime.

In the next regular season game between the sides, Lemieux and McCarty set up across from each other before the opening face-off. The moment the game started, they dropped their gloves and fought. Lemieux had been humiliated in the league for turtling and was determined to do better. This time their clash was less eventful, ending in a draw with no serious injuries.

As for feeling any remorse, McCarty has no time for that. In his mind, when he took out Lemieux he was serving justice. Every year, on the anniversary of that first fight, McCarty sits down at home and watches it.

Over the years, biting has begun to attract stronger penalties, perhaps because it keeps happening. In 1994, South African prop Johan Le Roux bit All Blacks player Sean Fitzpatrick's ear and received an eighteen-month suspension. This sentence had been reduced from an initial ruling of twenty months.

In an appreciative mood after the reduction, Le Roux said, 'For an eighteen-month suspension, I feel I probably should've torn it off.'

Biting opponents is one thing, but biting teammates is another, especially in the case of Spanish soccer player Francisco Gallardo. Playing Valladolid, when his teammate José Antonio Reyes scored,

Gallardo decided the best way to celebrate was to bite him on the penis.*

José Antonio Reyes said, 'I felt a bit of a pinch, but I didn't realise what Gallardo had done until I saw the video. The worst thing about it is the teasing I'm going to get from my teammates.'

I'm not sure the teasing was the worst bit.

Incredibly, it can get worse than being bitten on the penis. In 2002 in the Victorian Football League (VFL), Port Melbourne was playing Springvale when Port Melbourne's Peter Filandia bit Springvale's Chad Davis's testicles, puncturing them. Davis also needed a tetanus injection.

Filandia was suspended for ten matches, which to me seems incredibly light punishment.

When it comes to biting people, though, Uruguayan soccer superstar Luis Suárez is challenging Mike Tyson for the title of Most Famous Biter in Sport. Not once, not twice, but three times the Barcelona striker has bitten opponents.

So often does Suárez bite people that Ian Stedman, writing in the *New Statesmen*, worked out that opposition players have roughly a one-in-two-thousand chance of being bitten by Suárez. This was based on how many games he's played, how many opponents he's been on the pitch with, and of course how often he's bitten one of them.

To put those odds in perspective, you have a one-in-3.7 million chance of being bitten by a shark while swimming in the ocean and a one-in-ten-thousand chance of being struck by lightning. In other words, professional soccer players have a significantly greater chance of being bitten by Suárez than by a shark.

Suárez's first biting incident occurred on in 2010, when he was playing for Ajax and bit PSV Eindhoven's Otman Bakkal on the shoulder. He was fined and suspended, but, three years later, while

---

* Personally, I can think of a lot of better ways – a high-five is always nice.

playing for Liverpool, Suárez bit Chelsea's Branislav Ivanović. The incident drew condemnation from no less than then Prime Minster David Cameron, who said Suárez had set 'the most appalling example'.*

By this stage, Suárez's hobby of biting people was well known and ahead of the 2014 World Cup a betting agency offered odds of 175-to-1 that Luis Suárez would bite someone during the tournament. A total of 167 people took up that bet. They were richly rewarded when, during Uruguay's final group match, against Italy, Suárez clashed with Italian defender Giorgio Chiellini and – you guessed it – bit him on the shoulder.

Uruguay won the game, but Suárez was banned from the rest of the tournament. Without him, Uruguay lost their next match and found themselves out of the tournament.

You would think after undoing shoelaces, licking and then biting, we'd have reached the end of weird things people can do to each other on the sporting field. However, there is always an innovator who will go that extra mile, a visionary who does things like no one else before them. Great people like Galileo Galilei, Leonardo da Vinci, Thomas Edison, Henry Ford and, perhaps the greatest of them all, John Hopoate.

IT'S A CONTACT SPORT

In 2001, while Australia's John Hopoate was playing Rugby League for the Wests Tigers, he came up with a new way to distract an opponent. When I tell you what it is, you'll agree that it would certainly take your mind off the game.

Against the North Queensland Cowboys, Hopoate unveiled his new tactic. When he had an opponent in a tackle, he inserted his finger into their anus. He did this to three opponents in the match.

---

* When David 'let's have a referendum on Brexit' Cameron is questioning your judgement, you know you're in trouble.

Imagine doing that at *your* workplace.

Given this was all being shown on television, everyone knew what was going on. When the game was over, Hopoate was interviewed. He claimed he had just been giving the players wedgies.

Peter Jones, one of the players involved, wasn't buying it. 'It wasn't a wedgie. That's when your pants are pulled up your arse. I think I know the difference between a wedgie and someone sticking their finger up my bum.'

You know what? I reckon you would. Even if neither of these things have happened to you. It's just something instinctive in us as humans.

Hopoate was banned for twelve matches, but people were nervous around him ever after.

Untying shoes, kissing, biting, sticking your finger into an opponent's bum – players will break a lot of rules to disrupt an opponent's concentration.

But there's another tactic that is both the simplest and the most common: pure physical intimidation. And when that fails, it's time for out and out violence.

CHAPTER 6

INTIMIDATION

The art of intimidation has a long and proud history in sport. Playing hard and tough is all part of contact sport. Even if you don't actually hurt an opponent, just the threat of violence instils a healthy sense of fear in them – it might give them second thoughts about taking you on.

In many sports, physical intimidation is a big part of the game, a deliberate test of strength as well as skill. As New Zealand All Black Tana Umaga once said to a referee, 'We're not playing tiddlywinks here.'*

Gaining ground by taking shortcuts is nice and all, but sometimes nothing is more intuitive than just trying to hurt your opponent or, even better, significantly injure them.

---

* If you *are* playing tiddlywinks, refrain from contact. I once delivered a late hit on a family member during a game and Granny has never forgiven me. The greatest ever tiddlywinks player is Lawrence Kahn, who goes by the nicknames 'Horsemeat' and 'King'. He often plays with doubles partner Dave Lockwood, who he also has a rivalry with in the singles format of the game. *Sports Illustrated* once described their rivalry as akin to that of Muhammad Ali and Joe Frazier. It's not.

Over time, officials have cracked down on this type of behaviour more and more. Out and out violence has, in the main, been consigned to the past. As an investment in the future, sporting leagues try to encourage kids to pick up their particular sport, so they're not keen for parents to have to worry about their kid getting maimed on the weekend. These days no sporting code wants to be labelled a blood sport.

Nonetheless, League types now cry 'bring back the biff' and ex-Australian Rules players reminisce about 'the good old days' when you could punch someone behind play and get away with it.

Like gamesmanship, intimidation has always hovered around the grey area between legal and illegal. But as the following stories show, threatening behaviour often tips into the illegal – and then some.

UNORTHODOX INTIMIDATION

Hitting someone with a late tackle, punching an opponent behind play, targeting someone's legs, all these things are cheating if you look at the rules. However, within a lot of sports, there's not much between legal and illegal hits and tackles, and both are seen as simply part of the game. But some attempts at intimidation sail well past 'acceptable' and into the 'outright bonkers' category.

Take for example Dock Ellis, a pitcher for the Pittsburgh Pirates, who in 1974 came up with a plan to intimidate the Cincinnati Reds.

The Reds weren't an easy team to intimidate. They were the best team in baseball in the seventies, so dominant they became known as the 'Big Red Machine' and are considered probably the best team in the history of the sport. They won the National League Championship in 1970, '72, '75 and '76 and won the World Series in 1975 and '76.

This domination by the Reds made Dock Ellis angry. Not at the Reds, but at his teammates. He believed they were in awe of the Reds – scared of them, even – and didn't believe they could win.

When the two teams met on 1 May 1974, Ellis was the Pirates' starting pitcher, and he decided the best thing to do was reverse the situation. He wanted to intimidate the Reds and show his teammates there was nothing to be scared of.

His plan was elegantly simple. When the Cincinnati batters came up to bat, he would hit every single one of them with a pitch.

A pitcher intentionally hitting a batter with a fastball travelling at about 155 km/h is something usually only done when the two players are feuding, or in reprisal for a teammate being hit earlier. Even then it's not done too often, and pitchers only target the one batter. The batters on a team hate it when their pitcher hits an opponent, because they know they could be hit in return.

Ellis's plan to hit every single batter on the Cincinnati Reds was unprecedented, and has never been attempted since. It was such a left-field idea that he didn't even tell his teammates he was going to do it. But there were early signs of what Ellis would try, even before the game started.

The Reds legendary hitter Pete Rose* was standing near the batter's box, leaning on his bat, studying Ellis doing his warm-up pitches. Ellis had considered not hitting Rose, partly because they were friends and, secondly, because he thought no matter how hard he hit him, Rose would not allow himself to show any pain – he would make a display of not being intimidated. This would be counter to Ellis's aim.

Having weighed all this up, Ellis decided to throw at him anyway, despite this only being the warm-up. He only just missed. Rose looked on bemused.

---

* Pete Rose is one of the greatest baseball players ever. He's the all-time MLB leader in hits (4256), games played (3562), at-bats (14,053), singles (3215) and outs (10,328), and he won three World Series rings. However, while managing the Reds in the eighties, he was accused of betting on his team, and even against them. Rose only admitted that he bet on them to win. He was investigated and it was alleged he placed bets on fifty-two Reds games in 1987, wagering a minimum of $10,000 a game. To this day he has been deemed ineligible for the Hall of Fame as a result.

The game started and Cincinnati were the first to bat. Rose was the first batter and Ellis threw the first pitch, which flew just over Rose's head. The second went behind his back, but the third pitch hit him in the side.

As expected, Rose picked up the ball and made a great show of gently tossing it back to Ellis to show he wasn't fazed at all.

In baseball, when you're hit by a pitch, you get a free trip to first base. So with Rose now on first base, the Red's second baseman Joe Morgan stepped into the batter's box. Ellis hit him with his first pitch, right in the kidneys.

Now Morgan was at first base and Rose was on second, and the Reds hadn't even got a hit yet. It was at this point that Ellis' teammates cottoned on to what he was doing. They remembered Ellis had voiced such a plan to them before the season started, but they had all assumed that Ellis, known for being a weird guy, was just talking nonsense.

Now that plan was unfolding before their eyes, they watched on, horrified. Ellis was putting runners on bases without getting any outs.

The third batter Dan Driessen was the next target. It took Ellis two pitches to hit him and suddenly the bases were loaded.

Strangely, the umpire hadn't decided to eject Ellis from the game, which is what would have happened by this stage in the modern game. Nor did Ellis's manager Danny Murtaugh decide to pull him, which was even stranger.

But both teams had now realised what Ellis was up to, and both benches were on their feet.

Tony Pérez was the next batter up for the Reds. He didn't even try to bat, he just dodged Ellis's four pitches – all outside the strike zone – like this was a game of dodgeball at primary school, drawing another walk to first base. This drove in a run.

Ellis seemed indifferent to giving up a run, something pitchers usually care very much about. 'The next hitter was Johnny Bench,' Ellis said later. 'I tried to deck him twice. I threw at his jaw, and he moved. I threw at the back of his head, and he moved.'

At this point, Murtaugh finally pulled Ellis from the game. This crazy attempt at intimidation was over, and it didn't even work. The Reds won 5–3.

In 11 pitches, Ellis had hit three batters and attempted to hit another two. His punishment from the league? Nothing.

For Ellis, this wasn't even the strangest thing he'd done on a baseball field.

Before all this, in 1970, Ellis was starting against the San Diego Padres. The day before the game, he had visited a friend in Los Angeles, and they'd stayed up late into the night, drinking, talking and taking LSD. This isn't a recommended way to prepare for a game, but as we've seen, Ellis didn't behave like most professional athletes.

The next day, Ellis awoke about noon. For some reason he thought he wasn't playing until the next day, so, as you do when you've just woken up, he took three tabs of LSD.

It was then pointed out to him by his friend that he was in fact pitching in six hours. Ellis quickly made his way to San Diego. This involved a plane flight, which would have been fun under the influence of LSD. He just made the game on time.

Despite tripping his head off, Ellis began pitching rather well. His control wasn't perfect, he walked eight batters and hit another (this time not on purpose) but, as each innings passed, he was achieving something truly astounding: he wasn't giving up any hits.

In baseball, pitchers dream of pitching a no-hitter: a full nine-innings without giving up a single hit. The only thing better is a perfect game, where you don't walk any batters and there are no fielding errors, meaning no opponent even gets on base.

Since 1876, only 302 no-hitters have been pitched in the major leagues, and only twenty-three of those have been perfect games.

But Dock Ellis, high on LSD, was close to pitching a no-hitter. Not that Ellis was too aware of this. He was having his own troubles out on the mound. 'I started having a crazy idea in the fourth inning that Richard Nixon was the home plate umpire, and once I thought I was pitching a baseball to Jimi Hendrix, who to me was holding a guitar and swinging it over the plate.'

It's hard enough pitching a no-hitter, but having Richard Nixon umpire the game would be problematic – his judgement isn't the best – and Jimmy Hendrix was known as a decent contact hitter.

Another sign that Ellis wasn't fully aware of his surroundings was that when one ball was gently hit along the ground, Ellis jumped out of the way like it was a hard-hit line drive coming right for him.

Despite Ellis's tenuous grip on reality, he somehow managed to pitch all nine innings, and when it was over, he'd done it, he'd pitched a no-hitter. His Pirates had beaten the Padres 2–0.

After Ellis quit baseball, he spoke openly about his drug addiction. He was a prolific user of amphetamines too, but he straightened up and became a counsellor, focusing on helping prisoners kick their addictions.

Major League Baseball has never released the full footage of that LSD inspired no-hitter.

BECOMING THE VILLAIN

Pushing the envelope by acting tough is one thing, but some players are plain malicious. They go out of their way to not just give their opposition a hard time, they set out to injure them. They go for cheap shots on defenceless opponents.

Not only are these types of hits cheating, they often set off a chain of events that brings out the worst in sportspeople.

One of those players whose violence set off a chain reaction was soccer player Andoni Goikoetxea, a defender who joined Athletic Bilbao in 1975.

Goiko, as he was known, played in an era when referees were more like vaguely interested observers than enforcers of the rules. At that time, referees in Spain's La Liga were at the mercy of the big clubs – they could be blacklisted if the clubs were unhappy with their performance. The result was that crunching, studs-up tackles were often ignored rather than earning a foul, never mind a card.

Goiko joined a defence that prided itself on being brutal, with no repercussions, and he was determined to become the most brutal of them all. But in joining Bilbao, Goiko had also been dropped into one of the most passionate rivalries in Spanish soccer, between Barcelona and Athletic Bilbao; Bilbao represented the Basque Country, Barcelona represented Catalonia.

The two clubs had completely different philosophical approaches, which led to a healthy rivalry on the pitch. Bilbao had a defensive mindset and saw the game as a tough physical encounter, while Barcelona believed in attacking, beautiful football.

By the early eighties, terrorist attacks by the Basque separatist group Euskadi Ta Askatasuna (ETA) had thrown Spain into political turbulence. At the same time, the two clubs' on-field rivalry exploded into true hatred, and it was Goiko who struck the match that set it alight.

When the two sides met in the 1981/82 season, they produced a match that would long linger in the memories of fans.

Barcelona was not quite yet the superpower it is today, but they had won some titles in previous decades and the club was very much on the rise. They had a 21-year-old West German midfielder by the name of Bernd Schuster who had made a name for himself at the Euro 1980 tournament. Schuster had had a great season so far, and his future was bright.

During the game Schuster made a run that was tracked by Goiko, who went in with a late, brutal tackle, his foot held at knee height to do the most damage possible. And that's exactly what he did – Schuster fell to the ground in great pain, his cruciate ligament* torn.

The young midfielder missed nine months, including the 1982 World Cup in Spain. Goiko felt no remorse; he saw Barcelona as a bunch of showboaters.

To say the Barcelona team were unhappy would be putting it mildly. They were about as happy as I am when I go to a restaurant and find out the menu is all share plates.** Yes, Barcelona were that angry.

With Schuster out, the following season Barcelona signed up a young player from Argentina by the name of Diego Maradona. He turned out to be pretty good.

The season after that, in 1983, the two teams played their first game in Barcelona at the Camp Nou. The national political situation was still perilous, and it didn't help that before the game Barcelona's coach César Luis Menotti described his Basque counterpart, Javier Clemente, as an 'authoritarian' and his team as 'destructive'. I'm sure Clemente was trying to ease tensions when he responded by calling Menotti 'a hippy and a womaniser'.

On the pitch, Bernd Schuster was now back, although he was never the same player after the injury caused by Goiko. In sport memories don't fade, and Schuster was determined to get revenge.

An hour into the match, Barcelona led 3–0, but Schuster still had to settle another score. When he got his moment, he slid in hard on Goiko, who landed heavily. The Camp Nou exploded in rapturous applause.

However, where Goiko had spent a lifetime perfecting tackles

---

* This connects the thighbone to the shinbone – it's pretty important if you don't want your leg to have the stability of an infant's.
** The problem with share plates is that people order things to show off how trendy they are with food, while you order something you actually want to eat, like fried chicken. And what happens? Everyone eats the fried chicken, because everyone loves fried chicken. So you get almost none of what you want, but the other people all say, it doesn't matter, there's heaps of sautéed kale left over. Well, of course there is.

that resulted in serious injuries, Schuster was an amateur. Goiko sprang straight up, furious. He started storming around the pitch trying to get to Schuster. Goiko was one of those people who thought it was fine for him to end other people's careers, but not the other way around.

As the game paused for Goiko's tantrum, Maradona tried to calm him, saying, 'Take it easy, Goiko, chill out. You're losing 3–0 and will just get booked for nothing.'

Instead of taking this advice, Goiko became angry with Maradona as well.

Play finally resumed and, as Maradona received a pass in his own half, Goiko mowed him down from behind, aiming solely for his leg and not the ball. The force of this illegal tackle snapped Maradona's lateral malleolus bone,* rupturing every ligament around it.

When it came to maiming people, Goiko was world-class.

Maradona later said, 'I just felt the impact, heard the sound – like a piece of wood cracking – and realised immediately what had happened.'

He was immediately stretchered off, and didn't return for the season. In fact, there were very real doubts he would ever play again.

For that brutal and unnecessary tackle, which had possibly ended a player's career, the referee gave Goiko a yellow card. Not a red, a yellow. Even for Spanish football at the time, that was seen as too light a punishment. The Royal Spanish Football Federation handed Goiko a ten-match ban.

Menotti, the manager of Barcelona and Maradona's country-man, wasn't happy even with that, calling for a lifelong ban for Goiko, accusing him of belonging to 'a race of anti-footballers'.

---

* The lateral malleolus bone is the round bit on the outside of your ankle. All my knowledge of the parts of the human body comes from sport – if something never gets injured in sport, I have no idea what it is.

English journalist Edward Owen went even further, giving Goiko a nickname that would stick: the 'Butcher of Bilbao'.

Maradona sat out for three months in the end, but he was keen to get back out there and get revenge.* He managed to get back in time for the return match in Bilbao, where he scored both goals in a 2–1 win, again a very physical match.

But in the time Maradona had sat out, Barcelona had lost momentum. Athletic Bilbao went on to win the 1983/84 La Liga title, finishing a single point ahead of Barcelona.

Fate, though, would play one more hand: the two teams met for a third time that season, in the Copa del Rey final.

The lead-up was every bit as civil as you'd expect. Javier Clemente called Maradona 'stupid and castrated' and suggested that he had 'no human qualities whatsoever'. Barcelona's Menotti responded by saying, 'Barcelona is prepared to respond to a determined violence with the same violence'"

This didn't bode well for a calm, friendly atmosphere when 100,000 fans piled into Santiago Bernabéu in Madrid for the cup final. Even the king, Juan Carlos I, was in attendance.

Any hope of the match being a healing moment between the two sides was dashed before the game even started. A minute's silence for a group of Barcelona fans recently killed in a car accident was ruined by Bilbao fans who chanted, 'Qué se jodan!', which translates to the wonderfully sympathetic, 'F— them!'

The game itself was a rather dull affair in terms of the skill on display, suggesting that Bilbao's strategy of turning these games into a contest of physicality was effective at neutralising Barcelona's stars. Bilbao scored relatively early and then defended for dear life

---

* People say 'revenge is a dish best served cold', but I can't agree at all. I like my revenge hot – almost instantaneous if possible. Why would I want to wait years, even decades? Revenge is like soup: it's only good hot.

with brutal, dirty tactics. That one goal was enough – Bilbao had won the league and cup double.

In celebration, they were as graceful as ever. Unused substitute Miguel Ángel Solá gestured at Maradona as he was leaving the pitch and told him to, 'F— off.'

Maradona snapped. A year of provocation finally got to him. He ran at Solá, who was on his knees in celebration, and kneed him square in the face, knocking him out cold. He then turned and began attacking other Bilbao players, launching a series of high-flying kicks and roundhouse punches.

Suddenly it was on for one and all: players and support staff all punching and kicking whoever was wearing the opposition colours.

Riot police and paramedics entered the fray, stretchering people off. TV crews and photographers were innocent victims, hit by objects thrown by the crowd, knocking some of them out. Dozens of people were injured.

In the middle of the melee, Goiko – right in the centre of the vortex of violence he had instigated – still managed to kick Maradona in the chest.

This brawl marked the high point of the violence between the two clubs.

Barcelona's manager Menotti returned home to Argentina after the season. When Argentinian football seems the less violent option, you know things have gone a bit far.

After that season Maradona made his exit too, joining Italian club Napoli and going on to worldwide superstardom. He never forgave the Butcher of Bilbao and later in life he claimed that Goiko's tackle had led to the cocaine problems that plagued a lot of his career.

As for the Butcher of Bilbao, he showed all the remorse you'd expect. To this day, Andoni Goikoetxea displays at his home, in a protective glass box, like a trophy hunter showing off his spoils, the boots he wore when he injured Diego Maradona.

A DIPLOMATIC INCIDENT

While the political situation in Spain underpinned the sporting battles between Bilbao and Barcelona, acts of physical intimidation on the field can themselves turn previously friendly countries against each other, with cries of 'cheat!' rising to the highest levels of government.

Every now and then a sportsperson comes along who transcends their sport, performing at such a lofty level that they become iconic beyond their sport. Think Michael Jordan, Babe Ruth, Pelé, Wayne Gretzky and Muhammad Ali – they all fit this mould.

In cricket, it's Don Bradman. Bradman is so far ahead of any other cricketers, there's no one to even compare him to. It's him, then daylight, then the best players who have ever played cricket.

Bradman's test batting average is 99.94 runs per test, over fifty-two tests. Of any player who has ever played more than twenty

GOD'S HAND IN THINGS

One of the most famous incidents of cheating is Diego Maradona's 'Hand of God'.

Coming just four years after the Falklands War, tensions were high during the 1986 FIFA World Cup quarter final between Argentina and England.

Six minutes into the second half, Maradona rose for a ball against English goalkeeper Peter Shilton. With his left fist held close to his head, Maradona punched the ball into the net, putting Argentina up 1–0. The referee didn't see the handball and the goal stood. The English fans went ballistic.

Only four minutes later, Maradona received the ball in his own half, dribbled 55 metres and weaving past four English players, then slotted home a goal with one of the most ice-cold finishes you'll ever see. It became known as the goal of the century.

Argentina won the game 2–1. England were furious; the illegal goal had made the difference.

Maradona cared very little for the opinions of the English. He said that first goal was scored 'a little with the head of Maradona, and a little with the hand of God'.

tests, the closest to Bradman's mark is current Australian cricketer Steve Smith, who averages 62.84. That's quite a drop-off.

Even more impressive is that over his 234 first-class matches, Bradman averaged 95.14 runs. The next closest is Indian Vijay Merchant, who played 150 first-class matches with an average of 71.64 run.

If you're not familiar with cricket, being about thirty runs better than anyone else in the history of the game is just nonsense. If it hadn't happened, you wouldn't believe it.

It's quite possible that no one has dominated their sport quite like Bradman did his. The only time I've seen anyone come close to Bradman's level, in terms of outdoing the rest of humanity, was a guy I used to work with called Dave. His skill was putting people offside. He was on a whole other level – sometimes he didn't even have to talk. It wasn't a great skill to have in a sales role.

Bradman, off the field, was said to not be far off Dave in the personality stakes. But on the field, he was a living god. He terrified other teams, and they all came up with different strategies to deal with his exceptional batting.

Having a strategy rarely worked, though. English captain Walter Hammond once said, 'On one or two occasions, when he was well set, and when he saw me move a fieldsman, he would raise his gloved hand to me in mock salute and then hit the ball exactly over the place from which the man had been moved!'

When the English cricket team toured Australia for the Ashes in 1932–33, they'd developed a new strategy for dealing with Bradman: they were going to physically intimidate him and, if possible, hurt him.

England's captain Douglas Jardine ordered his fast bowlers, Bill Voce and Harold Larwood, to bowl short-pitched balls and aim them at the bodies of the Australian batsmen, and Bradman in particular.

The intimidation tactic was highly effective. As a result of these orders, Australia's batsmen were hit twenty-five times over the five-match series. Bradman was hit twice.

But when fast bowlers bowl a rock-hard ball at 150 to 160 km/h, things get dangerous very quickly. Add to that the fact that back then batsmen didn't wear helmets, and it meant the results could be fatal.* The bodyline strategy was legally questionable, but it was certainly not within the spirit of cricket.

On the second day of the third test, in Adelaide, the simmering anger at the ground was palpable. And then it erupted.

Harold Larwood hit Australia's Bill Woodfull in the heart, causing him to double over in pain for several minutes. The crowd almost rioted. Police had to come onto the boundary to stop a pitch invasion. With Woodfull bent over and in serious pain, Jardine simply said, 'Well bowled, Harold.'

The next day was equally fraught. Bert Oldfield mis-hit a hook shot off Larwood's bowling and fractured his own skull.

Off the field, things escalated quickly too. The Australian Board of Control for Cricket sent a cable to the Marylebone Cricket Club in London, who ran English cricket:

> Bodyline bowling has assumed such proportions as to menace the best interests of the game, making protection of the body by the batsman the main consideration.
>
> This is causing intensely bitter feeling between the players, as well as injury. In our opinion it is unsports-manlike. Unless stopped at once it is likely to upset

---

* An old cricket joke goes that the first box was used in cricket in 1874 but the first cricket helmet was only used in 1974 – it took men 100 years to realise that their head was also important.

the friendly relations existing between Australia and
England.

At that time the two countries did enjoy a very close relationship,
with many Australians proud of being part of the British Empire.
Bodyline is what changed that.

The English reacted with outrage at being called unsportsmanlike, and tensions rose to the highest political levels. The South
Australian governor took up the issue with the British Secretary of
State for Dominion Affairs, suggesting the ill feeling could affect
trade between the two countries.

Suddenly a trade war was on the cards, and it was because of
a game of cricket.

It got to the point where Australia's prime minister, Joseph
Lyons, had to step in. He told the Australian Board of Control
to withdraw the 'unsportsmanlike' remark, as the damage to the
economy would be severe if trade with Britain was affected. The
Board withdrew the remark and the series continued.

The English continued to use bodyline bowling in the final two
tests of the series. The English departed Australian shores with
a 4–1 win, and the Ashes. They also left hated by the Australian
public, with Jardine reviled to this day.

The use of bodyline tactics declined after this series and was
soon outlawed. Australia returned to England in 1934 and, with
bodyline banned, the Australians regained the Ashes, with Bradman
dominating the English bowlers.

BOUNTY HUNTERS

Sporting tactics designed to injure opponents didn't end with
Bodyline, of course. The NBA's Detroit Pistons, for example for-
mulated similar plans to deal with Michael Jordan, another
transcendent talent. Aside from some tactical points, the 'Jordan

Rules' mainly consisted of thumping him whenever he went near the basket.

But some sports just lend themselves better to injuring people, with American Football particularly coming to mind.

The NFL's NFC East division contains four teams: the Dallas Cowboys, the New York Giants, the Philadelphia Eagles and the Washington Redskins.*

What the NFC East lacks in adherence to geographical accuracy, it makes up for in bitterness and violence.

All four teams enjoy strong rivalries, but when head coach Buddy Ryan joined Philadelphia in 1986 there was one team he already hated: the Dallas Cowboys.

Former Eagles linebacker Seth Joyner, who played for Ryan, explained, 'Buddy hated Dallas before he even came to Philadelphia. He was the perfect coach to run this team. It was heightened, because he was pissed off that they self-proclaimed themselves "America's team".'

Like all bad nicknames, it was one they had given themselves.** In a 1978 highlight film the Cowboys produced, the narrator said, 'They appear on television so often that their faces are as familiar to the public as presidents and movie stars. They are the Dallas Cowboys, "America's Team".'

Adding to Ryan's hatred, during the 1987 player strike over the collective bargaining agreement with franchise owners, the Cowboys had run up the score on the Eagles. Several big-name players had crossed the picket line to play for Dallas and they beat up on an Eagles side made up of fill-in players, winning 41–22.

Running up the score is already very bad form in the NFL.

---

*   In 2020, the Washington Redskins agreed to drop the 'Redskins' part of their name due to its racist connotations. At the time of writing we don't know what their new name will be, but I'm excited to find out what minority group they're going to offend.

** Giving yourself a nickname is always a bad idea. Even if you get people to use it, they'll call you something different behind your back.

Doing it with players who many saw as scabs wasn't going to help, especially when you'd already committed the cardinal sin of giving yourself a nickname.

The next game between the two teams, with all the Eagles' players back on the field, Philadelphia were leading 30–20 with not long left in the game. The Eagles' quarterback Randall Cunningham took two knee downs, which ends the play but keeps the clock running down. It's normal to run the clock down like that at the end of games when you're leading, to avoid risking a turnover; it signals the game is really over.

On what everyone assumed would be a third knee down, and the end of the game, Cunningham passed instead, drawing a pass interference call, and then the Eagles ran it in for a touchdown, making the final score 37–20.

It was the football equivalent of spitting in someone's face.

The next year on Thanksgiving Day the two teams faced off again. During the second half kick-off the Eagles' Jessie Small, a 190-centimetre, 109-kilogram rookie linebacker, made a beeline for the Cowboys kicker, the 175-centimetre, 77-kilogram Luis Zendejas.

Small collided with Zendejas like an irresistible force meeting an incredibly movable object. Kickers aren't built for the physical side of American football, they're there to kick and nothing else.

In fact, Small had gone past several Cowboys he should have blocked as part of his defensive role in order to take out the one guy on the field who wasn't there to tackle.

Zendejas went down. Hard. When he got up, he could barely stand.

Today, a hit like that would get you suspended. But in 1989, Zendejas, who had crouched down to try to minimise the force of the hit, was penalised for a low block.

Zendejas had crouched down well in advance of Small's arrival because he knew the hit was coming before the play even started. He knew he was a target.

Zendejas had played for the Eagles before being cut from their roster. When he left Philadelphia, he hadn't left happy. He'd been furious that Buddy Ryan had got someone else to break the news to him that he was cut, publicly labelling Ryan as 'classless'. Then he'd joined the team Ryan hated the most, the Cowboys.

That was why he was a target for the Eagles, but the reason he knew about it was that he'd been warned by the Eagles' special-teams coach, Al Roberts. According to Zendejas, Ryan had promised the Eagles players $200 for anyone who took out the kicker; Zendejas had a bounty on his head.

Despite being very wobbly after the hit, Zendejas made his way toward the Eagles' sideline, yelling at the Eagles before some teammates restrained him.

Zendejas said after the game, 'If I could've stood on my two legs, I would've gone over and decked [Ryan]. We'll play again in two weeks. If I see him then, I'll deck him then. Honestly, I will.'

As the game ended, Dallas's head coach Jimmy Johnson, who was in his first year as coach, headed onto the field to confront Buddy Ryan. But Ryan had already left the field, skipping the traditional coaches' face-to-face that occurs after every NFL game.

When asked about Ryan leaving, Johnson told the media, 'Oh, I would have said something to Buddy, but he wouldn't stand on the field long enough. He put his big fat rear end into the dressing room.'

Ray Didinger of the *Philadelphia Daily News* was covering the game. He reported that Ryan hadn't fled to avoid Johnson. 'It was true Ryan left the field as soon as the game ended, but he did that every week. He didn't believe in post-game handshakes. Professional courtesy wasn't his thing.'

Didinger was also present after the game when Small approached Zendejas and said, 'I was just doing my job.' The Cowboys' kicker responded, 'You know what you were doing. You all know what you were doing.' When an Eagles' trainer then offered his hand to Zendejas by way of an apology it was slapped away.

Ryan was not in an apologetic mood after the game. He denied a bounty had been put on Zendejas, remarking, 'Why would I place a bounty on a kicker who can't kick worth a damn?'

In response to Johnson's insult about 'his big fat rear end', Ryan joked, 'I resent that. I've been on a diet; I lost a couple of pounds. I thought I was looking good, and he goes and calls me fat. I kind of resent that.'

Zendejas decided to double down on the fat shaming,* 'It's stupid to have a coach like that in the NFL, the fat little guy. He can't take you out himself so he pays somebody else to do it for him. That's about as low as you can get.'

Ryan was forced to admit he offered $100 'bonuses' to his players, but he said they were only paid for important events in a game. No one really believed this, and Ron Wolfley, who playing for the Phoenix Cardinals at the time, said he'd heard the Eagles had a bounty on him during the 1987 season.

It was also reported that in a game between the Eagles and the Chicago Bears in the 1989 season Ryan had put bounties on Bears' quarterback Mike Tomczak and their wide receiver Dennis McKinnon.

Even more surprising was that Ryan had allegedly put a bounty on Chicago head coach Mike Ditka, who he'd feuded with publicly in the media. Apparently Ryan had offered money to any player who took out Ditka while he was coaching from the sidelines.

Ryan never admitted to putting bounties on players, but years later a former player of his, Seth Joyner, was asked about what had by then been dubbed the 'Bounty Bowl' and said, 'I will not deny

---

* 'Fat shaming' didn't exist in the eighties. In fact, it was pretty much free rein back then.

today. I will confirm that there was a bounty on Luis Zendejas and it wasn't $200, it was for $10,000.'

THE WORST FANS IN THE WORLD

While the NFL began investigating the fallout from the Bounty Bowl, the two teams were scheduled to meet each other again in two weeks' time.

This time the game would be played in Philadelphia's Veterans Stadium. That's important because Philadelphia are considered to have the worst fans possibly in the world, but certainly in America.

Consider some of the things Philadelphia fans have done over the years:

- When a Santa appeared at half-time during an Eagles game, the entire stadium pelted him with snowballs.
- When the Washington Redskins' controversial unofficial mascot Chief Zee once visited Veterans Stadium he was attacked in the stands. The feathers that he wore in his headdress were ripped off his head and tossed away. Then, after the game, he was attacked by Eagles fans in the parking lot. They broke his leg.
- In two separate incidents, different Eagles fans punched police horses.
- While being ejected for poor behaviour, a fan made himself vomit on an 11-year-old girl and her father. The dad was an off-duty cop.
- When the Dallas Cowboys' star receiver Michael Irvin sustained an injury in a 1999 game and wasn't moving on the field, the Eagles fans cheered. Even the Eagles' players tried to get them to stop. They didn't. They cheered again when a cart came on to the field to take Irvin off. It turned out he had suffered a spinal injury that ended his career.

- In 2016, when Philadelphia Phillies slugger Ryan Howard was struggling, a fan threw a beer bottle at him.
- When fans of the Philadelphia Flyers were given commemorative wristbands in honour of Flyers owner Ed Snider, who had passed away from bladder cancer a week before, they threw them all on the ice. The game had to be stopped so they could be removed and the Flyers received a delay-of-game penalty.
- Philadelphia fans have thrown D batteries at players, including St Louis Cardinals outfielder JD Drew and, more surprisingly, the Eagles' own quarterback, Doug Pederson.

This being the circumstances surrounding the Cowboys' visit to Buddy Ryan's Eagles, just two weeks after the hit on Zendejas, the media helped calm things down – CBS promoted the game as 'Bounty Bowl II'.

Unlike the first game, there were no big hits. But the Eagles fans, in the snow-filled stadium, pelted the Cowboys players, the NFL officials and even their own players with snowballs – hard, icy snowballs.

They even pelted the CBS commentary team, with commentator Verne Lundquist remarking during the call, 'I gotta tell you what a joy it is to come to Philadelphia and stand here and dodge ice balls – not snowballs, but ice balls – about twenty-five of which have been thrown into the booth in the last three minutes. This is really fun.'

THE SAINTS COME MARCHING IN

While the Bounty Bowls became the most famous incident of bounties being put on players, there had long been a culture of teams and individuals doing it.

The NFL has always frowned on this practice, in part because they don't want players to get injured, but mainly because payments outside the salary cap upset them. To understand the NFL, always remember they put money above everything else. It makes their decisions incredibly easy to understand, and they don't do very much to hide it.

In 2009, rumours that the New Orleans Saints were running a bounty scheme began to surface publicly. People within the league already thought it existed, but that season's NFC Championship game made the media and public sit up and take notice.

The game was between the New Orleans Saints and the Minnesota Vikings, with the winner going on to play in the Super Bowl. Indeed, the Saints won this game and went on to win the Super Bowl, but it was the way they had gone out of their way to try and hurt Vikings quarterback Brett Favre that drew a lot of interest. The Vikings complained to the NFL about it, who launched a two-and a-half year on-again-off-again investigation.

What it ultimately revealed was that the Saints operated a rather sophisticated bounty system. Between twenty-two and twenty-seven defensive players put money into a pool, out of which the bounties were paid.

The mastermind behind the scheme was defensive coordinator Gregg Williams, who had been hired by the Saints to turn around one of the worst defences in the league. Williams relished this task – he was determined to make the Saints defence feared – and the bounty system was key to that.

Players could make money for legal plays, like causing a turnover, but also for injuring opponents. If you took a player out of the game with a hit, you got $1500. If you got a 'cart off' – a player having to be helped off the ground – you got $1000.

The scheme targeted star quarterbacks such as Aaron Rodgers, Cam Newton and Kurt Warner. Williams would take the money, recording everything in a ledger, and then stand up in front of the defensive team the week after a game and hold up envelopes full of cash. As he handed them out for the various actions on the field, the players would chant, 'Give it back! Give it back! Give it back!', with players regularly paying the cash back into the pool and increasing the payouts.

By the time of the NFC Championship game against the Vikings, in January 2010, the stakes had risen to the point that defensive captain Jonathan Vilma offered $10,000 to any player who knocked Brett Favre out of the game.

As the investigation slowly gathered steam, with leaks and documents confirming the details of the scheme, an audio tape was leaked of Williams addressing his defensive unit before the 2011 wildcard game against the San Francisco 49ers. Williams urged his players to injure various key players on the 49ers.

On Michael Crabtree, the 49ers wide receiver, he said, 'We need to decide whether Crabtree wants to be a fake-ass prima donna or he wants to be a tough guy. We need to find out. He becomes human when we f— take out that outside ACL.'

And on quarterback Alex Smith: 'Every single one of you, before you get off the pile, affect the head. Early, affect the head. Continue, touch, and hit the head.'

This isn't the sort of thing the NFL or their broadcast partners were keen on the public hearing. It had been a long time since marketing a game as a 'Bounty Bowl' was considered a good idea.

Finally, in March 2012, the NFL came down hard on the Saints. They were fined $500,000 – the maximum amount allowed by the NFL's constitution – and had to forfeit their second-round draft picks in 2012 and 2013. Their head coach, Sean Payton, was suspended for the entire 2012 season for not doing enough to stop the scheme.

Several players also received suspensions, but this was eventually overturned, with the NFL believing the real blame lay with the Saints organisation.

As for Williams, he was suspended indefinitely. Although it turns out in the NFL 'indefinitely' means twelve months. He was back as a senior assistant defensive coach for the Tennessee Titans by 2013 and is now the defensive coordinator for the New York Jets. It might seem amazing that he was ever allowed back in the game, but others would argue having to work for the Jets is a significant punishment in itself.

Williams later apologised for his role in the scheme. 'It was a terrible mistake, and we knew it was wrong while we were doing it. Instead of getting caught up in it, I should have stopped it.'

Fair enough, we've all been caught up in a scheme to maim people in the workplace at some stage in our lives.

Williams certainly got caught up in this culture of cheating – well before this iteration of the scheme, in fact. Years before 'Bountygate', in 1990, Williams' first job in the NFL was as the special-teams coordinator for the Houston Oilers. His boss back then? None other than Buddy Ryan.

ICING AN OPPONENT

Purposefully injuring someone on the field is something NFL players and coaches have mastered over the years, but they're actually light-weights in this field of endeavour.

Waiting till you're on the field leaves a lot to chance. A better way to make sure someone is unable to compete – and to show you're truly committed to winning at any cost – is to injure them off the field.

You won't find that level of aggression in American Football, though. For Mafia-like hits, you have to turn to that most brutal of sports: Olympic figure-skating.

Nancy Kerrigan and Tonya Harding had been teammates on the US women's team at the 1992 Olympics, and as the 1994 Winter

Olympics* approached they were once again battling it out for a spot on the team.

The two were very different skaters. Kerrigan was seen as graceful, the perfect image of a figure-skater, while Harding was powerful – she was the first American woman to perform a triple axel, an incredibly complex move.**

Kerrigan was always portrayed in the media as an upper-class American princess, but she actually had a working-class background. While Harding's background has been exhaustively profiled, Kerrigan continues to be misunderstood. She worked incredibly hard to become a world-class skater and her father worked three jobs to fund her career.

The two were often played off against each other. Kerrigan was dressed on the ice by fashion designer Vera Wang, while Harding wore homemade outfits. But this was mainly because Harding had always been a controversial figure – she was not exactly easy for sponsors and designers to deal with.

As the Olympics approached, both skaters were preparing for the US Figure Skating Championships, where positions on the Olympic team would be decided.

Days out from the championships, on 6 January 1994, Kerrigan had just finished training at the Cobo Arena in Detroit when a man approached her and hit her with a metal object just above her knee.

A camera caught the aftermath: Kerrigan on the ground, screaming in pain, yelling through tears, 'Why? Why? Why? Why me?' The footage was soon running on every news channel as the world became obsessed with this sporting whodunnit.

---

*   The 1994 Winter Olympics Games were the first to be held in a different year from the Summer Olympics, meaning that year they occurred only two years after the previous Winter Olympics.

** I should know. I tried it once at the local ice rink and took out six kids having a lesson. People were very upset. It was the first and last time I tried ice skating.

In the days following the attack, an FBI investigation into the attack on Kerrigan took place at the same time as the US Figure Skating Championships continued.

For Kerrigan, the news was much better than first expected. The blow had landed above her knee, causing extensive bruising, but it hadn't broken any bones. Participating in the national championships was impossible – they started two days after the attack – but there was a chance she would be ready in time for the Olympics.

Meanwhile, Harding easily secured her place in the US Olympic team, winning gold at the national championships. But there was good news for Kerrigan, too; despite being unable to compete, the other skaters agreed to give her a spot on the Olympic team. Both Harding and Kerrigan were off to the Olympics.

A MOTLEY CREW

There was good news for the FBI, too. Their investigation had made a breakthrough.

The day before the championships, a woman refusing to identify herself had phoned the Detroit deputy police chief Benny Napoleon, who she'd seen on TV discussing the case. The woman claimed to have heard a tape where four men planned the attack on Kerrigan.

Napoleon made a note of the names of the men and began investigating. It was an interesting group the anonymous woman had presented him with.

First on the list was an unemployed man named Jeff Gillooly, Tonya Harding's ex-husband – although the two seemed to be back together.

Then there was Shawn Eckhardt, a long-time friend of Gillooly's. He was head of World Bodyguard Services, a business so successful he ran it from his parents' house. His only real client was Harding, and even that was more of a favour.

Next was another friend of Gillooly's, Derrick Smith, who was also unemployed but had a plan to open a 'paramilitary survival school' in the Arizona desert.

The last person on the list was Smith's nephew, Shane Stant, a high school dropout and not much else. He had an interest in bodybuilding but, beyond that, Stant had managed to fail at everything he'd ever done.

It was a crew right out of a Coen brothers movie.

With a promising group of suspects now identified, the FBI began applying pressure to the men, who collapsed faster than Kerrigan's knee. As the details of their plan were revealed, the FBI soon realised that these were not the most sophisticated criminals.

The plan had begun simply enough, with Gillooly complaining to Shawn Eckardt about the possibility of Harding not making the Olympics. This was something Gillooly was intensely concerned about. Harding was his avenue to money. Her missing the Olympics would result in some terrible outcomes for him, like having to get a job.

Eckardt was very understanding. Harding was technically his only client, and he was almost as invested in her success as Gillooly was.

What happened next is contested, but one of the men came up with the idea to take out Harding's main competitor, Nancy Kerrigan. Eckardt warmed to the idea quickly. He had the notion that an attack on a top figure skater would have other skaters flocking to his World Bodyguard Services. It could help him realise his dream of not living with his parents.

Derrick Smith rang Eckardt not long after this discussion, about something else entirely, but Eckardt couldn't help himself and told Smith all about the plan. Smith refused to do it himself, but he knew the perfect person for the job.

It was a loose use of the word 'perfect'; Smith had in mind his nephew, Shane Stant. It was like saying you had the perfect person to paint the Sistine Chapel ceiling when you were referring to your unemployed nephew who had never held a paintbrush in his life.

Smith briefed his nephew about the very loose plan and Stant expressed interest. He was offered $6800 to do the job and he accepted.

This is how terrible things happen: several different layers of stupidity all come together to create something spectacularly stupid.

With the crew now assembled, planning got underway. Discussions turned to what to do to prevent Kerrigan participating in the national championships. Eckardt was keen to do something drastic; he floated the idea of running Kerrigan off the road, but this was shot down by the others. Stant recalled later, 'There was initial talk of cutting her Achilles tendon, which obviously would cripple her. I didn't think it was necessary. I wasn't willing to do that.'

Both Gillooly and Stant told the FBI that Eckardt said to them, 'Wouldn't it be easier to just kill her?' and talked about where he could position a sniper with a rifle. This suggestion was ignored.

Eventually the plan to cripple her landing leg was agreed upon. Stant went to a store called Spy Headquarters and purchased a black, 21-inch retractable tactical baton for $58.56.

The only remaining problem was that they didn't know where Kerrigan was. Gillooly claimed that Harding assisted with that, something Harding denied.

According to Gillooly's FBI statement, Harding called Vera Marano, a journalist, asking for Kerrigan's home address. She said she had a bet about where Kerrigan trained and that she also needed her to sign a poster.

Marano was later interviewed by the FBI and confirmed this call. She said she managed to get details of where Kerrigan trained – Tony Kent Arena on Cape Cod – and passed on this detail to Harding by leaving the information on her answering machine. Marano said she never passed on Kerrigan's home address.

It still took some time for Smith and Stant to track down Kerrigan. She'd moved from training at Cape Cod to Detroit, and Smith and Stant drove back and forth trying to locate her in a comedy of errors.

Eventually Stant arrived in Detroit, where he stayed at a Super 8 motel, cleverly using his real name. He also used his credit card to rent a VHS player* and some X-rated movies.

The next day Stant made his way to the Cobo Arena for surveillance. He found security to be almost non-existent and spent forty-five minutes wandering around, heading down to ice level and also into the corridor leading to the skaters' locker rooms. No one said a thing to him.

He also found an exit with Plexiglas doors and decided that would be his escape route – he told Smith that he should wait outside those doors with the car.

The next day, Stant arrived in time for Kerrigan's practice, and being the absolute professional that he was, he didn't recognise her and had to ask a spectator to point her out. When Kerrigan finished her skate, Stant followed her down the corridor to the locker rooms. Kerrigan was chatting with a newspaper reporter.

This was his chance. He approached, walked between his target and the reporter, pulled out the retractable baton, and quickly struck at Kerrigan's knee. She screamed. Despite being the perfect guy for the job, he missed her knee. He also hit her just once, because then he panicked and ran.

When he got to his exit point, the Plexiglas doors, unlike the day before, they were locked with a chain. Stant got through them

* For younger readers, a VHS player was a machine that played 'tapes' with movies on them. This was before streaming. If you wanted to watch something, you usually had to go somewhere that rented out movies on these cassettes. If the movie wasn't there, you couldn't watch it. None of this 'watch whatever you want whenever you want'. We had it tough back then. It once took me six weeks to track down a copy of *The Fugitive*, but that sort of struggle has made me the man I am today.

by ramming his head into them several times and crawling through the hole he made.

Outside he briefly lay on the footpath, recovering, and then picked himself up and ran, throwing the baton under a parked car. Naturally he ran in the wrong direction – away from where Smith was waiting with the car – and Smith had to go get him.

But the job was done. Not perfectly, but the fact that these guys had actually pulled it off shocked even them; none of them had ever come through on anything in their lives.

Crimes, though, are like a triple axel: you have to nail the landing for it to count.

SOMEONE ELSE'S TRASH

Unfortunately for this super slick crew, by 11 January, not even a week after the attack, Gillooly had confessed everything to the FBI. Charges were laid against all four men.

Part of the reason the FBI tracked down the four men so quickly was that Eckardt, he of 'World Bodyguard Services' and an obvious high-level operator in the security industry, 'couldn't stop bragging to everybody that he had planned the attack.' Even before the actual attack took place, he had a friend listen to an audiotape of the four men discussing their plan, telling him he'd made the recording in case he needed to blackmail the other three.

As soon as the FBI started interviewing him, Gillooly implicated Harding in the planning of the attack. He claimed Harding's only reservations had been about Eckardt being able to organise such a plan.

Harding denied all accusations she had any prior knowledge of the attack, issuing a statement that said, 'Despite my mistakes and rough edges, I have done nothing to violate the standards of excellence in sportsmanship that are expected in an Olympic athlete.'

Meanwhile, in Portland, a woman by the name of Kathy

Peterson had discovered that someone had dumped their trash in the dumpster behind her restaurant, the Dockside Saloon. This happened often enough to drive Kathy mad, and she opened up the bag to see if she could identify whose trash it was. She found a cheque stub from the US Figure Skating Association made out to Tonya Harding and an envelope containing handwritten notes about where Nancy Kerrigan practised and when.

Peterson had heard all about the attack – it was the leading story in the news – and called the FBI. The FBI would later prove the handwriting was Tonya Harding's.

While this was all going on, the US Olympics Committee had decided to bar Harding from competing in the Olympics, but Harding sued them for $25 million dollars. The committee, while deeply suspicious of Harding's denials, backed down; there was no clear evidence she had any prior knowledge of the attack. The FBI said they were still building their case.

Harding, despite all that had gone on, was allowed to compete at the Olympics.

In Lillehammer, the games were finally getting underway, and Kerrigan and Harding had to share the ice during the American team's practice session.

The two skaters coming together for the first time since the attack resulted in a media frenzy, with 700 journalists showing up at the practice. So over the top was the coverage that *Sports Illustrated* calculated the closest the two skaters come together was 31 inches (78.74 centimetres).

Kerrigan had made a miraculous recovery just to be there. Immediately after the attack she had committed herself to an exhausting rehabilitation regime, and she seemed to skate well during the practice.

In a sign she didn't believe Harding's protests of innocence, at the training session, in front of the world's media, Kerrigan wore the outfit she had been wearing when she was attacked. Asked about it afterwards, she told the media, 'Humour is good, it's empowering.'

Finally, on the night of competition, Harding started her program but stopped midway through to show the judges that the laces on one of her skates had broken. The judges allowed her to redo her routine, but she performed nowhere near her usual level, finishing eighth.

Kerrigan did the opposite: she skated one of the best programs of her life, an amazing response after all she'd been through. The crowd responded with a standing ovation and threw flowers on the ice as she skated off in full contention for the gold medal.

However, the fairytale ending much of the world had been hoping for was upended by the sixteen-year-old Ukrainian Oksana Baiul, who beat Kerrigan by a tenth of a point. Despite only receiving silver, the mental and physical strength Kerrigan showed in her comeback made hers one of the all-time great Olympic performances.

A fortnight after the Olympics, Harding pled guilty to 'conspiring to hinder prosecution'. Her story, after denying any knowledge for months, was that she knew about the attack only after it occurred, but then didn't tell police about what she knew. Harding was sentenced to three years' probation and received a $160,000 fine.

Both Gillooly and Eckardt plead guilty to racketeering to avoid heavier charges. Gillooly was sentenced to two years in prison and Eckardt was sentenced to eighteen months. Smith and Stant both plead guilty to conspiracy to commit second-degree assault and were sentenced to eighteen months in prison.

Who would have thought such a cunning plan could come undone so easily?

THE REAL VICTIM

What stands out when reviewing the Tonya Harding story is that it is the Tonya Harding story. Nancy Kerrigan, the actual victim, is given a very small role in the way the story is told.

The 2017 film *I, Tonya* goes out of its way to paint Harding as a victim in the whole saga, when a closer examination rips that idea apart.

Harding's long-held position that she knew nothing about the attack has always been laughable at best, but she stuck to the story all through the FBI investigation. She even refused to admit she knew who had committed the attack until after the Olympics. That's extraordinary.

These denials were all happening while Gillooly was implicating her in the entire plan. Now, you have to take Gillooly's claims with a grain of salt – he and Harding had a highly combustible relationship, including accusations of violence, which he has always denied. But, overall, Gillooly's FBI statement is very accurate and aligns with what the other accomplices said, as well as the statement given by journalist Vera Marano, who confirmed it was Harding who rang her to track down Kerrigan.

The handwritten notes of Kerrigan's practice times, written by Harding, add further weight to Gillooly's claims that she was in on the plan.

Then there is the fact that, in an ABC News' two-hour special that aired in 2018, *Truth and Lies: The Tonya Harding Story*, Harding completely changed her story, for the first time admitting she 'knew something was up' before the attack.

Harding told ABC News she suspected something about a month or two before the attack. 'I did, however, overhear them talking about stuff, where, "Well, maybe we should take somebody out so we can make sure she gets on the team." And I remember telling them, I go, "What the hell are you talking about? I can skate."

'This was, like, a month or two months before [the attack]. But they were talking about skating and saying, "Well, maybe somebody should be taken out so then, you know, she can make it."'

After claiming for fourteen years she had no knowledge of the attack, suddenly Harding admitted on national television that she had some knowledge of it. It makes you question her entire story. Which version is the truth? Is either of them true?

And, as always happens, it's the cheat that gets all the attention. Nancy Kerrigan had devoted her life to becoming a great skater, and despite being attacked just months out from the Olympics, she overcame enormous physical and mental challenges to come within a tenth of a point of winning gold.

It shouldn't have to be said, but Nancy Kerrigan is the victim. Tonya Harding is the epitome of the morally corrupt cheat, who let someone else do her dirty work instead of being an honest competitor.

We are always more fascinated by bad behaviour than good, but Nancy Kerrigan should be the name we remember.

CHAPTER 7

DODGY EQUIPMENT

While injuring people is fine for some, not everyone has the stomach for it. A simpler way to gain an advantage, and one that works in many sports, is to ensure you have better gear than everyone else.

If there's equipment in sport, you can count on the fact that people have tried to modify it – making it longer, shorter, heavier, lighter, stronger, more flexible, faster. You name it, they've done it.

And, in response, sporting bodies have gone out of their way to stop competitors from modifying equipment, passing new rules and regulations, and going to all sorts of lengths to catch the cheats. But often people aren't strictly cheating with their equipment, they are just pushing the envelope on what's allowed. And, sometimes, the modification of equipment is so clever that even those enforcing the rules have to marvel at it.

THE REGULATORY WALTZ

Sometimes, fiddling with the equipment forces the rules to be changed. The design of tennis racquets and golf clubs constantly tests the regulations, and swimming has had similar issues with full-body swimsuits.

Take for example NHL Hall of Fame goalkeeper Tony Esposito, who in 1969 sowed a piece of mesh between his legs to stop pucks from going through them. It basically formed a web and took away a common avenue to goal. It was genius, and not even illegal at the time. During a game, however, a shot went into this web, only to slingshot straight back out and almost take off the shooter's head.

The NHL quickly moved to ban such equipment, but NHL goalies have never stopped trying to innovate with wider pads and bigger sticks.

Ice hockey skaters are no different. There are regulations on how curved and how long their sticks can be, but players find ways to get around them.*

Jamie Baker, who played for numerous NHL teams over a ten-year career, said when he played he just had three sticks. 'One stick was for regular play; it was probably illegal. I had one stick I was sure was legal, for the end of the game. And one stick for penalty killing – it was too long.'

In any sport, the back and forth between athletes, equipment manufacturers and administrators is a regulatory dance – a dance that will never end.

Rally car driving, like all motorsports, involves enormous amounts of tuning and tweaks to the car, given the equipment is arguably the most important part of the sport. Race car design is in itself an attempt to beat other people, and rules brought in to make things safer or more even are tested constantly.

---

* Depending on the type of curve, players can get greater control when carrying the puck across the ice and greater control when launching wrist shots.

In the mid-nineties, the Fédération Internationale de l'Automobile (FIA), the governing body of motorsport, wanted to slow down the rally cars a bit. Watch any rally event and you'll understand why. It's incredibly dangerous; curvy roads, often unmade, lined with trees and rocks and, even worse, spectators.

Standing next to a road where almost-out-of-control cars are being driven at breakneck speed seems to me to be natural selection at work, but the FIA decided they needed to do something about it. They slowed the cars down by mandating that the turbocharged engines had to be fitted with a restrictor plate, which would limit the amount of air the turbo could draw in, reducing the engine's power.

In 1995, the clever engineers at Toyota Team Europe, as required, installed a restrictor plate in the Celica GT-Four that they were using in the World Rally Championship. But their restrictor plate had an artfully subtle tweak to it.

When examined by the FIA, it was completely legal – it met all the requirements. And the FIA testers knew what they were doing; they could tell that the part was a proper restrictor plate. The Toyota Team Europe's car was fully inspected and passed with flying colours.

The tweak, though, was that their restrictor plate was designed to disengage when installed – installation changed the internal geometry of the part. When the part was taken out to be examined, it clicked back into being a perfectly normal restrictor plate. The very act of taking the plate out to inspect it made an illegal part legal.

The benefits of this were huge. By disengaging when inserted, 25 per cent more air flowed into the turbo engine, giving the car 50 horsepower more than if it worked as it was meant to. In 1995, WRC cars had about 300 horsepower in total, so 50 horsepower was a massive advantage.

So beautifully designed was the part that the FIA only found out about it because someone told them – it was never picked up through inspection.

FIA president Max Mosley seemed almost in awe of the cheating:

> It's the most ingenious thing I have seen in thirty years of motorsport.
>
> Inside it was beautifully made. The springs inside the hose had been polished and machined so not to impede the air which passed through. To force the springs open without the special tool would require substantial force. It is the most sophisticated and ingenious device either I or the FIA's technical experts have seen for a long time. It was so well made that there was no gap apparent to suggest there was any means of opening it.

The Toyota Team Europe was banned for the rest of the 1995 season and the 1996 season too, but the cleverness of their cheat has never been forgotten in motorsport.

However, not all equipment cheats are so clever or so elegant.

MISSION IMPOSSIBLE

Some baseballers modify their bats by placing cork inside them. The theory is it makes the bat lighter to swing, and the spongy nature of the cork makes the ball fly further.* Corked bats are banned, but they can't always be detected, so players routinely try to get away with using them.

Perhaps the most famous incident of a player using one was

---

* Despite this long-held belief, over the years various scientists have tested this theory and discovered that corked bats are worse than normal all-wood bats. It shows you that athletes will do things that don't help them so long as they *think* they will. I guess we all do that sometimes.

when the Chicago Cubs' Sammy Sosa's bat shattered on a pitch, littering the infield with pieces of cork.

Yet that wasn't the weirdest example of someone being caught with a corked bat.

In July 1994, Cleveland Indians slugger Albert Belle was playing the Chicago White Sox. The White Sox's manager, Gene Lamont, had been tipped off that Belle's bat was corked and he told the umpire, Dave Phillips, of his suspicions. It was early in the game, so Phillips confiscated the bat to be investigated once the game finished.

The Cleveland Indians knew this was a problem, because everyone on the team knew Belle's bat was corked. The bat was being kept in the umpire's locker, and as the game progressed the Indians began wondering how to retrieve it.

Indians pitcher Jason Grimsley would later say, 'As I was sitting there, the thought came to my mind: I can get that bat.' He had noticed there was a hatch in the ceiling of the Indians' clubhouse and wondered if there was one in the umpires' dressing room too.

The problem was he couldn't replace the confiscated bat with another one of Belle's because *all* of them were corked. So he got one of Paul Sorrento's, another teammate. He then climbed into the ceiling duct with a flashlight in his mouth and made his way to the umpire's room, like he was a spy in a movie.

It took him between thirty-five and forty minutes to make his way through the hot, dark ventilation duct. At one stage he miscalculated where he was and lifted a tile to the wrong room. 'There was a groundskeeper in there, sitting in there on a couch. I put the tile back down, but he had to know. Thank goodness he didn't say anything.'

Finally arriving at the umpire's room, he dropped down onto a refrigerator and replaced Belle's confiscated bat with Sorrento's, then climbed back into the ceiling and replaced the tile.

'As soon as I got back up, somebody came back in the room. I had to sit there for about two minutes; I was about 20 or 30 feet from somebody.'

It had taken him four innings to pull off the heist.

But it was all for nothing. The minute the game ended, the umpires went back into their room and saw that the floor was covered in plaster dust from the ceiling. They checked the bat and, like all major league bats, it had the owner's name written on it: Paul Sorrento.

Major League Baseball (MLB) threatened to call in the FBI, but said that if the Indians returned Belle's bat they would not ask who had made the switch.

The Indians returned the bat and the MLB made Belle and the Indians' general manager John Hart watch as they sawed into it, proving it was corked. Belle was given a ten-game suspension, reduced to seven games on appeal.

Perhaps most surprising was that anyone was willing to go to such great lengths for Belle, who treated Jason Grimsley to a round of golf for his efforts. Baseball writer Buster Olney once wrote of Belle:

> It was a taken in baseball circles that Albert Belle
> was nuts . . . The Indians billed him $10,000 a year
> for the damage he caused in clubhouses on the road
> and at home, and tolerated his behavior only because
> he was an awesome slugger . . . He slurped coffee
> constantly and seemed to be on a perpetual caffein-
> ated frenzy. Few escaped his wrath: on some days
> he would destroy the post-game buffet . . . launch-
> ing plates into the shower . . . after one poor at-bat
> against Boston, he retreated to the visitors' clubhouse
> and took a bat to teammate Kenny Lofton's boombox.

Belle preferred to have the clubhouse cold, below 60 degrees, and when one chilly teammate turned up the heat, Belle walked over, turned down the thermostat and smashed it with his bat. His nickname, thereafter, was 'Mr Freeze.'

GLUE SNIFFERS

While some baseball players put cork in their bats, professional table tennis players use something a bit more dangerous.*

The illegal practice is known as 'paddle doping', and it has as much of an impact on performance as doping does in other sports. Although I would be careful using the phrase 'paddle doping' without providing some context.

While corking bats is relatively harmless and of dubious benefit to baseballers, paddle doping has enormous benefits and is far from harmless.

In 1978, Hungarian player Tibor Klampár, who went on to have a highly successful career, was training with his brother. He wasn't playing well and, in frustration, he decided to do the table tennis equivalent of a pit stop in racing: he ripped off the rubber on his paddle and attached a new one, hoping that would help. Replacing the rubber on a paddle is a regular thing top players do, it's like restringing a tennis racquet.

But the new rubber didn't help Klampár in this instance – he was still playing poorly. So he ripped off that rubber and used some glue to put the old rubber back on. This time, when he hit the ball, it made a clicking sound.

---

* The table tennis paddle has several names. In the USA they call it a paddle. In Europe and Asia, it's called a bat. The International Table Tennis Federation decided to not side with anyone and officially called it a racket. I call it a paddle in this book because it's funnier.

I noticed that my original rubber had suddenly become much more effective. I was getting greater spin and speed in my strokes. I immediately realised that this had something to do with the glue, and from that moment I began gluing before every training session and before every match. On some occasions I was doing it six times a day.

What Klampár had stumbled on by complete accident was a chemical process that transformed the rubber on the paddles, a revelation that changed table tennis forever.

'It was as if I'd won the jackpot,' Klampár later said.

Solvents from certain types of glue enter the rubber and, in doing so, expand it equally in all directions, providing better grip on the ball when striking it. The larger surface area and greater softness of the rubber gives more control and more spin, but also mean that when you hit the ball the rubber tightens more than usual, making the ball go faster.

The simple act of reapplying this kind of glue to the rubber on your paddle can give you up to 30 per cent more speed and spin. If the process works, it produces that clicking sound Klampár heard.

This is why athletes will push the limits of equipment: sometimes small tweaks can produce enormous outcomes. Paddle doping did that, and it was legal.

Once Klampár discovered paddle doping and started using it in competitive play, the practice spread. Before long, everyone playing at the top level was doing it. Players pushed the process further and further – the more volatile the chemicals in the glue, the stronger the effect. At first it started with the glue used to repair bike tyres, but then volatile organic compounds such as benzene, octane and n-hexane were added.

The practice soon became known as 'speed gluing', due to the fact it made the ball leap off your paddle faster.

Suddenly you had professional table tennis players traveling on planes to tournaments carrying a variety of flammable chemicals and then spending hours in their hotel rooms gluing their paddles.

Every store that sold table tennis equipment at a serious level had more glue than a hardware store, and they were selling it in huge amounts. Even young players started to do speed gluing, emulating the professionals.

By 1992, the practice was widespread. But several worrying developments forced the International Table Tennis Federation (ITTF) to consider the legality of it.

One was an incident at the Scottish Championships where a player knocked over a can of glue and the vapours caused another player to collapse. That wasn't that surprising: these chemical glues were also the type people sniffed to get high.*

Even worse for the ITTF was that scientific research was starting to show the harmful effects of speed gluing. Christian Palierne, a former physician to the French national team, had delivered the report from a research project into speed gluing, and it was scary:

> It has been proved beyond doubt that inhaling solvents during the speedgluing process has side-effects. The trainers must ask themselves whether they really can be answerable for allowing 11–13-year-olds to use speedglue.

Speed gluing, the report revealed, endangered a person's nervous system. It gave them headaches, concentration problems and poor

---

* A table tennis shop in Japan was raided by police because teenagers were buying glue there to do just that.

awareness. Palierne went as far as recommending that anyone gluing their paddles should wear a gasmask.

Other evidence suggested the chemicals often used were linked to cancer.

That was enough for the ITTF. They announced speed gluing would be banned from 1 January 1993.

The response was not what you'd expect: the players reacted furiously. They argued against the ban, believing that it was impossible to enforce. How would the ITTF know what type of glue people were using? The players argued nothing would change, it would just make a legal practice into an illegal one, turning everyone into cheaters.

In response to the players' protests the ITTF backflipped; just two months into the ban they overturned it.

There was truth in the players' argument – there were no reliable ways to measure the chemicals in the glue used on a paddle. Instead the ITTF decided to pass rules that allowed players to use only certain approved glues, ones that were not quite as toxic as the worst of them.

But these glues didn't last as long; they would lose the speed glue effect much more quickly. To compensate, players began to speed glue much more frequently. At tournaments, there would even be an official gluing room, with built-in ventilation systems.

The whole practice was starting to make table tennis look bad. Well-known Swedish player Stellan Bengtsson said:

> In my local club in Falkenberg, on the west coast of Sweden, the top players held their training sessions directly after the beginners. So when parents came into the changing room to collect their youngsters, they saw a dozen guys in track suits wearing gas masks. The bewildered parents thought they'd opened

the wrong door and had stumbled into a chemical warfare defence exercise.

Finally, in 2004, the ITTF again banned solvents in paddle glues and this time they stuck to their decision, despite the players protesting again. Testing machines were introduced that could break down chemicals into ions under an ultraviolet light, which gave a reading of what glues had been used.

In response, a new market sprang up for 'boosters' – substitute glue products that got through the testing machines. These boosters were not without their own problems. One Japanese player who used them suffered a serious reaction and had to be rushed to hospital.

Another problem was that the boosters expanded the rubber a lot more than the earlier glues had, which meant many of the paddles became illegal in another way: exceeding the maximum legal width of the rubber, 4.0 millimetres. This was a big deal; it might not sound like much, but even an increase of 0.2 millimetres is a huge advantage to a professional player.

In 2008 the ITTF took it all a step further, banning all additions to paddles beyond water-based adhesives. Boosters were now banned as well. Better detectors were also brought in for the London 2012 Olympics.

But the arms race between substances that can pass a test and newer detectors continues – the benefit of speed gluing is too great for players to stop trying to do it.

Former world number one Timo Boll said, in 2018, that about 80 per cent of international players were still practising some form of speed gluing. 'The rubbers are treated with chemicals to increase the catapult effect when hitting.'

In response, ITTF president Thomas Weikert admitted it was difficult to detect speed glue, due to the testing process being costly and because the paddle dopers were outpacing those doing the detecting. 'The fact is, at the moment, there is no testing method to detect [what Boll was alleging].'

So next time you go to watch a table tennis match, consider taking a gasmask.

COLD COMFORT

One thing a study of cheating in sport does is teach us that pressure does weird things to people. And it can't always be traced back to inhaling too much glue.

Most cheating, you would assume, is done by athletes struggling to stay up with the competition, or to get that final edge to make them the best. Illogically, this isn't always the case. Quite regularly it is the best athletes who cheat, even though they're already good enough to beat everyone else.

Other times the cheating can be explained away because someone is simply an awful person. They are taking every shortcut they can find, and often have a heap of problems away from the sporting arena too. But this is not always the case either.

Sometimes cheating just makes no sense. Sometimes it can only be explained by the fact that, under pressure, people do strange things. And nothing is stranger than the case of former Soviet pent-athlete Boris Onischenko.

A three-time world champion, Onischenko was a top-level pent-athlete in the seventies. He'd won silver at the 1968 Mexico City games as part of the Soviet team and at the 1972 Munich games he'd led the Soviet team to gold while also capturing silver in the individual category.

The modern pentathlon is a sport steeped in military tradition. It was designed to emulate the original pentathlon from the Ancient Olympics, which featured running, discus, javelin, wrestling and the long jump, skills believed to represent the perfect soldier back in ancient Greece. For the 1912 Olympics it was decided the pent-athlon would be updated to represent the skills of a cavalry officer caught behind enemy lines making his way back to his own side: horse riding, swimming, fencing, pistol shooting and running.

A rumour was Baron Pierre de Coubertin, the founder of the modern Olympics, invented the sport because he was so appalled by the performance of the French army in the Franco–Prussian War (he concluded French men had become weak).

The modern pentathlon was such a militaristic sport that women weren't even accepted into the discipline until after the 1976 Olympics in Montreal.

Leading into the Montreal games, the Soviets were again expected to take gold. The pentathlon began with show jumping, then moved on to the fencing on the second day. The Soviet Union started the day in fourth place, just behind Great Britain. This was no problem at all, there were four events to go and they were well in contention.

Within each team, certain members specialised in particular events. Boris Onischenko, for example, was the best fencer in the entire competition. His first fencing match was against Adrian Parker from Great Britain, who was in their team mainly for his swimming expertise.

British team captain Jim Fox was watching on and was not surprised when Onischenko made short work of his teammate. But the manner in which it happened surprised him. It seemed Onishchenko's épée* had registered a hit on Parker despite, to Fox's eye, not touching him.

In épée events, an electric system is used to score hits. When the tip of the weapon is depressed with a force of 750 grams, it closes an electric circuit, which registers the hit and awards a point.

---

* The sport of fencing has three types of swords: foil, épée and sabre. The épée is the heaviest and in the event where it's used your opponent's entire body is a target, unlike the other two, where strikes only count above the waist.

Fox was next to face Onishchenko. On the Soviet's first thrust, Fox dodged straight backwards and Onishchenko's blade missed him by about 15 centimetres. Despite this, a hit was registered.

The obvious explanation was that Onishchenko's épée was malfunctioning. Fox mentioned this to the officials, who took it away and replaced it with another.

Onishchenko, despite the swap, continued to dominate, defeating Fox. Hardly surprising given he was the best fencer in the competition. But Fox recalled that later, as the two passed each other, Onischenko said to him, 'Jim, I am very sorry.'

This confused Fox, but it soon became clear why Onischenko was apologising. The judges, who had been inspecting what they believed to be a malfunctioning épée, determined that it had in fact been modified on purpose. Onischenko had rigged his épée with a switch hidden in the guard on the handle. All he had to do was press on this switch and it registered a hit.

Quite ingenious, really, but for what purpose? There was no doubt that Onischenko was the superior swordsman in the competition. Even when his modified épée was removed and replaced with a normal one, he easily bested Fox.

On top of that, Onischenko didn't seem the cheating type. Everyone in the sport was fond of him, and in the moments after he was caught and promptly disqualified, he was deeply apologetic, especially to the British team.

'We weren't bosom pals, but we'd often drunk vodka together in the evenings at various competitions, so there was a relationship between Boris and me,' said Fox, who was thrown by the whole thing. He said he was very down after the Onischenko's disqualification – he fenced badly for the rest of that day, then had a terrible day at the pistol range the next. Eventually he rallied, leading the British to the gold medal.

Onischenko's cheating didn't seem to be part of some Soviet

plot, either. His teammates were reportedly furious – they had no chance of winning without him. The Soviet volleyball team threatened to throw him out of a window at the athletes' village.

There was talk Onischenko would be sent to the Siberian salt mines for disgracing the Soviet Union. Instead he was forced to appear before Soviet leader Leonid Brezhnev for a berating and was fined ₽5000 (A$7326).

Brezhnev's dressing down was possibly the biggest clue as to why Onischenko had cheated at an event he dominated anyway. With the Montreal Olympics taking place in the middle of the Cold War, the clash between the Soviet bloc and the Western world was the leading narrative at the games, and the pentathlon meant more than most events because of its military background.

The earliest modern pentathlon was contested only by military officers, and even in 1976 many of the competitors were still in the military.

'What you have to remember is that I was very publicly a member of the British Army and Boris was a half-colonel in the KGB,' explained Fox. '[His disqualification] became a huge international incident. At one stage, I was told the whole Eastern bloc was going to pull out, and it was down to me. It's not ideal material for a competitor to be thinking about, is it?'

Jim Fox believed that political pressure – the fierce antagonism of the Cold War – had pushed a well-liked man and the best swordsman in the competition to think he needed to cheat. It's possible Onischenko felt leaving victory to chance wasn't an option, that even the tiniest percentage chance of losing was not an acceptable risk.

But we can only speculate. Once Onischenko got Brezhnev's telling off he was dismissed from the KGB and disappeared from public view, never to explain what drove him to cheat.

CHAPTER 8

BALL TAMPERING

Fiddling with your equipment, while not appropriate in polite company, is widespread in sport. But it's not as widespread as ball tampering. That's because in sports where a ball is used, especially baseball and cricket, tampering with the ball significantly changes the way it behaves. An average pitcher or bowler can become pretty much unhittable if they're allowed to do whatever they want to the ball.

How much can changing the ball affect the way it behaves? A lot, it turns out. But the repercussions of ball tampering can go way beyond a game. They can rip apart the cultural heart of a nation.

ON TOP OF THE WORLD
To see what ball tampering can do, we should first examine a natural occurrence that meant one major league ballpark behaved differently to every other.

The Major League Baseball team the Colorado Rockies draws its name from the mountain range that skirts Denver. The Rockies were an expansion team that joined the league in 1993, moving to their current home, Coors Field, in their third season.

The Denver ballpark quickly developed a reputation as a great place to hit home runs. Being the highest park in the majors, at 1580 metres above sea level, the thin air provided little resistance to any balls hit towards the fences.

In the 1999 season, 303 home runs were hit at Coors Field, beating the 1961 record of 248, set at the Los Angeles Angels' original home of Wrigley Field.

The Rockies moved the outfield fences further back, but this just led to more triples and doubles being hit, plus the home runs kept coming anyway. This was a real problem for the team. Almost everyone loves home runs, but pitchers don't – and no pitcher worth their salt wanted to play for the Rockies. The way the ball behaved at Coors Field basically took pitching almost out of the game; it was all offence.

The other problem was that when the Rockies went on the road, without the thin air, not only did their sub-par pitchers continue to get belted, their batters lost their Superman-like hitting powers and reverted to being pretty average.

It seemed there wasn't much to be done. The thin air was just a result of having a team in Denver.

But one day an electrician at Coors Field, Tony Cowell, went elk hunting, as folks in the Rockies tend to do. As he hunted, he noticed his feet hurt terribly. The boots he was wearing hadn't been worn that summer and the dry desert air* had dried out the leather, causing it to constrict.

'I wondered if the same thing was happening to the baseballs,' he said. 'If the leather cover of the ball shrinks up like my boots,

---

* Denver is both high and arid, although it does get plenty of snow. Marijuana is legal there, too; each adult can have up to one ounce on them when out and about. That's almost a day's worth.

it would squeeze the wool yarn winding more tightly, and pull the laces tighter and lower, and the ball would be smaller and harder, and fly farther.'

Perhaps it wasn't the air pressure that was the problem.

Baseballs get delivered to the major league parks in bulk and then sit in storage for months. Cowell performed some tests and found the dry Denver air had sucked so much moisture out of the Rockies' store of balls, they came in below the mandated legal weight for a baseball (between 142 and 149 grams).

Because the woollen seams and the leather were being stretched, the baseballs were harder, lighter and more difficult to grip. All this combined to make them perfect for hitting home runs. It was as if nature was doctoring the balls for hitters.

Cowell, being one of those annoying people who actually knows how to build things with his hands, turned a large aluminium case normally used to store beer kegs into a moisture-controlled storage unit for the baseballs, ensuring they once again met the major league standard.

These new balls were put into play for the 2002 season, without the players being told about the change. That year, the Rockies hit thirty fewer home runs than their average over the past seven years.

Suddenly, Coors Field played like a normal baseball field. A small change in the balls – the moisture component – changed the way the sport was played.

AN ALARMING AMOUNT OF SPIT

Players, however, are not as clever as nature. Their attempts at ball tampering tend to be less subtle, and they involve a lot of lubricant.

Baseball is one of the rare sports that has had to ban players from spitting on the ball, such was the frequency with which they did it. The practice even gave rise to a specific type of pitcher, the spitball pitcher, and an entire era in baseball is named after it: the spitball era.

People don't need more evidence to prove that men are disgusting, but here is a truckload anyway.

Early in baseball's history, pitchers figured out that holding the ball in different ways caused it to curve, dip or just go very fast. Certain grips ensured the ball would rotate in certain ways, producing curveballs, sinkers and sliders.

But another discovery – right up there with the discovery of penicillin – dating back to at least 1884, was that spit allowed to you create two different changes to the way the ball behaves in flight.*

The first is that when throwing with a fastball grip, if you put a bit of spit on your finger, when you release the ball it slips a little and therefore has almost no spin, meaning it dips down suddenly as it reaches the batter. This significantly throws off the batter – it seems to be a normal fastball, but it's slower and then drops right before they swing at it. A similar effect is achieved with the knuckle-ball grip.

The other way is to have spit on one side of the ball, changing the ball's aerodynamics. When thrown, the ball will curve towards the side the spit is on, but unlike a curveball it travels at the same speed as a fastball, a big advantage.

The success of spitting on the ball led to numerous 'spitball pitchers' plying their trade in the late nineteenth century and early twentieth century.** Spitting on the ball was such an advantage, the sport was dominated by pitching during this era, with runs hard to come by. It was the reverse of what happened in Colorado.

---

* No one really knows for sure what great hero discovered spitting on the ball helped your pitching.

** Eventually spitball pitchers or 'the spitter' became a term for any pitcher that loaded up a ball with a foreign substance, not just spit.

In 1920, this all changed, after a game between the Cleveland Indians and the New York Yankees in which the spitball pitcher Carl Mays hit Indians shortstop Ray Chapman. Spitballs behave in unexpected ways, making them impossible to read sometimes – Chapman didn't even see what the ball was doing, he just stood there in the batters' box and didn't try to get out of the way.

The pitch hit Chapman in the side of the head.

Back then helmets were not in use. Chapman went down, with blood streaming out of his ears, nose and mouth. He was revived after several moments and carried off the field, but later died in hospital.

The response from the league was swift. Adding spit, grease or any other lubricant to the ball was banned, as was trying to rough up one side of the ball, which used the same principle of making the ball curve by increasing drag on one side. Using the same ball for most of the game was also out. Instead, new baseballs were used throughout, with any scuffed or dirty balls taken out of rotation.*

The rule changes showed just how widespread the practice had become. The new rules read in part that pitchers could be 'disbarred from the game' for applying 'rosin, paraffin, liquorice or any other foreign substance to [the ball], or damaging or roughing the same with sandpaper or emery paper.' Even more telling was that Major League Baseball gave seventeen spitball pitchers exemptions from the ban, allowing them to keep using the pitch until the end of their careers.**

In 1934 Burleigh Grimes became the last person to throw a legal spitball in the majors. Fourteen years after Chapman's death and finally the spitball era was over.

---

* You'd think another move would be to introduce helmets, but this didn't happen for another twenty-one seasons.
** A strange little exemption. It was like allowing people to keep drink driving after it was made illegal so long as they'd been caught doing it in the past.

Yet it wasn't, really. Pitchers just went from doctoring the ball legally to cheating.

A book detailing all the times pitchers have illegally doctored the ball would be so big you couldn't just use it to prop up a wonky table, it would *be* a table. But some of these incidents are so ridiculous, we have to cover them.

Perhaps one of the most well-known cheats was Hall of Fame member Gaylord Perry, who pitched from 1962 to 1983. In 1982 he was finally suspended for doctoring the ball, but people had suspected him of doing this for years.

Perry's favourite substance was vaseline. His catcher Gene Tenace once remarked that Perry loaded up the ball so much that sometimes it was so slippery he couldn't even throw it back to the mound after a pitch.

When questioned about Perry's illegal tactics, Indians president Gabe Paul said, 'Gaylord is a very honourable man. He only calls for the spitter when he needs it.'

In 1987, New York Yankees pitcher Joe Niekro was pitching in California when the umpire visited him at the mound – the ball had been doing strange things. At that very moment an emery board fell out of Niekro's pocket. It was then discovered that he also had some sandpaper fitted to one of his fingers.

While suspended, Niekro appeared on *Late Night with David Letterman* carrying a power sander and wearing a carpenter's apron, the pockets of which were overflowing with sandpaper and emery boards.

An umpire once said of Niekro, 'The guy was so blatant, it was like a guy walking down the street carrying a bottle of booze during Prohibition.'

Another Yankees pitcher, Whitey Ford, had several ways of cheating. He would cut the ball with his wedding ring, but he would also place small piles of mud around the mound and then rub that mud on the ball. Ford admitted later, 'I used enough mud to build a dam.'

Ford even filled a deodorant can with glue to use on the ball. Once, the legendary Yankees catcher Yogi Berra unknowingly used this 'deodorant', resulting in his arms being glued to his sides.

While using a spitball was chiefly dangerous for batters, it could also be hazardous to some pitchers.

Rick Honeycutt was in a severe slump while pitching for the Seattle Mariners, so when he passed a noticeboard and saw a thumbtack on his way to the mound one day, he took the tack and stuck it to his thumb.

During the game an opponent spotted the tack and alerted the umpire, who approached Honeycutt and found it. Even worse, Honeycutt had gashed his forehead when he had absentmindedly rubbed it, forgetting the tack was there. He later said that in another inattentive moment he'd also almost poked his eye out.

Kevin Gross was another pitcher who was caught and suspended for having sandpaper in his glove, which was confiscated. Three years later, Gross rang the commissioner's office at MLB headquarters, asking if he could have it back.

In baseball, being caught tampering with the ball is likely to be taken with good humour, like a naughty boy caught doing something a bit cheeky. Those who have been caught cheating don't always react with the shame you'd expect; as well as Niekro's appearance on *Letterman,* Gaylord Perry published an autobiography called *Me and the Spitter*, which was published in 1974. He didn't stop playing until 1983.

They're examples of how culture partly informs how much cheating there is in a sport. If cheating is accepted as being widespread, it tends to encourage more of it. And if the penalties are small and the culprits don't become pariahs, others are less afraid to take the risk.

But these things shift with time, or through a clash of cultures. As the Australian Cricket team once found out.

SHINY BALLS

Cricket differs from baseball when it comes to ball tampering. For a start, in cricket you're allowed to shine the ball, which produces 'swing bowling' – the ball gets some sideways movement in the air.*

Unlike baseball, in cricket the ball isn't regularly swapped out for a new one. In test cricket the same ball is used for 80 overs,** at which point the fielding side can choose to take a new ball.

Shining the ball is important because a cricket ball that's had the shine completely taken off it is very easy to hit, giving the bowlers little chance of getting anyone out. Cricketers are therefore allowed to use sweat and spit to shine the ball, but they can't use foreign substances to do it, nor can they use foreign objects to rough up one side. In fact, in cricket managing the condition of the ball is part art, part science, with key players often assigned the job of shining the ball and others taking care of the unlawful ball manipulation.

No less a person than the current prime minister of Pakistan, Imran Khan, was once caught tampering with the ball. Khan was one of Pakistan's greatest ever players, so think of it like Michael Jordan becoming president of the United States, or John Eales becoming prime minister of Australia.

But in 1981, in a county game in England, Khan admitted to ordering a bottle cap be brought onto the ground, which was used to rough up the ball. Khan showed no remorse, saying it was part of the game and everyone did it. This was the first indication Khan would go on to have a highly successful career in politics.

---

* You shine one side and let the other side get rough as play goes on. The rougher side drags in the air and the shiny side doesn't, making the ball 'swing' left or right through the air if the bowler uses the right grip.
** About five and a half hours, depending on how much stuffing around is going on.

He certainly wasn't wrong when he said everyone did it. The English had used mints to doctor the ball, South African players have rubbed the ball on the zippers in their pants, Pakistan star Shahid Afridi once bit into the ball (a move not recommended by nine out of ten dentists, and the tenth dentist works out of a shed). That's just a small sample.

Perhaps the most interesting case of ball tampering is what became known as 'Sandpapergate', which occurred in South Africa in March 2018. What happened isn't that interesting, but what it demonstrates is how different people and countries view cheating, or, more accurately, themselves.

Ball tampering cases in baseball and cricket get a lot of attention, but the penalties are mainly pretty light. Like low-level speeding, so many people do it, you can't jail everyone – half the population would be locked up.

In baseball, a ten-day suspension is pretty common, while in cricket you would expect to get a fine or miss one or two test matches.

But when Australian player Cameron Bancroft was caught on camera using sandpaper to doctor the ball against South Africa in 2018, Australia lost its mind. It was the number-one news story for weeks – radio stations had callers ringing in who were in tears over the incident.

Bancroft's biggest mistake was forgetting that he was playing cricket with about forty high-definition cameras watching him. The stupidity of the plan was a big part of the reason the entire country was so angry with him, captain Steve Smith, who tried to cover up the plan, and vice-captain David Warner, who came up with it.

I had countless people saying to me at the time, 'Can you believe they've been so stupid?' Which I could, having spent some time with groups of Australian men. This isn't even in the top 100 stupid plans I've heard.

In the cricket community, a certain amount of ball tampering is accepted and expected. No one wants to talk about it, but there would be few teams who have never at least pushed the limits. In the main, cricketers don't see much wrong with it. To them, it's games-manship – pushing the limits of the rules to gain an advantage – and most would refrain from calling it cheating.

After the Sandpapergate incident, in a media conference, then Cricket Australia CEO James Sutherland avoided using the word 'cheating', despite being directly asked about it numerous times. This was such an obvious evasion I felt like I was watching the break-up of a relationship.

Precedent suggested that Warner, Bancroft and Smith would have been expecting to face a one- or two-test ban for their actions. What they ended up with were twelve-month bans for Smith and Warner, and a nine-month ban for Bancroft. Cricket Australia's CEO and chairman were soon gone from the organisation as well.

Ian Gould, the TV umpire for the match, said later that he was surprised at the reaction. 'Under the rule book they would have got a one-game ban, but I just think the Australian public had simply had enough of the team.'

Gould was referring to the fact that the Australian cricket team had been behaving badly for some time – not cheating, but abusing and intimidating their opponents. Also, David Warner had been behaving like a right galah for his entire career.

Yet the Australians had been performing well on the field for over a decade and, so long as they kept winning, the Australian public had written it off as the cost of doing business.

The real problem was that the Australian cricketers were trapped between two completely different cultures: the culture of cricket, which considers ball tampering an embarrassing but low-level misdemeanour, and the culture of Australia, which views any form of cheating as a cardinal sin, a black stain on an athlete's soul that usually can never be washed off unless there's lots and lots of winning.

The United States has the myth of American exceptionalism – that it is inherently different from other countries because of how it was formed, its enormous natural resources, its size and its culture.

Australians believe in a similar exceptionalism: that they are uniquely blessed when it comes to sport. And there is some truth to that – Australia does perform exceptionally well on the world's sporting stage. Starting at the 2000 Olympics, the country has finished fourth, fourth, sixth, eighth and tenth at the summer games, which isn't bad for a nation ranked fifty-third in the world in terms of population.

This obsession with sport and the importance it holds in Australia's culture also comes with a firm belief that Australians don't cheat at sport.* Cheating would undermine the belief that Australia's sporting success is a result of superior ability and hard work, that the country's success was somehow a myth, based on fraudulent foundations.

When others are caught cheating, it only further entrenches in Australian minds the exceptionalism of the Australian athlete who does not need to resort to such shortcuts to win.

That's why when Bancroft was filmed cheating, so clearly trying to sandpaper the ball, Australians were shocked. That image contradicted the view the country had of itself. It seemed to suggest that perhaps Australia was not exceptional; that it was like all the other countries who've cheated at cricket, as the English, Indians, Pakistanis and South Africans all have.

The public reaction reflected this. It escalated to the point where then prime minister Malcolm Turnbull rang the chairman of Cricket Australia to express both 'disappointment and concern'.

---

* All sorts of Australian athletes have cheated, of course, but this is conveniently forgotten not long after it happens.

It's one thing to be disappointed, but a prime minster concerned about a twenty-year-old rubbing some sandpaper on a leather ball?

The thing is that Malcolm Turnbull is not a sports fan, so he didn't live in the world of cricket culture. But he did understand Australian culture. He understood that the Australian populace was angry because their perceived exceptionalism was being threatened.

Cricket Australia wasn't so quick on the uptake. As an organisation they were steeped in cricket culture, and so they spent days wondering what the big deal was. The same goes for the players.

Before long, the reality of the situation came crashing down on them all. Sometimes cheating is measured not against the standards of the sport but by a country's culture. As Turnbull put it, 'Cricket is "synonymous with fair play".'*

This is what happens: a sport develops a culture where certain types of cheating become minimised in people's minds, but eventually – through fans, politicians and sponsors – the culture of the broader world is brought to bear and everything in that sport changes.

Yet the universe always has a sense of humour, showing there's one thing that's always more powerful than human culture: nature.

The outbreak of COVID-19 has forced the International Cricket Council (ICC) to reconsider its stance on allowing players to use sweat and spit to shine the ball. Way before the pandemic, non-cricketers always thought this was a disgusting habit. Now the ICC is wondering if having eleven blokes spitting and sweating on a ball and then passing it around between themselves might be a bad idea.

One idea being considered is to ban shining the ball with spit and sweat, but allowing bowlers to use a foreign substance to shine

---

* This statement is factually incorrect, but Turnbull was right in the sense that it's how cricket is perceived. Like all great nation-building cultural myths, it's more something to strive for than something that actually happens.

the ball so that the game doesn't become decidedly stacked against bowlers.

Still, it will be a sad day when you're no longer allowed to share spit and sweat with your teammates in the refined, gentlemanly game of cricket.

THE MAIN EVENT

William Gilbert Grace, known as WG Grace, was arguably the first major sports star. In his prime, it was said only the Queen was more famous.

From 1865 to 1908, he dominated the cricketing world like no other, inventing new ways of batting. Crowds flocked to games just to see him play, and this established cricket as the number-one summer sport in England and its many colonies.

Grace was also a massive cheat. He made enormous amounts of money from what was then still an amateur game. He actually played off his amateur status, making a big song and dance about how he worked as a doctor throughout his career, despite sometimes declining to go on tour if he wouldn't be making any money out of it.

He would also often refuse to leave the field when he was given out, instead bullying umpires and opponents. Famously, when he was bowled in one exhibition match, he simply reset the stumps and told the bowler, 'These people have not come to watch you bowl. They have come to watch me bat.'

This didn't always work. In one game, when he had his bails knocked off, he said to the umpire, ''Twas the wind which took the bail off, good sir.'

To which the umpire replied, 'And let us hope the wind helps thee on thy journey back to the pavilion.'

So well known was his cheating that once, with Grace actually walking off the ground after being bowled, the bowler said to him, 'Surely you're not going, doctor? One of the stumps is still standing.'

CHAPTER 9

SCHEMING

The more complicated efforts at cheating involve schemes. Some of these are clever, and some should have been thrown in the bin the minute they crossed whatever was passing for a mind. Most cheating schemes in sport highlight not only the lengths people will go to in order to win but also that there's a lot of not very bright people in sport.

That's not always the case, though. Some schemes are so clever they make you think that if these people put the same amount of effort into worthwhile legal schemes, they'd be rich and famous.

Lucky for us they didn't, because nothing's funnier than when a scheme comes undone.

THE RACE DAY THAT WASN'T

In July of 1898, a well-dressed man in a suit and top hat entered the offices of the London newspaper *The Sportsman*, identifying himself as Mr G Martin. He brought details of an upcoming horseracing day to be held at Trodmore Racecourse in Cornwall on 1 August – a public holiday.

The newspaper said they were already struggling to cover all the various race days occurring throughout the country – sending someone to cover Trodmore would be impossible.

But Mr Martin helpfully suggested that if *The Sportsman* could publish the race card to help drum up some interest, he would be happy to telegraph them the results for a small fee. The paper said that would work for them and it was all agreed.

On the morning of the race, the paper published the Trodmore race card and then waited for Mr Martin to send them results.

The only problem was that the entire day's racing was a complete fiction. None of the horses on the card existed, and neither did the jockeys, and so all the odds were made up too. In fact, there wasn't even a Trodmore Racecourse. It was all a ruse.

But with the card now published in a respected newspaper, the gang behind the scam took the paper to various bookies around London to place bets. Many bookies were only too happy to accept the word of *The Sportsman* and took the men's bets. The gang bet on horses with odds of about 5–1, not long enough odds to raise any suspicions, but enough for a decent return.

As promised, that afternoon Mr Martin telegrammed the results to the paper, which they then printed the following day. Amazingly, all the horses the gang had bet on went on to win their races.

The gang went to collect, and many of the bookies paid up, but some didn't. They were confused because the rival racing paper, *Sporting Life*, hadn't published the results from Trodmore.

'Mr Martin' was quick to organise for *Sporting Life* to publish the results the day after that, only for them to make a misprint for a particular winning horse, Reaper. They put the winning odds as 5–2 instead of 5–1 as *The Sportsman* had printed.

This made the bookies seek to clarify what the correct odds

were. But attempts to contact Trodmore Racecourse proved fruitless, mainly because it didn't exist. This led the bookies to contact the police, who do exist, and they quickly determined that the whole thing was a work of fiction.

A fraud investigation commenced, but Mr G Martin and the gang had disappeared – along with £100,000 – never to be seen again. They had concocted a perfect scam, and if not for a misprint they would have made a lot more, and possibly run the scam again and again.

ALL IN A NAME

Horseracing always produces a lot of cheating because there's a lot of money to be made and it's filled with some of life's more 'colourful' characters.

One colourful character was Bob Skelton, known as 'The Baron' in the twenties and thirties. He was not only one of the biggest punters Sydney had ever seen, he owned a lot of horses too.

One day at Kensington Racecourse – a real racecourse in this case – one of Skelton's horses was to be ridden by an unknown jockey listed as John Nugent. Jockeys have a huge impact on a horse's performance and the punters weren't keen to risk their money on someone they'd never heard of, so the odds drifted out significantly.

Skelton, however, was seemingly unconcerned by his horse being ridden by an unknown jockey. He bet heavily on the horse and its odds shortened so much that, by the time the race started, it was the favourite.

Once the race got underway, the untested jockey easily piloted the horse to a victory. Skelton celebrated.

But, in the winner's circle, the punters noticed that John Nugent bore more than a passing resemblance to Mick Hayes, one of the era's top jockeys. They called on the stewards to launch an inquiry.

John Nugent looked so similar to Mick Hayes because he *was* Mick Hayes.

The stewards hauled both Skelton and Hayes before them and began asking some tough questions. Skelton, grinning ear to ear, produced a document. It was a legal document showing that Mick Hayes had changed his name to John Nugent by deed poll the day before the race.

Skelton asked the stewards to show him what rules he'd broken. They couldn't. Correct weight was awarded, and Skelton took home all his money.

The next week, Skelton paid for John Nugent to change his name back to Mick Hayes.

A SCHEMING MASTER

Some schemers blur the lines between legal and illegal to the point where the rules become irrelevant – their schemes are so entertaining almost no one cares.

When it comes to breaking the rules in this way, one man stands head and shoulders above almost every other schemer. Bill Veeck owned three different Major League Baseball teams in his life* and while he sometimes broke the league's rules to win, mainly he did it to entertain the fans. He took unbridled joy in this, and it drove the other owners crazy.

Veeck once said, 'I try not to break the rules but merely to test their elasticity.'

He was a man full of energy who just thought differently than other people. He served in the United States Marine Corps during World War II, where recoiling artillery crushed his right leg, forcing it to be amputated above the knee. As a result he wore a wooden leg for the rest of his life, which he cut a hole in to use as an ashtray.

---

* The Cleveland Indians, St. Louis Browns and Chicago White Sox.

Veeck was a born promoter. At games he gave away live animals and birds, and once a 200-pound block of ice. He scheduled morning games so night-shift workers could attend and held weddings at home plate – anything to get fans to the ballpark.

On one occasion he held a 'Good Old Joe Earley Night' for a fan by that name who had written a letter to the local paper complaining that Veeck was honouring everyone but average people.

Veeck's love of the fans was deep. At the Cleveland Indians, when he tried to trade the popular shortstop Lou Boudreau, word got out and the fans were outraged. In response, Veeck called off the trade and visited all the bars in Cleveland to personally apologise to fans and let everyone know the trade was off.

Aside from entertaining the fans, Veeck was about winning. At Cleveland, in 1946 he had a portable centre-field fence built that could move by about five metres. He would have it moved in or out depending on which team was better at hitting home runs.

It was a trick he'd learned while he owned the then minor league team the Milwaukee Brewers. He'd done a similar thing in right field, but unlike at Cleveland – where he only moved the fence in between games – in Milwaukee he'd move it during innings, pushing it back when the visiting team was batting and pulling it forward when the Brewers came up.

In Cleveland he got away with it for a year, but in the following season the major leagues passed a law banning teams from changing the distance of the fences mid-season.

Perhaps Veeck's most creative streak came while he owned the St Louis Browns. In 1951 the Browns were having one of their worst seasons ever, leading Veeck to flick the switch to vaudeville.

On August 19 the Browns were playing a double-header against the Detroit Tigers, another struggling team, and Veeck was determined to attract a crowd. It was also the fiftieth anniversary of the American League, one of the two leagues that make up the major leagues, so Veeck decided to throw a party: attending fans would receive a piece of birthday cake.

But the biggest surprise was still to come. Before the second game (the Browns had lost the first), a giant birthday cake was wheeled out onto the field for the manager, Zack Taylor, only for a three-and-a-half-foot dwarf dressed in a Browns uniform and elf shoes to jump out of the cake.

The man was Eddie Gaedel, who Veeck had recruited. Veeck announced that Gaedel would play in the second game of the double header, to the roar of the crowd.

Veeck had proposed the idea to Gaedel by saying, 'Eddie, you'll be the only midget in the history of the game. You'll be appearing before thousands of people. Your name will go in the record books for all time. You'll be famous, Eddie. You'll be immortal.'

As the second game started, the first to come up to bat was Gaedel. It was here that Veeck's plan was revealed to have another layer, beyond pure entertainment for the crowd.

In baseball, to earn a strike you have to throw the ball through the strike zone, which is defined by the width of the home plate and the armpit and knees of the batter. Given Gaedel was only slightly taller than a baseball bat, and was crouching down in a batting stance, the strike zone was tiny – almost impossible for a pitcher to target.

Detroit's manager immediately protested to the umpire, but Veeck produced a valid playing contract showing he'd signed Gaedel to the team earlier in the week. Veeck had also technically lodged the signing with Major League Baseball: he'd mailed it to them, ensuring it arrived on a day when they were closed.

The umpire conceded that Gaedel was a valid player.

Given the near impossibility of a pitcher throwing three strikes to Gaedel, Veeck had told him not to swing and instead to wait for four balls, drawing a walk to first base. Just to make sure Gaedel didn't get too excited up there and try to swing for the fences, Veeck also told him he'd placed a sniper on the roof.

The first pitch was thrown and it was perfect strike, right down the middle of the plate. Or it would have been, except for Gaedel it was a ball. The second pitch was the same, and the pitcher, Bob 'Sugar' Cain, decided it was all too ridiculous. He just threw the next two pitches high above Gaedel's head. Veeck's plan had drawn a walk.

Gaedel jogged to first base, tipping his cap to the adoring crowd – who gave him a standing ovation – before being subbed out for a pinch runner. He would later say, 'For a minute, I felt like Babe Ruth.'

The Browns still lost the game 6–2. And while the crowd loved the move, it was condemned by others. Priests, the newspapers, other team owners, they all screamed that the stunt was making a mockery of baseball. A new rule was passed that the Commissioner of Baseball had to approve all contracts before a player entered a game.

With the baseball world in a fury, Veeck waited all of five days before pulling another stunt.

This one started with Veeck calling for fans to vote on the starting line-up for a game. A form was printed in the newspaper and those who filled it out got a ticket to the game, sitting behind home plate.

It was called Grandstand Manager's Day, and instead of manager Zack Taylor calling the plays, the fans in those sections of the stand voted on what the team should do at certain points in the game. Veeck held up signs asking things like 'should the player bunt' or 'should he try to steal a base' or 'should we change the pitcher' and the crowd would hold up signs with a thumbs up or a thumbs down.

While this all happened, Zack Taylor sat in a rocking chair, puffing on a pipe.

As managers, the fans turned out to be pretty good. The Browns won 5–3, ending a four-game losing streak.

TAKING THE PATH LESS TRAVELLED

While all sorts of sports see people coming up with schemes, the marathon seems to produce an alarming number of them. Perhaps it's the herculean size of the task that makes people come up with ways to avoid having to do the entire thing.* And there are so many ways to cheat.

In 2018, at a marathon in Shenzhen, China, a competitor discovered a shortcut across a wooded area and set off down it. Their fellow competitors, instead of protesting, followed them, also taking the shortcut. This resulted in the disqualification of 258 runners, the Chinese media deeming it 'deeply shameful'.

All those years ago, when Fred Lorz hopped in a car for part of the 1904 St Louis marathon only to jump out and 'win' it, he probably didn't think he was creating a template for others to follow. But he did. Taking a shortcut or using another form of transport to complete a marathon has become its own flourishing subset of cheating.

But Lorz wasn't even the first to cheat in the Olympic marathon. At the 1896 Athens Olympics, the first modern games, third-place finisher Spyridon Belokas was later disqualified for completing part of the course in a horse-drawn carriage. Even back then that was against the rules.

Using another form of transport is a common occurrence in the marathon. In 2019 a woman was disqualified from the Xuzhou marathon in China for using a bike for parts of the course. Running part of the race, she would jump on a bike for certain sections,

---

* There's an easier way to avoid having to run a marathon: just don't. Some would say you miss out on the sense of achievement, but is there any greater satisfaction than getting out of having to do something?

then hop off while someone else drove the bike to the next section. Despite all this she still took over five and a half hours to reach the finish line, which makes you wonder why she'd even bothered.

Plus, it turns out riding a bike along the course in your full marathon gear isn't the smartest idea – it tends to leave a lot of witnesses.

If riding a bike seems a bit too much like hard work, there are other options. At a marathon in Berlin in 2000, thirty-three runners decided to catch the train for part of the route, ducking down to the subway to shorten the distance. The only problem was that every runner had a microchip in their uniform, making it easy to detect the subterranean detour.

Another runner caught taking a shortcut was no less than Roberto Madrazo, a Mexican politician and former presidential candidate. Madrazo 'won' the men's 55–59 category in the 2007 Berlin Marathon, with a truly impressive time of 2:41:12.

When he crossed the line a photographer, Victor Sailer, noticed something was off, and he notified the race organisers. 'It was so obvious to me. If you look at everyone else that's in the picture, everyone's wearing T-shirts and shorts, and the guy's got a jacket on and a hat or whatever.'

Once again the microchip data was quickly checked and it showed that Madrazo skipped two checkpoints, completing one 14.5-kilometre section in just twenty-one minutes. This would mean Madrazo had run at a speed of 40 km/h for twenty-one minutes, which is difficult to believe. Usain Bolt only averaged 37.8 km/h in his world-record breaking race at the 2009 World Championships, and that was over only 100 meters.*

For Mexicans, Madrazo's cheating just reinforced the view that many of their top politicians were corrupt. Madrazo had suffered a humiliating defeat in the presidential election the year before, but

---

* Usain Bolt's fastest ever competitive speed was 44.72 km/h, in the same race, but he hit it only briefly, between meters 60 and 80.

pretending you ran part of a marathon faster than Usain Bolt can run 100 metres is even more humiliating.

SEEING DOUBLE

Taking a train or a shortcut is all well and good, but another way to cheat in a marathon is to have someone else run part of it for you. This is an option I'm keen on.

The Comrades Marathon is an ultramarathon over 90 kilometres, more than double the length of a normal marathon. It winds its way from Pietermaritzburg in in-land South Africa to Durban on the coast.

South African Sergio Motsoeneng was an excellent long-distance runner who decided to tackle the race in 1999, finishing eighth. It was an impressive effort for his first attempt.

But another competitor, Nick Bester, had suspicions about Motsoeneng's performance. He reported him to organisers, who examined the timesheets at the various checkpoints and found Motsoeneng had passed all of them, so he was cleared of any wrongdoing.

Despite being cleared by the race officials, *The Beeld*, an Afrikaans newspaper, investigated further. They found two photos of Motsoeneng from different points in the race. Strangely, it seemed he had switched his watch from his left wrist to his right wrist. This could have been explained away: perhaps the watch had been causing him some discomfort.

Harder to explain was the fact that between the two photos being taken he'd somehow managed to grow a scar on his left shin.

The answer was simple enough: the person in the second photo was Sergio Motsoeneng's identical twin brother, Fika. The two men had switched clothes forty-five minutes into the race, and then swapped several more times throughout the race.

Both men were banned from the race for years, but Sergio

returned in 2010, this time running the race all by himself and finishing in third place. A wonderful story of redemption.

Until of course he returned a positive drug test.

THE CASE OF THE DISAPPEARING MOUSTACHE

The sad thing is that most of us don't have an identical twin to swap places with during a marathon, much less a scar-less one. That being the case, the next best thing is to find someone who bears a passing resemblance to you.

This is what Algeria's Abbes Tehami did when he won the 1991 Brussels marathon. There were a few flaws in his brilliant plan, though. See if you can spot them.

The man who started the Brussels marathon running under the name Abbes Tehami was in fact his coach, Bensalem Hamiani.

Hamiani ran the first 12 kilometres of the race, then ducked into the woods and swapped his marathon bib with Tehami, who re-joined the race.

Before the switch, organiser Milou Blavier had seen Hamiani struggling, but later he spotted him powering along and catching the leaders, who he went on to beat. 'I said, "Gee, that is some comeback",' Blavier later recalled.

But there were a few subtle differences between the two men that eagle-eyed spectators managed to pick up. The first was that the man who finished the race was slightly taller than the one who had started it. But another clue was that the man who started the race had a moustache, while the man who finished did not.

This seems to be a significant oversight by Hamiani and Tehami – shaving a moustache off isn't that hard. Although I understand that once you've grown one you may be reluctant to undo the hard work.

Still, it gave the game away. As Tehami crossed the line, many of the spectators were laughing at such a clumsy ruse. The two men, sensing the jig was up, hastily fled.

FINE COTTON

It's been tried many times in horse racing, but never this badly: swapping a bad horse for a good horse without letting anyone know.

In August 1984, a group of men decided to swap a rather bad racehorse, Fine Cotton, with a superior horse that looked exactly the same, Dashing Solitaire. The problem was, when it came time to race, Dashing Solitaire was injured. The men decided to use a horse named Bold Personality instead. Unfortunately, Bold Personality looked nothing like Fine Cotton.

No problem, thought the men. To mimic Fine Cotton's coat and markings, they dyed the horse's hair using off-the-shelf human hair dye and painted it with white house paint.

A betting plunge on the day of the race had already made stewards suspicious. The fact that by the time the horse was taken to be weighed the paint was starting to run then gave the rather odd scheme away.

A REAL SPUD

Sometimes the motivation for cheating can be boredom. While starting a marathon with a moustache and finishing it with a different person, moustache-free, may come across as a rather ill-conceived plan, it's not the worst cheating scheme in the history of sports.

This is.

Dave Bresnahan was a minor league baseball catcher who came up with a truly bizarre way to cheat. In 1987, Bresnahan was playing for the Williamsport Bills, the Cleveland Indians' Double-A affiliate. His plan was to trick a baserunner by misthrowing the ball over the third baseman's head and into the outfield, prompting the runner to take the opportunity to run home, only for Bresnahan to then tag him with the ball at home plate.

How would he produce this bit of trickery? By not throwing the game ball to third base but instead something that looked like the ball.

Bresnahan decided the best thing to do was to use a potato.

I know, it's the obvious answer.

Before the game, Bresnahan got a potato, peeled it, and carved it to look a bit like a baseball. No photos exist so I can't speak to how realistic it was, but I don't think it was in the class of Auguste Rodin.

Bresnahan put his plan into action, and in the moment it worked: the potato soared above the third baseman's head, the runner set off for home, only to be tagged out with the game ball by Bresnahan.

As all hell broke loose, a bewildered umpire retrieved the potato. After he'd worked it all out, the umpire awarded the baserunner a run.

Bresnahan's manager pulled him from the game immediately, and the next day the Cleveland Indians cut him. He never played again.

But Bresnahan wasn't too fussed. He knew he was on the cusp of being cut anyway, and his motivation was to lighten up a long season.

Despite all this, many appreciated his attempt as a comedic endeavour. The *Chicago Tribune* named him their '1987 Sports Person of the Year' and the following year the Williamsport Bills held a 'Dave Bresnahan Day', retiring his uniform number 59.

Each fan in attendance was given a free potato on entry.

CHAPTER 10

DOPING

I want to begin this chapter on doping by letting you know that everyone caught doping is innocent. Only on the rarest occasion does an athlete who tests positive say, 'Yep, I was doping to improve my performance and you got me.' There is always either a flat-out denial, a madcap explanation or an excuse.

As Morgan Freeman's character Red says to Andy Dufresne in *The Shawshank Redemption*, 'Everyone in here is innocent.'

Dufresne is truly innocent, but there aren't too many Andy Dufresnes, in prison or in sport. Almost all the players who are caught cheating and then deny any knowledge of it are eventually found to be lying. I know, I was shocked too.

One piece of equipment that every athlete has in common is their body. They can improve it through training, of course, but unfortunately genetics can curb anyone's dreams of sporting glory, no matter how hard they work. I've discovered this early and repeatedly in my life.

This leads to another option, especially for those who value winning above everything else in life: not accepting your biological limits. And that requires a little outside help.

EVERYONE IS INNOCENT

When it comes to excuses, there's almost nothing that hasn't been tried. A popular approach to explaining away a failed drug test is to claim that the drug that was found wasn't, in fact, used to enhance performance or mask another drug.

Cricketer Shane Warne, when found to have taken a prohibited diuretic, said it was given to him by his mum to help him get rid of a double chin.

US sprinter LaShawn Merritt was apparently also worried about his appearance: he claimed traces of dehydroepiandrosterone found in his system were the result of a penis enlargement supplement, wonderfully named 'ExtenZe'.*

A similar approach was taken by a member of the Japanese billiards team, Junsuke Inoue, who after testing positive for methyl-testosterone said it was for improving his performance in bed, exclaiming, 'My wife is entitled to be satisfied.'**

Romance seems to be linked with an enormous number of failed doping tests. French tennis player Richard Gasquet escaped sanction in 2009 when he claimed that the traces of cocaine found in his test were the result of the drug being in the mouth of a woman, known only as 'Pamela', who he'd kissed the night before in a Miami nightclub.

It's a reminder to always conduct a drug test before kissing someone.

US sprinter Dennis Mitchell also claimed that love explained his high levels of testosterone. He said the night before the drug test

---

* I'm not sure a purposefully capitalised 'Z' in a brand name screams 'medically safe'.
** This is actually a pretty strong argument.

he'd had 'five bottles of beer' and sex with his wife 'at least four times', because 'it was her birthday and the lady deserved a treat'.

And to think I thought a night of watching *Midsomer Murders* was an exciting birthday treat.

When you can't cite romance as a reason for your positive drug test, blame something else. Mitchell's five bottles of beer aren't that impressive when compared to British cyclist Jonathan Tiernan-Locke's story; he claimed abnormal findings in his results were due to the thirty-three drinks he'd had the night before, which seems like a lot given the world championships were just days away.

The Dutch cyclist Adri van der Poel tested positive to strychnine in 1983 and claimed it must have come from his father-in-law's racing pigeons, which had been made into a pie.

But you can get even more creative than that. Cyclist Tyler Hamilton claimed the reason he had someone else's red blood cells in him was because of a 'vanishing twin', who had been in the womb with him but had died and then been partly absorbed by Hamilton. Later, after admitting to doping regularly, Hamilton said that this excuse wasn't his idea but that some of his doctors had come up with it.

When several players on a team all test positive for the same thing, you have to get really creative. In 2011, the North Korean women's soccer team had five players fail a drug test. Their excuse was a beauty: apparently they'd all been struck by lightning and to recover had taken a traditional Chinese remedy involving deer musk glands. It seems traditional Chinese medicine has a cure for everything.

Claims of a conspiracy are another tried and true approach. Cuban high jumper Javier Sotomayor tested positive for cocaine at the 1999 Pan-American Games and the Cuban media claimed it was the result of a plot concocted by either the CIA or the anti-Castro Mafia. Even Fidel Castro himself defended Sotomayor.

In 2001, however, Sotomayor again tested positive, this time for nandrolone. He said, 'I know that every time there is a doping case, everyone generally says they are innocent,' he said. 'But in my case, I really am innocent.'

THE DRUGS DO WORK

Drugs can do all sorts of wonderful things. They can make you faster, stronger, reduce your heart rate, increase your heart rate and boost your endurance. No wonder some athletes turn to them.

Just some of the things athletes have put in their things include: caffeine, cocaine, amphetamines, modafinil, ephedrine, laudanum, nitroglycerine, methandrostenolone, nicotinyl tartrate, atrychnine, benzedrine, mephedrone, ephedrone, fluoroamphetamines, metandienone, stanozolol and erythropoietin.

No one outside of sport, aside from Keith Richards, has pumped as many different chemicals into their bodies as athletes have.

It's hardly risk free, either. Many of these drugs can kill you and, even worse, some of them cause baldness. Other side effects can include hallucinations, acne, liver damage, heart failure and an enlarged head.* In men they can cause both impotency and an increased sex drive, which must be an incredibly frustrating combination. Women can develop irregularities with their menstrual cycle and their clitoris can become enlarged beyond normal proportions.

Despite these risks, doping continues to be the most common way of cheating in sport. It's impossible to cover all the doping that has gone on, it's so widespread. Baseball, for example, didn't just have a spitball era, it also had a steroid era.

---

* You'd think risking an enlarged head would be reason enough not take steroids, but you'd be wrong.

THE ONES YOU LEAST EXPECT

If I told you weightlifters dope, you'd not be the least bit surprised. Pure strength can obviously be helped by a big dose of testosterone. The sport is constantly engulfed in doping scandals. Even the weightlifters that aren't on drugs look like they're on drugs.

But what if I told you the sport of curling had been rocked by a doping scandal? Some of you would respond, 'What's curling?', while the rest of you would be wondering why anyone in curling would need to take drugs, except perhaps to stave off the boredom.

Curling originated in Scotland in the early sixteenth century and involves two teams, each made of up of four people, who slide a stone along ice towards a target some distance away.

These polished granite stones have a handle, which allows them to be 'curled' along the ice by turning them as they're released. Then two teammates use brooms to sweep the ice ahead of the stone, which decreases the friction of the ice and makes the stone travel further, or makes it go straighter. The team needs to coordinate the arc of the curve when it's released with the sweeping that's done as it travels along the ice. Fans of the sport marvel at its strategy, calling it 'chess on ice'.*

To be fair, curling is hypnotising to watch. Every Winter Olympics I find myself watching hours of it, wondering why, but also transfixed. But fascination aside, if I had to guess a sport where doping doesn't occur, curling would be right up there.

That was until the 2018 Winter Olympics in Pyeongchang, when Russian curler Alexander Krushelnytsky was caught using the drug meldonium.

Meldonium might sound familiar, and that's because it's the drug tennis player Maria Sharapova tested positive for in 2016, leading to her suspension. Showing that Sharapova is a wonderful

---

* I have something entirely different in mind when I hear the phrase 'chess on ice'.

spokesperson for any product, not just watches and luxury cars, meldonium had a spike in sales after she was caught, mainly in Russia and Latvia, where it can be purchased over the counter.*

Meldonium is a drug used to treat various heart conditions and diabetes. It expands the arteries, helping to increase blood flow and the distribution of oxygen through the body.

When Sharapova was caught using it, she claimed she was taking it for a heart condition. But the manufacturer of the drug says the appropriate course of treatment for a heart condition is to take it for four to six weeks – Sharapova said she took it for ten years. I guess you can't be too careful with a heart condition.

The fact that both Sharapova and Krushelnytsky are both Russian is relevant, because meldonium has a long history in Russia. It was first used by the Soviet army in the mountains of Afghanistan in the eighties, during their rather unsuccessful invasion.

The inventor of the drug, Latvian chemist Ivars Kalvins, explained, 'If the soldiers are to operate in the mountains, there's a lack of oxygen. The way to protect against damage is by using Mildronate.'** Kalvins said that during the Soviet invasion the Latvian firm Grendiks, who make the drug, shipped hundreds of metric tons of Mildronate to the Soviet army.

Athletes that claim that meldonium provides no benefit to physical performance are obviously ignorant of what its first use was.

This was hardly the first time an army had used drugs; the Nazis gave their soldiers crystal meth to fuel the Blitzkrieg that swept the German army through France in 1940. Not having to sleep and being filled with a manic energy can give you a real edge.

Unlike the Soviet approach, where drugs were first used by soldiers before being taken up by athletes, the Germans went the

---

* Sharapova even has her own brand of candy, but I understand it is just actual candy.
** Mildronate is the brand name for meldonium.

other way. They had learned a lot from doping their athletes with Benzedrine* at the 1936 Olympic Games and then worked out you could give it to soldiers too.

From Soviet soldiers to Russian tennis players and then to curlers, meldonium had really gathered an eclectic group of fans by 2018, when Alexander Krushelnytsky was found to have traces of it in his body after winning the bronze medal in the mixed-doubles curling at PyeongChang. He'd won the bronze with his wife; as they say, the couple that curls together stays together.**

When the news broke, the curling community and the wider world reacted with shock. That is, disbelief that someone in curling would need to use drugs. Danish player Madeleine Dupont said, 'I think most people will laugh and ask, "What could you possibly need doping for?", as I am thinking. I'm not even sure what use doping would be for in curling. There is probably something with strength, I'm not sure, it's not down my alley.'

Norwegian former silver medallist Thomas Ulsrud agreed. 'For me it's tough to see doping in curling. Maybe as a brusher, but come on, hit the gym, you know.'

Despite the strangeness of the case, Krushelnitsky got a four-year ban. Unlike when Sharapova was caught, I'm not aware of it resulting in a spike in sales of meldonium.

THE DIRTIEST RACE OF THEM ALL?

If there is one event that really brought doping to the public's attention, it was the 1988 Seoul Olympics 100-metre sprint.

It was hardly the first time an athlete got caught doping, and it certainly wasn't the funniest, but it was the highest profile case up to that point and it stunned the world. And while the immediate

---

* Another methamphetamine, in the same family as crystal meth.
** I'm not sure they do say this, but I think it would be true. Who would want to hook up with a curler except for another curler?

fallout was spectacular enough, later revelations have made this 'the dirtiest race in the history' – not that many other events haven't tried to claim that title.

In 1980, at the Junior PanAms, two sprinters raced each other for the first time. One was Carl Lewis, from the United States and already one of the brightest talents in athletics, the other was Ben Johnson, a Jamaican-born Canadian who was so skinny he looked like a gust of wind could knock him over.

Lewis won the race easily, in 10.43 seconds; Johnson came sixth in 10.88. At the time there was nothing to link the two men, nothing to hint that they would be linked for the rest of their lives.

By the time of the 1984 Los Angeles Olympics, Carl Lewis was a superstar of athletics, an American competing on home soil. He attracted further attention by announcing he would attempt to match Jesse Owens' legendary four gold medals at the 1936 Games in Berlin by competing in four events – the 100 metres, the long jump, the 200 metres and the 4×100-metre relay.

The 100 metres was first, which Lewis won; Johnson took bronze. The gap between the two men was closing, but most people didn't notice. Lewis was the focus, and for good reason – he also won gold in his remaining three events, tying Owens' record.

This should have made Lewis a massive star, but there was one problem: people didn't like him. He had Muhammad Ali's arrogance but none of the charm. *Sports Illustrated* described him as 'vain, shallow and self-absorbed'. At a time when the sports media tended to lionise stars, Lewis must have worked really hard to earn that description.

Some of his arrogance was on display after he won the 100 metres in 1984. The very next day *Time* magazine had him on the front cover with the gold medal around his neck – an extraordinary turn around in the days before digital photography and printing.

The reason it was so quick was that Lewis had actually done the photo shoot days ahead of the race.

To understand Lewis's complete lack of self-awareness, all you need to do is look up his 'music career' with his band Electric Storm. The film clip for the song 'Break It Up' is worth a watch on YouTube if you want to see someone who has no idea how others perceive him.

Following the LA Olympics, Lewis didn't get the big bump in sponsorships any other athlete would have gotten after winning four golds. The was a rumour that Lewis was homosexual and that this drove advertisers away from him, but Coca-Cola had offered him a sponsorship before the games. The trouble was that he'd turned it down, believing he'd get more money from them after the games.

But by the end of the Olympics, Lewis's brash character had managed to annoy most Americans. In fact his confidence, which he thought was both necessary for a top athlete and good show-manship, rubbed almost everyone up the wrong way – the media, teammates, opponents, children, pets. That was probably the main reason most sponsors weren't keen.

The lack of adulation and sponsorship grated on Lewis, and on top of that over the next few years he came under increasing pressure on the track from that once skinny Canadian kid, Ben Johnson. While Johnson's bronze wasn't really noted by the general sports fan, in the athletics world it announced him as a serious com-petitor. He had bulked up significantly and was starting to turn in some eye-catching performances.

By 1987, as the world championships in Rome approached, Lewis and Johnson had begun a true rivalry. Lewis, so long untouchable, had lost to Johnson four times ahead of the champi-onships. After the fourth loss, the simmering tension resulted in the two of them yelling at each other and having to be separated. This only drew more attention from the media, and piled the pressure onto Lewis.

Rome was no different – Johnson torched the field with a new world record of 9.83 seconds. This catapulted him to superstardom and, unlike Lewis, Johnson's quiet demeanour made him an easy sell for sponsors. The public adored him, further angering Lewis.

Lewis, already a bad winner, became an even worse loser. He said, 'There are a lot of people coming out of nowhere. I don't think they are doing it without drugs.' He hadn't named Johnson, but the inference was there.

Many didn't believe him; in their minds Lewis was a sore loser and his arrogant persona meant most people were thrilled that someone had taken him down a peg.

Johnson responded simply. 'When Carl Lewis was winning everything, I never said a word against him. And when the next guy comes along and beats me, I won't complain about that either.'

When the 1988 Seoul Olympics arrived, the world's eyes were on the 100 metres and the clash between Johnson and Lewis. Many were looking forward to Johnson handing Lewis another embarrassing defeat.

The race was stacked with other top runners, including former world record holder Calvin Smith and future gold medallist Linford Christie. But the world was only interested in the animosity between the brash American and the quiet Canadian. And after Lewis accused Johnson of being a drug cheat, the event had the feel of a heavyweight title fight.

The race itself was a brutal display of power by Johnson – he took off with an explosive start and was never bettered. Lewis never got closer to him than a metre.

The scoreboard flashed Johnson's time: 9.79 seconds. It was another world record. Lewis had run 9.92, which would have been a world record if Johnson wasn't around. Linford Christie took the bronze.

Johnson was the darling of the sporting world; Canadian prime minister Brian Mulroney called Johnson on live television and thanked him for 'a marvellous evening for Canada'.

After the race, Johnson made his way to the doping control room to do a routine test. As he entered, he received applause from those working there, and was surrounded by the staff who got autographs and photos with the new Olympic champion. The supervising IOC member of the doping control room, Dr Arne Ljungqvist, made sure he too got a photo with Johnson. The mood could not have been more jubilant.

Johnson told the media after the race, 'I'd like to say my name is Benjamin Sinclair Johnson Jr, and this world record will last fifty years, maybe 100. A gold medal – that's something no one can take away from you.'

Two days later, he was proved wrong on both accounts.

The first sign of trouble for Johnson came the following day. His 'A' urine sample was flagged as positive for the anabolic steroid stanozolol. Carol Anne Letheren, the head of Canada's delegation, was informed by the IOC at 1.45 a.m. By midday, the 'B' sample had also been confirmed as positive.

Dick Pound, then the IOC vice-president, was the only lawyer in Canada's Olympic delegation, so he was pressed into service to defend Johnson at the hearing. He said that Johnson denied he'd taken performance enhancing drugs and that the sample was tainted, arguing that there had been a 'mystery man' in doping control.*

This was a fairly weak defence. Even worse, the German IOC member Manfred Donike stated that an unofficial test showed Johnson was a long-time taker of anabolic steroids. This wasn't

* This turned out to be Andre Jackson who, unbeknown to Johnson, was friends with Carl Lewis. Jackson drank beers with Johnson and even took photos with him. Even after Johnson confessed to doping, he maintained that in 1988 Jackson had sabotaged this test, claiming he hadn't been using the particular drug he'd tested positive for. Johnson says that in 2004 Jackson confessed to him he'd done it; when approached for a comment by journalists, Jackson cryptically responded, 'Maybe I did, maybe I didn't. What has been carried out in 1988 cannot and will not be invalidated.'

allowed to be entered into evidence, but despite some inconsistency in the process, Johnson was stripped of his gold medal.

But that wasn't the only drama in doping control. Britain's Linford Christie, who had come third, also tested positive, for pseudoephedrine. But he was cleared in a split decision by the IOC medical commission – he had argued that his positive test was a result of drinking ginseng tea.

When news broke that Johnson would be stripped of his medal, the world was shocked. Except for Carl Lewis. Lewis felt completely vindicated.

Years later Lewis would say of the race, 'In the old Westerns they had the guy in the white hat and the black hat. I felt like the clean guy going out and trying to win. I was the guy in the white hat, trying to beat this evil guy.'

Lewis was awarded the gold medal and his time was recognised as the new world record, while Linford Christie received the silver.

The fallout for Johnson continued, starting with the announcement of an inquiry back in Canada to look into the whole mess. At the Dubin Inquiry, Johnson admitted to doping in the past, and implicated his coach.

CAN'T BEAT 'EM

Seven years earlier, in 1981, Ben Johnson had a conversation with his coach, Charlie Francis, that would change his life.

Francis was a former Canadian sprint champion himself, and the two had been working together for a year. While Johnson had all the talent in the world, Francis tried to convince him that he needed something more if he was to have any chance of becoming a true great of the sport.

Francis himself had made the second round of the 100 metres at the Munich Olympics in 1972. According to Francis, he'd raced clean for most of his career, but then realised it was impossible to win when everyone else was doping. The 1976 Montreal games, which saw East Germany power ahead of everyone else on the back of doping, only confirmed his view.

Francis said, 'I'm not going to have my runners start a metre behind', meaning *not* using drugs.

It was these beliefs that saw him pressure Johnson into adding steroids to his training regime. Francis's view, which he reiterated later in life, was that 'steroids could not replace talent, or training, or a well-planned competitive programme. They could not transform a plodder into a champion. But they had become an essential ingredient within a complex recipe.'

It was at this point Johnson chose to take the path that led him to global disgrace – he agreed to start a program of steroids, which continued right up to the Seoul Olympics.

At the Dubin Inquiry, Francis seemed most annoyed by one inference: that he didn't know how to dope his runners properly. Francis argued strongly that he was well aware of exactly how long it took to flush drugs from Johnson's system to beat a urine test, and that Johnson was completely free of any traces of doping on race day in Seoul. He said the only way Johnson could have failed the test was if there had been a conspiracy at the doping centre.

This seemed to miss the whole point. Taking steroids for years enables an athlete to train harder and for longer, increasing muscle mass faster and reducing recovery times – being drug-free on the day of competition doesn't mean too much.

Later, in a book he wrote, Francis added that there was no way Johnson could tested positive for stanozolol, because Francis had given him a completely different steroid. Not the best defence.

GLASS HOUSES

As the years passed, the narrative of the 1988 race became just as Carl Lewis had framed it: he was the clean, good guy athlete, overcoming the rising tide of drugs that was personified by Ben Johnson.

Slowly though, reality – as it so annoyingly does – started to poke holes in this triumph of virtue. Like leaves falling from a tree in autumn, runner after runner from the Seoul race was linked to doping.

Third placed Linford Christie, who had then been awarded the silver medal, tested positive for drugs in both 1988 and 1999. Of course, he initially claimed he was innocent. Another Canadian, Desai Williams, who had come sixth, was found by an inquiry to have received steroids at the games. Dennis Mitchell, who came fourth, tested positive for testosterone in 1998.* The United States' Ray Stewart – eighth – was in 2010 banned for life by US Track and Field for trafficking banned substances to athletes.

But the biggest to fall was none other than Carl Lewis himself. He who had been so vocal about the use of drugs in sport and had modelled himself as the shining beacon for all clean athletes.

In 2003, Wade Exum, the United States Olympic Committee's director of drug control administration from 1991 to 2000, released documents to *Sports Illustrated* revealing some 100 American athletes who failed drug tests from 1988 to 2000. Lewis was named in the documents.

In the lead-up to 1988, Lewis had tested positive three different times: for pseudoephedrine, ephedrine and phenylpropanolamine. Interestingly, Lewis's training partners Joe DeLoach and Floyd Heard had also tested positive for the same drugs.

But the whole affair was covered up at the time. When confronted, Lewis had said the failed test was the result of a potent herbal tea, and the US Olympic Committee accepted this.** But

---

* He was the man who explained the test result as being a result of his wife deserving a birthday treat.
** Herbal supplements and teas seem to pop up regularly when athletes test positive for performance-enhancing drugs, making you wonder why they take them.

under international rules, Lewis should have been banned from the Seoul Olympics.

After the document leak in 2003, Lewis maintained that he had only taken a herbal supplement. Defending the decision that allowed him to compete, he said, 'There were hundreds of people getting off. Everyone was treated the same.'

Roger Kingdom, the winner of the 110-metre hurdles in Seoul, wasn't buying Lewis's excuses, recalling that all athletes had extensive briefings on how what went into their bodies was their personal responsibility. 'He should not have been allowed to compete, plain and simple,' Kingdom said. 'You can't plead ignorance; it didn't roll. Obviously, it goes back to show you favouritism was involved. At the time Carl was Mr Track and Field, and what a black eye it would have given the US not to have your top dog there.'

Of the remaining field, only two runners have never had any accusations of doping levelled at them. US sprinter Calvin Smith, who originally finished fourth, and Brazil's Robson da Silva, who finished fifth.

That's two out of the eight competitors. Unfortunately, it seems Charlie Francis wasn't wrong when he said to compete at the top-level back then you had to be doping.

Ben Johnson never really accepted his fate as the most high-profile doper in the world, always believing he was the true winner in Seoul. A comeback in 1993 was short-lived – he tested positive again.

He went on to work for Libyan leader Muammar Gaddafi, coaching his son, Al-Saadi Gaddafi, who dreamed of joining an Italian football club. And he managed it, too, joining Serie A team Perugia in 2003. But this was short-lived too – the younger Gaddafi lasted one game before being sacked for failing a drug test.

As for Charlie Francis, disgraced for his role in the whole affair, in 2002 he was recalled to coaching by Tim Montgomery and Marion Jones. This certainly raised a few eyebrows. As it should have. Jones was later stripped of all five of her medals from the 2000 Sydney Olympics for doping, and Montgomery was banned for two years for doping offences.

Time marches on, but it seems athletes are destined to repeat the mistakes of the past.

EQUALITY

In this wonderful new world of equality, we've learned women can do anything men can. And the women's 1500 metres at the London Olympics in 2012 showed that women could match the exceptional efforts of the men in 1988. As I write this, six of the top nine finishers have now been caught doping.*

Aslı Çakır Alptekin from Turkey, who won the gold that day, had already served a two-year ban for doping before London. It was therefore a shock to all when she was caught again and received an eight-year ban and had her gold stripped.

Her countrywoman Gamze Bulut, who won silver, is currently serving a suspension for doping. Russian Tatyana Tomashova, the fourth placed finisher, had previously been caught substituting a urine sample, which was indeed found to contain someone else's urine when tested.

Abeba Aregawi of Ethiopia (fifth) later turned in a positive test, as did Natallia Kareiva of Belarus (seventh) and Ekaterina Kostetskaya of Russia (ninth). It seems to suggest that the world hasn't really moved on since 1988. But then, 1988 hadn't really moved on from all the Olympics that came before. The fight against doping is like the war on drugs: the drugs are winning.

As for Ethopia's Abeba Aregawi, her test showed she had meldonium in her system, so perhaps the problem there was that she had been spending too much time with curlers.

* I had a really funny joke here, but the lawyers cut it because they are unreasonably risk-averse and don't have a sense of humour, and that's why no one likes them.

CHAPTER 11

A MASTERCLASS IN CHEATING

Now you've been privy to so much cheating in the glorious world of sport, you might think you've heard it all. But we've just been warming up. Now you're ready to be immersed in a whole new dimension – and it's quite a step up.

You probably think of the Tour de France as a bike race, but soon you'll share my view that the race itself is just a platform for the cheating. Le Tour is actually the world's top cheating competition.

I suppose you could swap it out for something else, but cycling has proven to work incredibly well as a test of who can cheat the best. The riders cheat, the teams cheat, the organisers cheat and the spectators cheat. Every form of cheating has been tried over time: transport, sabotage, violence, illegal equipment, substance abuse and systematic doping programs are as much a part of the race as the beautiful French scenery. If a ball was involved, it would have been tampered with by now.

And disabuse yourself of the notion that the cheating escalated over time as the race became more competitive, more high profile and more lucrative. In fact, there has quite possibly never been a clean Tour de France. While there appear to be winners who were clean, you have to wonder about that once you know the race's full history.

IT'S JUST LOGIC

While athletics has had huge problems with doping, as have many other sports, cycling is probably the one that jumps into most people's minds when it comes to doping. But why? Are cyclists simply morally shadier than everyone else? I'm tempted to say yes, but I don't think so. Culture explains a bit, given that, as we'll see, taking substances to boost performance has been part of the Tour since it began, but that alone doesn't explain it all.

Perhaps the biggest reason is just that the Tour is so gruelling.

Anyone who completes the Tour de France is a freak. The average fit person could be pumped with all the drugs in the world and they still wouldn't be able to complete it, let alone in the times these athletes do. The modern Tour de France goes for twenty-one day-long stages, spread over twenty-three days, in which the riders cover approximately 3500 kilometres.

The first thing to consider is the flat parts. These would appear to be the easy bits, but riders have to maintain a brutal average speed of about 45 km/h, before sprinting the last 5 to 10 kilometres at 60 km/h. At the very end, as they sprint for the line, they get up to about 80 km/h.

To put this into perspective, you have to consider the power a rider must output to reach and maintain those speeds. Cycling is one sport where the athletes' efforts can be easily measured – they are essentially putting power into a machine, so you can measure the watts produced at any given moment.

On the flat stages, to reach the speeds required to compete you need to produce between 2000 and 2500 watts (W). How does this compare to what a normal fit person can produce on a bike? Well, the average is around 800 watts for men and 600 watts for women. Tour de France riders aren't just a bit better than most cyclists, they're in another universe.

Then the riders have to tackle the mountains, which means climbing up as high as 2500 metres above sea level, depending on the route, often with multiple ascents per stage. At this height altitude sickness can certainly occur, and the lack of oxygen reduces your athletic capacity by up to 15 per cent.

To climb these mountains, you need to produce an average power output upwards of 450 watts, and you need to do that for thirty to sixty minutes per climb. An average cyclist who cycles regularly on the weekend for good distances might be able to produce 450 watts for a maximum of between 30 and 120 seconds.

This sort of energy output means riders have to take in a lot of energy to maintain their weight and muscle, with most riders finishing the Tour pretty close to the weight they started at. To do that, they take in about 6000 calories per day. The average male needs between 2000 and 3000 calories a day.

All this adds up to a race that, in terms of what it demands of the human body, is right on the cusp of what's possible. Racers have often said you need to take something just to get through the entire ordeal, and there may be some truth to that.

Ultimately, though, the most significant reason for cheating being so prevalent in cycling is the simplicity of the sport. Aside from team tactics and reducing wind resistance, which every team tries to do, the only thing separating competitors is their power output.

The more power a cyclist can produce, the better they will be. It's that simple. Boost your power and you'll finish higher up the standings.

And consider this: not much separates Tour de France riders.

It's not like the winner has produced orders of magnitude more power throughout the race, it's usually only a tiny fraction more than their fellow competitors.

The smallest change in power output can massively impact the results. For example Chris Froome of Great Britain won the 2015 race in 84 hours, 46 minutes, and 14 seconds. If sixteenth-placed Thibaut Pinot of France had improved his power output by just 1 per cent, he'd have come first. By 12 minutes.

Just 1 per cent.

In sports such as soccer or basketball, a 1 per cent improvement, even across an entire team, is not going to change things that much. It's not going to turn the sixteenth-best Premier League team into champions.

But like sprinting, which is decided by hundredths of a second, in cycling a 1 per cent increase can make all the difference. These tiny margins mean the temptation to dope is huge; and it seems few competitors can resist.

What this all means is that doping in the Tour de France, while morally reprehensible, is an incredibly rational action. It helps you handle a sport that operates at the extremes of human ability, and it can make the difference between being in the middle of the pack or first.

And if large amounts of your competitors are doping, it is almost impossible to win if you don't – the margins are just too tight.

This is not to say I approve of doping, or that it exonerates those who have done it – obviously it doesn't – but it does answer the question of why cycling has a greater doping problem than most other sports.

POSSIBLY THE WORST PERSON IN SPORT

Let's begin with Lance Armstrong. If you ask a group of people to name the biggest sports cheat of all time, almost all of them will name the Texan. Wonderful human being Lance is often held up as the pinnacle of cheating, not just in Le Tour but in all sport.

Lance Armstrong wasn't always Lance Armstrong. When he was born in 1971, in Plano, Texas, his given name was Lance Edward Gunderson. 'Gunderson' came from his father, who left the family when Lance was two. A year later his mum married Terry Armstrong, who gave Lance his now famous surname.

'Live Strong' does sound better than 'Live Gunderson'.

Lance's first name was chosen by his parents in honour of the American football player Lance Rentzel. Naming him after a sports star could seem prophetic, but like all things with Lance, there was a lot going on under the surface.

Armstrong's parents had decided to name their son in honour of Rentzel just one year after he had been arrested for exposing himself to a ten-year-old girl. This may well be the weirdest Lance Armstrong fact in existence, just ahead of Armstrong once dating Ivanka Trump.

Armstrong began his sporting career as a triathlete. He dominated the cycling segments of races, leading him to eventually commit to cycling full time. By 1992 he was a professional.

It only took him three years to begin doping, starting in early 1995, but this was of course unknown at the time.

In 1996, Armstrong received the news that he had potentially fatal metastatic testicular cancer. His doctor told him he had a 20 per cent chance of surviving, but later admitted he just said that to give Armstrong hope – he believed he had no chance.

Lance's obsession with cycling was on display even during his cancer fight. He refused bleomycin, a powerful chemotherapeutic drug, because it can damage the lungs. Armstrong wanted to be able to race after he beat the cancer.

The enormity of Armstrong's cancer fight can't be overstated. Not only were his chances of survival extremely slim, he had to undergo extensive chemotherapy and had brain surgery to remove lesions in his brain.

Part of the mythology around Armstrong sprang from his battle to overcome cancer. It made his subsequent feats seem that much more amazing, and his work raising money through his Livestrong Foundation made him seem much more than an athlete.

The great unknown, though, was whether Armstrong's early doping actually caused the cancer. In the 2020 ESPN *30 for 30* documentary on Armstrong, 'Lance', even he admitted he couldn't rule out that possibility.

'I don't know if it's yes or no, but I certainly wouldn't say no,' Armstrong conceded. 'The only thing I will tell you is the only time in my life I ever did growth hormone was the 1996 season.' This was the year Armstrong was diagnosed with testicular cancer. 'So, just in my head, I'm like, "Growth, growing hormones and cells, if anything good needs to be grown it does, but wouldn't it also make sense that if anything bad was there it too would grow?"'

A COMEBACK FOR THE AGES

Overcoming cancer is one thing, but Armstrong's ability to come back and dominate his sport was key to his legend. Returning to the sport in 1998, he won the Tour de France seven years in a row – an astounding feat in itself, but on the back of almost dying of cancer, it was as close to superhuman as you can get.

This comeback was such a great story, at the time it seemed like a fairytale. And it was. Because it wasn't true.

When it came to cheating, Armstrong was ahead of all his competitors in both the breadth and organisation of his doping.

The first thing to remember when listening to Armstrong defend himself in one of his many self-serving interviews is that he not only doped himself, he pressured all those who raced in his team to do it too. If you didn't go along with him, if you refused to follow his strict doping regime, you were out. This was despite the fact that he suspected doping had contributed to his own cancer.

Armstrong's team, US Postal Service, ran a sophisticated scheme that involved erythropoietin (EPO), testosterone, cortisone, human growth hormone and blood transfusions. His medical team worked out a rigid system that ensured he and his teammates balanced what was in their blood and urine in a way that would help them get past the tests.

A simpler part of the plan was just avoiding the tests all together when they could. This proved to be laughably easy. Armstrong turned drug testing into a game of hide and seek.

To start with, there was a surprising lack of testing. Armstrong used to proudly claim he passed up to 600 tests over fourteen years, but the truth was the USADA only tested him sixty times in that period and the International Cycling Union tested him about 200 times, although many of these were for a health program, not doping tests.

I know, it's surprising that Armstrong would not be completely factual in how he presents himself.

To avoid the tests they did have to do, the US Postal team exploited the rather shambolic arrangements that were in place. Outside of competitions, professional cyclists have to inform the national drug authorities where they'll be. Failure to provide your whereabouts can result in warnings, and three of these in the space of eighteen months means you get the same punishment as failing a drug test.

But the US Postal riders discovered that you just had to tell the testers what city you'd be in. If they showed up at the address you'd given them, you could pretend you weren't in and you wouldn't get a warning for that.*

---

* This seems like a very simple strategy – it's hardly that of a criminal mastermind at work. Pretending no one's home when someone knocks on the door is standard operating procedure in my house.

Armstrong would also deliberately submit the details of his many trips at the last minute, often on the day he was leaving, making it almost impossible for the testers to keep up with him. Other times he stayed in a remote hotel in Spain where it was almost impossible for the tester to surprise him.

Armstrong also expected his teammates to look after him and warn him of any tests. In one case, his teammate George Hincapie sent him a text message warning him that the testers were at the team's hotel. Armstrong promptly dropped out of the race to avoid being tested.

When a test couldn't be avoided, like during competitions, the team would simply time when they took the drugs to ensure they were clean when a test happened.

This wasn't always foolproof. At the 1998 World Championships, testers surprised the team – which is sort of their job, they just usually weren't very good at it.

Armstrong knew he'd doped too recently to pass the test; it was not looking good. His teammates volunteered to go ahead of him to try and buy him some time. While this was going on, a member of his medical team managed to smuggle a bag of saline past the testers under his raincoat and quickly gave Armstrong a saline infusion.

The saline managed to get Armstrong's blood levels back to normal, but it had been a close-run thing – Armstrong's comeback was almost over before it began.

The next year, Armstrong came even closer to being undone, testing positive for a corticosteroid during the 1999 Tour de France. His teammate Tyler Hamilton later said in a sworn affidavit that the positive test prompted 'a great deal of swearing from Lance'.

But Armstrong again escaped, his team arguing the result was because of a cream Armstrong was using for saddle sores, an argument that was accepted by the authorities. The only problem was, he hadn't been using the cream; his team had managed to get a prescription backdated to make the claim appear to be true.

Perhaps the most amazing thing about Armstrong's entire career is that, despite the many rumours that swirled around him, he never got caught while he was still competing. It raises a few questions. Were the testers really that bad? Or was Lance really that good? It does make you wonder how badly the various cycling authorities wanted to take him down, given he was their biggest star.

Did they really have no idea that he was cheating for all those years? It's possible, but it's also a bit like Pakistan not knowing Osama bin Laden was living in a town that also happened to have the Pakistan Military Academy located in it.

BEING HORRIBLE

The second thing to remember when listening to Armstrong defend himself is how he treated those who tried to expose him. It was this side of him that made a mockery of the Armstrong legend, and showed the corrosive effects of cheating, beyond denying those who compete clean their rightful victories.

The immense force of will directed towards winning at the highest level is often on display in the greatest legends of a sport. Michael Jordan is often lauded for his ruthlessness, while acknowledging that it contributed to making him not the nicest person on the planet. Likewise Don Bradman, who dominated cricket perhaps even more than Jordan dominated basketball, famously didn't get along with his teammates.

Perhaps it's impossible to be that driven and also care about the feelings of those around you. Yet unlike Bradman and Jordan, Armstrong turned this mindset into covering up his extensive cheating. In this regard he was relentless; he sought to end people's careers in order to protect his own, even though he knew those critics were telling the truth.

Armstrong's approach was that the best defence is a strong offence. He did a Nike commercial that attacked those who suggested his victories may have relied on more than him and his bike.

When media suggested he doped, he sued or threatened them.

Fred Dreier of the magazine *VeloNews* said Armstrong went after him and the publication, urging sponsors to steer clear of the magazine after they put a hypodermic needle on their cover.

Reed Albergotti of the *Wall Street Journal* said that, after he wrote some negative stories, '[Armstrong] told my boss that I was a terrible journalist and that he had a dossier on me of my earlier articles. He would message my editor insulting things about me, including stuff about the way I looked. He knew I was a cyclist and he said I was too fat to be a cyclist.'

Armstrong also attacked former teammates who testified against him. Frankie Andreu and his wife, Betsy, had testified under oath that they were in a hospital room in 1996 when Armstrong told a doctor he was using EPO, human growth hormone and steroids. They were also critical of Armstrong's relationship with his long-time doctor Michele Ferrari, who had been previously linked to doping.

In response, Armstrong worked to have Frankie's contract with bike manufacturer Trek ended and attacked the couple publicly. At one point, Betsy received a voicemail from one of Armstrong's associates, saying, 'I hope somebody breaks a baseball bat over your head. I also hope that one day you have adversity in your life and you have some type of tragedy that will . . . definitely make an impact on you.'

When Armstrong famously confessed to his doping in 2013, in a tell-all interview with Oprah Winfrey, he admitted he had called Betsy a 'crazy bitch' but hastened to add that he 'never called her fat'.

Greg and Kathy LeMond also found out what it was like

to be on the receiving end of an Armstrong attack. Greg, a top cyclist who had won the Tour de France three times (1986, 1989 and 1990), had also criticised Lance's relationship with Michele Ferrari. In response, Armstrong got Trek bicycles to drop LeMond's bicycle brand.

Kathy explained the impact this had on her family: 'We lost our livelihood and we spent $4 million in legal fees defending ourselves.' It took years for the LeMonds to recover, and they only really got their lives back on track when Armstrong eventually came clean.

Italian cyclist Filippo Simeoni also incurred Armstrong's wrath for going against Michele Ferrari. Simeoni had testified that Ferrari had shown him how to dope, but Armstrong defended Ferrari aggressively, calling Simeoni a liar. In response, Simeoni sued him for defamation, although he later dropped the case.

When next they raced against each other, Armstrong rode up to Simeoni and said, 'You made a mistake when you testified against Ferrari and you made a mistake when you sued me. I have a lot of time and money and I can destroy you.' He then made a zipping-his-lips motion towards the TV camera. It wasn't exactly subtle.

Armstrong also went after Emma O'Reilly, the former masseuse of the US Postal Service team, who had given an interview that formed the basis of a book by sports journalist Pierre Ballester, *L.A. Confidentiel*, which outlined much of Armstrong's doping.

Armstrong began the character assassination immediately, claiming O'Reilly hadn't resigned from her position but was sacked because of 'inappropriate' issues in the team. He said O'Reilly was afraid 'we were going to out her . . . as a whore, or whatever, I don't know'. He testified in a deposition for a libel lawsuit against her that she was an 'alcoholic whore'.

O'Reilly later said, 'The traumatising part was dealing with telling the truth.'

The person Armstrong went after the most was his former teammate Floyd Landis, who in 2010 had emailed the CEO of USA Cycling, Steve Johnson, a complete outline of how he and his US Postal team had doped.

In 2012, after two years of investigation, USADA brought doping charges against Armstrong. After initially contesting the charges, Armstrong dropped his defence but maintained his innocence – until that calculated Oprah interview in 2013. But the damage had already been done. Sponsors had fled and Armstrong stood down as the chairman of his charity. He was stripped of his seven Tour de France titles and an Olympic medal, and he was banned from cycling for life.

Landis had also filed a whistleblower lawsuit under the federal False Claims Act. In this he alleged Armstrong and his team had defrauded the government by taking the US Postal Service sponsorship money while doping. This was the lawsuit that was later joined by the US government, with the two parties settling out of court in 2013. In the end Armstrong lost over $100 million in sponsorships, legal fees and settlements.

But even now, with everything proven to be true, Lance still attacks Landis. In that ESPN documentary, which screened in 2020, Armstrong said about moving from Texas to Colorado, where he now lives, 'Could be worse. I could be Floyd Landis, waking up a piece of shit every day.'

That's the thing with Lance. Even after the truth came out, he's continued to show he's a terrible person. He even used his cancer as a defence when people were attacking him, confessing in the documentary, 'I'll admit, I used cancer occasionally as a shield.'

The thing is, no matter how bad we all think Lance Armstrong's actions were, he cannot be fully understood without knowing the history of cycling and doping, most specifically in relation to the Tour de France.

He may be a terrible person, but Armstrong was no anomaly in the sport when it comes to doping. He stands on the shoulders of giants. Doped up, scheming giants.

IT BEGINS, ESPECIALLY THE CHEATING

The first Tour de France, in 1903, was a marketing exercise to boost the circulation of the newspaper *L'Auto*. At the time the paper's numbers were plummeting, losing ground to its competitor, the long-standing *Le Vélo*. The two papers were locked in a bitter battle.

L'Auto editor Henri Desgrange was pitched the idea to hold a race around France by his employee Géo Lefèvre; he knew something big was needed to change *L'Auto*'s trajectory. So if you think of the Tour as essentially a publicity stunt, a lot of what's coming will make sense.

Planning began for a six-stage race that would leave from Paris and travel through Lyon, Marseille, Toulouse, Bordeaux and Nantes, then return and finish back in Paris. Each stage was 400 kilometres long, with competitors using bicycles that usually had no gears and were much heavier than today's with their ultralight frames. This made it a gruelling race, even if it didn't travel through the mountains that the modern race is so famous for.

Riders also had to do their own repairs along the way, which sounds like fun.

But there was a lot of optimism around the race – it was a chance to display the beauty of racing across France, and top riders had signed on. The favourite to win was one Maurice Garin. He certainly set the tone for the Tour's future – and makes Lance Armstrong look like a choirboy.

THE CHIMNEY SWEEP

Maurice-François Garin was born in 1871 in the town of Arvier, in north-west Italy, in the French-speaking Aosta Valley. Being so close to the French border, Garin always saw himself as French, and later in life he became a naturalised citizen.

Life was hard for Garin. He was one of nine children, and the family was poor. He was small of stature, which eventually led to him moving to France at the age of fifteen: there was plenty of work for chimneysweeps in northern France, and it turns out that being small is a real advantage if you have a job that involves being shoved down a chimney.

His family agreed for him to be smuggled across the border to work as a chimneysweep. In return, they received a wheel of cheese.* A fair swap.

Before long Garin found himself working in factories, often running errands on a bicycle. He realised he had a love for cycling, and some talent.

Soon he was riding regularly in amateur races, and eventually he decided to enter a race in Avesnes-sur-Helpes, not far from his home. Upon arriving he discovered the race was only for professionals. He tried to talk his way into competing but was firmly told no.

Rather than heading home, Garin came up with a plan. As the race started, he waited for a moment, then took off after the professional cyclists, ignoring the officials telling him to stop.

Despite giving up an enormous head start, Garin overtook all of the professionals and won the race, the crowd cheering him on. The organisers refused to pay him the F150 prizemoney, so the crowd raised F300 for him.

In Garin's first ever professional race, he broke the rules. This established a lifelong pattern.

Garin was hooked. Soon he was racing professionally all over France, becoming known as 'le petit ramoneur' – The Little Chimneysweep. When it comes to nicknames, it's hardly The Butcher

---

* Getting a wheel of cheese for selling your kid off into indentured servitude is frowned upon these days, which is a shame – everyone loves cheese.

of Bilbao. Despite this, he endeared himself to crowds and the iconic image of him racing with a lit cigarette dangling from the corner of his mouth was splashed across newspapers the length of France.

Smoking while riding wasn't strange at the time – most of the cyclists smoked, there was a belief that it 'opened the lungs'.* It was not uncommon before a gruelling part of the race for all the cyclists to quickly stop and suck down a few ciggies, believing it would help them.

As well as smoking while riding, Garin was famous for what he ate during races. He would eat oysters and consume several litres of tapioca, washing it all down with hot chocolate and red wine. Alcohol was basically compulsory in the races of the day; none of the riders would have passed a breath test if they'd existed back then.

Putting aside the oysters, wine and cigarettes – certain to make anyone a top professional cyclist – he was also ruthless. Journalist and author Peter Cossins said of Garin, 'Lance Armstrong was a modern day Maurice Garin. That's what Maurice Garin was like. He intimidated everybody. He wanted everybody to do things in the way that he saw was fit. He wasn't subtle about what he was doing at all.'

By 1903, Garin was at the peak of French cycling, a master without peer. The inaugural Tour would show just how far Garin was willing to go.

KICKING OFF

Sixty cyclists left Paris on 1 July 1903. Almost immediately the big race was beset by controversy. Hippolyte Aucouturier, one of the favourites, had to stop in the opening stage due to stomach cramps.

The cause of the cramps was revealed to be a spiked bottle of lemonade that had been handed to him by a roadside spectator.

---

* I'm not a doctor, but I don't think this is true. Unless 'open up the lungs' means during an autopsy.

The first dodgy event of the Tour had happened, the crowd had gotten involved, and they hadn't even finished the first stage.

But other cheating had been arranged before the race even started.

Teams make a huge difference in cycling. When riders are at the front of the pack, everyone behind them rides in a slipstream, which is much easier going. It's a massive aerodynamic advantage – studies have shown drag reductions of between 27 and 50 per cent. In teams, the star's teammates will sacrifice themselves to allow him to save energy for the mountain stages and sprints, or to allow him to break away from the pack to win.

But Henri Desgrange had mandated that the Tour would be a test of individual strength and stamina, meaning that teams were banned. No one would be getting that kind of assistance in the first tour – in fact, teams weren't fully legal until 1930.

Garin, however, had no interest in the niceties of the rules. He'd put together a team, or as they called it, a 'group', named La Française. They didn't acknowledge this was what they were doing, but they would protect and help each other during the race. At least, that was the idea.

In the fifth stage, four members of La Française had broken away from the field. Garin was leading, and he told the group that he would be winning the stage, only for one of the group, Fernand Augereau, to argue, 'Well, I think I can win. Why should I let you win?'

Garin was furious. He had expected complete loyalty from his team. He ordered another member of La Française to knock Augereau off his bike, which he promptly did.

Augereau hit the road, but he pulled himself up, got back on his bike and chased them down. Garin saw him coming and issued the same order.

Again, Augereau hit the road. But this time Garin stopped. He got off his bike and jumped up and down on Augereau's wheels until they were completely smashed, rendering the bike unusable.

This wasn't exactly subtle, and it was also done in front of spectators, who watched on in amazement as Garin obliterated Augereau's bike before riding off again.

One of the spectators was so appalled, he handed his own bike to Augereau, who took off in pursuit, catching his former team-mates once again. This time, both Augereau's tyres blew out before any further brutality could occur. La Française powered ahead and Garin won the Tour de France.

Augereau, however, wasn't about to let this injustice stand. He presented his story to the organisers; after all, he had witnesses.

The organisers listened to his case intently, then ignored him completely. The whole thing was about boosting the circulation of *L'Auto* and here they had the most popular rider in France winning what had been a very successful race. None of the organisers wanted to change the outcome. Running the Tour had been a risk that had paid off – why ruin it?

So from its very beginnings the Tour de France had a winner who cheated, violently so, and had it covered up by the organisers.

In their eyes, the end justified the means. The circulation of *L'Auto* increased more than six-fold during and after the race – a stunning turnaround. By 1905, their competitor *Le Vélo* was out of business.

GUNS, BLOCKADES AND TRAINS

Excitingly for us, the next Tour delivered behaviour that was much, much worse. It was a beauty.

Just weeks before a certain St Louis marathon was run, the second Tour de France kicked off on 2 July 1904, following the same route as the previous year. Thanks to the success of the first race, and the star power of Garin, interest had skyrocketed. Spectators lined the course and cheered on the riders, especially when they rode through their home town. With passions heightened, the race turned into a brutal battle between the riders, but also involving the spectators.

The cheating got underway immediately. Some riders put itching powder in other cyclists' shorts, others sabotaged their competitors' bikes. Compared to what lay in store, this was all good clean fun.

The first stage saw riders try all manner of tricks to get ahead. One caught a ride in a car for forty-five minutes, another rode in the slipstream of a car and a third, Ferdinand Payan, was disqualified for being assisted by other riders.

Hippolyte Aucouturier, he of the poisoned lemonade during the first tour, was also caught cheating. He tied a length of string to a car and attached a cork to it, which he gripped between his teeth. He was pulled along in this way for some time, miraculously avoiding dental damage, as far as we know. His one mistake was that the car drove too fast – he arrived at the end of the stage almost at the same time as a bunch of race officials who were travelling by car.

A new thing the riders in the second Tour had to deal with was hostile spectators who were keen to assist their favourite riders. Garin became concerned about this early on – he preferred violence that he was orchestrating. During the race he remarked, 'If I'm not murdered before we reach Paris, I'll win the Tour de France again.'

He wasn't exaggerating – being murdered wasn't out of the question for any of the riders. Before the first stage ended, four masked men in a car attempted to run Garin and his rival Lucien Pothier off the road. The cyclists managed to escape to safety, but it was a sign of things to come.

Further controversy arose when it became known that Garin had received food along the route, as riders were only supposed to get food at designated points. But the organisers couldn't punish him – they were the ones who had provided him with the food. Garin had threatened to drop out of the race if they didn't feed him along the way and the organisers, worried about losing their biggest star, had relented.

It had been an eventful start to the race, and only the first of six stages had been completed.

THE BATTLE OF SAINT-ÉTIENNE

The second stage in 1904 was arguably the most dramatic in the entire history of the Tour de France.

Between Lyon and Saint-Étienne, Andre Faure was pushing ahead of the field when he entered his home town. The townsfolk had lined the roads to cheer him on, and they decided to give him a bit of assistance.

After Faure passed, 200 of them blockaded the road. They wouldn't let any other rider through, attacking them instead. Soon a riot had broken out, with the townsfolk yelling 'Kill them!' as they rushed the cyclists.

It was hand-to-hand combat, the cyclists fighting off the stick-wielding townsfolk.

Géo Lefèvre – the man had come up with the idea of the Tour De France – arrived in a support car. Assessing the situation, he pulled out his gun and fired several shots into the air until the mob dispersed.

The brawl was no laughing matter. Garin sustained a hand injury and finished the stage using only one hand. Another rider, Paul Gerbi, was left unconscious on the side of the road and had his fingers broken. He did not continue the race.

After the blockade was cleared, the riders continued on, only to find another obstacle: the road ahead was covered in nails and broken glass, causing numerous punctures and delaying them even further.

As the second stage finished, the confusion was so great that the control post forgot to record the correct finishing times of the cyclists who had finally made it through the gauntlet.

The riders complained that the whole stage should be voided, but there was no budging from the organisers.

STICKS AND STONES

You'd think things would settle down after all that drama, but the third stage was no better. The Tour entered Nîmes, near the home town of Ferdinand Payan, who had been disqualified during the first stage for receiving assistance from others, including riding behind a car for large parts of the stage.

His fans now demanded that the decision be overturned, but the race organisers refused. The result was that the crowd barricaded the road to stop the entire Tour and began pelting the riders with rocks. Several were injured.

Again, the organisers had to step in and brandish firearms to persuade the crowd to disperse. It was now becoming a bit of a tradition: 'We begin the stage with the now traditional building of the barricade and the firing of the warning shots.'

Another emerging tradition was observed when the riders encountered more nails and broken glass all over the road, forcing them to continue on foot, carrying their bikes for much of the way.

It had been another eventful day. Most of the riders hadn't had a chance to cheat, they had been so busy avoiding being murdered by angry mobs.

Both the organisers and the riders needed a quiet next stage, and luckily, they got it. But that didn't mean no cheating.

JUST THE TICKET

Stage four got underway without any angry mobs, and Garin used the relative quiet to increase his lead. We don't know exactly when but somewhere along the route he caught a train for part of the stage.

The Tour was so big and spread out, it was hard for organisers to survey all of the stages properly. This time, instead of jumping in cars or being towed, riders had decided to catch the train. Garin didn't actually admit he'd caught the train until he was an old man. But he was hardly alone – at least nine other riders had jumped on the train, and numerous others took shortcuts.

A lack of major crowd violence and a nice train journey saw the riders somewhat refreshed for the fifth stage, but once again they were beset by nails on the roads, causing numerous punctures. As outside assistance wasn't allowed, the riders had to stop and fix their own tyres as best they could, wasting precious time. Young cyclist Henri Cornet couldn't fix his tyres because the damage was so bad, so he rode the last 40 kilometres of the stage on two flat tyres.

By now, Paris was in sight, and it came down to a battle between Aucouturier and Garin. Aucouturier won the final stage, but Garin, who'd come second in the final stage, won the Tour overall.

The little chimneysweep had done it again – two Tour victories in a row.

But this time the cheating had been too widespread. Everyone knew the whole race had been a complete mess. The getting in cars, the catching of trains, the sabotaging of other riders' bikes, even the itching powder in the shorts – it had all made it into the media. There had been riders working in teams, physical altercations and threats. It was a delightful mess.

Almost immediately an investigation was set up, and they received testimonies from dozens of competitors and witnesses.

Henri Desgrange despaired. His marketing exercise looked like it was backfiring. In *L'Auto*, he proclaimed, 'The Tour is finished, and I am very afraid that the second edition will be the last. It will have been killed by its own success, driven out of control by blind passion, by violence and filthy suspicions worthy only of ignorant and dishonourable men.'

Four months after the race, the investigative committee announced that the top four finishers would all be disqualified.

Twenty-nine other riders were also punished. The reasons for the suspensions were never released, and the records were lost during the war, meaning we will probably never know the full extent of the riders' skulduggery.

But we can get some sense of the level of cheating that was going on by who was eventually declared the winner: Henri Cornet, who had finished one stage on two flat tyres. He was just shy of his twentieth birthday when he won, and is still the youngest man to ever win the Tour de France.

Cornet himself had been warned for receiving a lift in a car during the race, but this was deemed to be not serious enough cheating, which means the four disqualified riders ahead of him must have done far worse things.

It was a case of another tour, another tainted winner.

Despite all this, Desgrange's concern that blind passion would end the Tour was unwarranted. The cheating was all part of the fun; it was a feature rather than a critical weakness. The passion really was blind – blind to all the rule-breaking – but that served to make the Tour even more popular.

Garin himself never raced again; he retired to Lens and bought a service station. When he was a very old man, his mind started to go. He would wander the streets asking, 'Where is the control? Where is the control?' referring to the checkpoints where riders signed in during the first two editions of the herculean, flawed, Tour de France.

SCALING THE PEAK

If the race organisers expected the 1905 edition of the Tour to be cleaned up, they were quickly disabused of this notion when an estimated 125 kilograms of nails were scattered along the first day's route, from Paris to Nancy. Only fifteen of the sixty starters made it through, and organisers had to allow the riders who had been forced to complete the stage by train or car back into the race.

But the crowd violence lessened over the years that followed the 1904 debacle, and this allowed riders to focus more on finding advantages rather than putting all their energy into staying alive.

In 1910, with the introduction of mountain stages, competitors needed new ways to help them get through an even harder race. One rider was known to ride up to Henri Desgrange's car on the mountain stages and pick a fight with him over the rules.

He'd say something like, 'Rule 72, sub-section four, paragraph three, doesn't make sense.'

Desgrange, an authoritarian, was a stickler for the rules and would respond with a passionate defence of that particular rule. The entire time, the rider would be subtly holding onto the car's door handle, getting a free lift up the mountain.

The 1911 Tour saw another case of poisoning. Given that there hadn't been one since the inaugural 1903 race, it was probably overdue.

Paul Duboc, a rider who had just won two stages in a row, collapsed with stomach pains while climbing in the Pyrenees. He lay on the ground for over an hour in complete agony.

Duboc survived, and even continued the race, but it had cost him the lead. Suspicion fell on Gustave Garrigou, the man who now led the race. Unfortunately for Garrigou, the course was about to take them through Rouen – Duboc's home town.

The night before the Tour arrived, signs were put up that said: 'Citizens of Rouen! If I had not been poisoned, I would be leading the Tour de France today. You know what to do when the Tour passes through Rouen tomorrow.'

Duboc had nothing to do with the notices, but it spelled trouble for Garrigou. He changed the colour of his bike and riding googles to try to throw the crowd off his scent. Tour organisers also sent three cars with bodyguards to act as barriers between Garrigou and the crowd. Amazingly, he got through unscathed, which was just as well.

Later on it was discovered that another rider, François Lafourcade, had been the one who poisoned Duboc. Garrigou had been completely innocent. He went on to win the Tour.

Over the years, riders decided poisoning was too much trouble and came up with other clever plans. One of the smartest schemes was that of Jean Robic, who won the 1947 Tour de France. Robic was small and light, which helped in some instances, but was a hindrance on the mountain descents, which are all about speed. At the top of each mountain he would grab a drink bottle from his support team that was filled with either lead shot or mercury, giving him extra weight and making him faster on the way down. Once finished, he would discard the bottle.

But other riders had something far more dangerous in their bottles.

BAD FISH

Doping pre-dates the Tour de France, and it has caused all sorts of problems for riders from the very beginning of cycling as a sport. From the earliest race, riders were putting all kinds of things in their bodies because there were no rules stopping them from doing so – it was all legal.

In the late nineteenth century, the American champion cyclist Major Taylor was racing in New York when the cocktail of drugs he was on caused him to start hallucinating. He stopped racing and, when asked if he was alright, answered, 'I cannot go on with safety, for there is a man chasing me around the ring with a knife in his hand.'

For the start of the Tour, caffeine, strychnine, cocaine and alcohol were all there. And huge quantities of alcohol – drinking wine dulled the pain – remained part of the race right up until the sixties.

The first time the public became aware of the amount of drugs being used in the Tour was when brothers Francis and Henri Pélissier* took a journalist through their bags while competing in the 1924 race. Pulling out various packages, they said, 'Cocaine to go in our eyes, chloroform for our gums, and do you want to see the pills? We keep going on dynamite. In the evenings we dance around our rooms instead of sleeping.'

This wasn't something the authorities were turning a blind eye to; it was all legal, and they didn't care. Drugs were so much part of the sport that the 1930 rulebook, given to all riders, reminded them that drugs would not be provided by the organisers.

Riders would regularly go down from tainted drugs, often en masse. The excuse given to the media was that they had eaten 'bad fish', which happened so often that 'bad fish' became code for any doping scandal.

The next major shift for the Tour came with the arrival of amphetamines. The drug first used by the Nazis, and later other armies in World War II, found a whole new market in the public – and athletes were big consumers.

In a television interview the winner of the Tour in 1949 and 1952, Fausto Coppi, admitted openly that he had used a special cocktail he called 'la Bomba', which he put in his water bottles. It certainly would have given him a significant boost: it contained amphetamines, caffeine, opiates, ether, cocaine, chloroform and alcohol.**

Asked when he used it, he said, 'Only when I have to.'

Asked when that was, he responded, 'Almost all the time.'

He was hardly alone in having his own cocktail of drugs. Five-time Tour champion (1957, 1961–64), Jacques Anquetil, would inject morphine to dull the pain in his body and then take amphetamines to prevent the lethargic effects of the morphine.

---

* Henri won the 1923 Tour.
** I think this was also a cocktail on offer at a suburban nightclub I frequented in my youth.

He once remarked, 'You would have to be an imbecile or a crook to imagine a professional cyclist who races for 235 days a year can hold the pace without stimulants.'

Elsewhere, Anquetil stated, 'For fifty years bike racers have been taking stimulants. Obviously, we can do without them in a race, but then we will pedal 15 miles an hour instead of 25. Since we're constantly asked to go faster and to make even greater efforts, we are obliged to take stimulants.'

Other riders used a variety of analgesics to manage their pain, with opioids being particularly popular.

The dangers of all these drugs became particularly obvious during the 1960 Tour, when Roger Rivière was descending the Col de Perjuret and went off the road and into a ravine. He had broken his back and had to be helicoptered out.

Rivière blamed his mechanic, arguing that his breaks had failed, but doctors had found palfium – a powerful analgesic – in his pockets. They believed the drugs had numbed his fingers, making it impossible for him to feel his break levers.

He would later admit to taking other drugs, such as amphetamines. After the crash, he never regained the use of his legs, spending the rest of his life using a wheelchair.

This was not necessarily a wake-up call for the Tour organisers, more of a light stirring, but the widespread use of drugs was starting to be seen as a little problematic.

TESTING THE TESTERS

By this time, most teams had a 'soigneur'. This was someone who helped with transportation and supplies, but more often than not they were also responsible for providing the drugs. Some soigneurs were sought out specifically for their expertise in mixing certain drugs.

This could sometimes become a real problem, because one soigneur could be servicing numerous cyclists – if something went wrong with the drugs, it really went wrong. In the 1962 Tour, twenty riders went down with an unknown illness. Once again, 'bad fish' was given as the reason, but really, they'd all received a concoction from the same soigneur.

These cases and numerous others finally forced the Tour organisers to act. Behind the scenes, doctors had quietly been saving riders' lives after drug-related collapses for years, but they'd had enough. As of 1 June 1965, performance-enhancing drugs became illegal.

For the first Tour under the new rule there was no testing, so it was completely ignored. Riders focused only on avoiding getting caught in the actual act of taking drugs.

But in 1966, drug testing finally arrived at the Tour de France. Following the eighth stage, rider Raymond Poulidor was required to give the first-ever urine sample. The riders saw this as degrading and an invasion of their privacy so the very next day, not long after the start of stage, they walked for five minutes in protest.

That was the end of testing for that year.

The following year, as the Tour started, most riders just outright refused to be tested. The Tour, realising they couldn't suspend everyone, basically let them.

The year everything changed was 1967. The leader of the British team, Tom Simpson, was three kilometres from the top of Mont Ventoux when he collapsed.

Simpson had already been struggling. Earlier he'd had 'excessive diarrhoea', never a good thing, but pushed himself to keep going. Not long before he collapsed, he'd fallen off his bike but got back on, drinking some brandy to fortify himself.

But the second time he fell, Simpson didn't get back up. He was airlifted to hospital, where he died soon after.

In his pockets, doctors found three empty vials and plenty of pills. The post-mortem examination found both amphetamines and alcohol in his system. Simpson had pushed his body further than it could go, and when it told him to stop, he'd taken drugs and alcohol to push through the barriers of human performance.

Simpson's death hung heavily over the Tour. Both the organisers and the riders had resisted tackling the issue for decades, and now a popular rider, one of Britain's best, was dead.

Drug testing was something riders could no longer say no to. But they had always known the risks of taking performance-enhancing drugs, so a death, while tragic, wasn't going to stop them doping. And so began the now time-honoured tradition of trying to beat the tests.

The seventies continued to see riders using drugs, and positive test were still rare. The science wasn't as sophisticated as it is now, and many riders learned how to time when they took drugs to make sure they had cleared out of their system ahead of any possible test.

They also developed other, more elaborate ways to cheat the tests, with urine substitution a popular method.

The lengths that riders would go to were exposed in 1978, when Belgian rider Michel Pollentier, one of the top riders, was caught trying to deceive a drug test. It was a massive story at the time – he had the leader's yellow jersey at the end of stage 16.

Drug testers watched riders as they passed urine, to ensure the person giving the sample was indeed the rider. But Pollentier had rigged up a condom filled with someone else's urine and placed this under his armpit. It was attached to a tube that was threaded down to his shorts, through which Pollentier planned to empty the urine into the drug test.

Unfortunately for Pollentier, another rider had used the same method earlier in the day, but his 'equipment' malfunctioned and he was caught in the act. So the testers were looking out for it, and Pollentier was caught too.

Pollentier was kicked off the Tour and, in the public's mind, drugs were now seen as something the top riders used. Not that this was really a new revelation.

It seems that time and again the sports world is shocked to learn about the extent of drug use on the Tour, but the only thing that's shocking is our ability to forget, the ability to be shocked repeatedly, when in reality, it's never stopped.

Pollentier being caught was not a wake-up moment for the sport either. Instead, teams just became more sophisticated in how they went about doping. This is the thing about cheating: when an individual does it, it's often simplistic, but a team-based approach brings a whole new level of endeavour to the dark arts. You can achieve so much more when you're working as a team.

By the eighties, doping was turning into a science. Teams had doctors travelling with them who would put riders on drips to rehydrate them, and they would have centrifuges 'cleaning' riders' blood overnight. A Tour de France rider's hotel room would look like an intensive care unit.

In 1991, the entire Dutch PDM team went down with a fever. There were televised images of all the riders shivering uncontrollably as they were helped back to their hotel. The spectre of drugs had risen over the Tour once again.

'Bad fish', the media reported with glee.

The team eventually blamed the fever on the riders being given incorrectly stored 'Intralipid'. Intralipid is an extract of the soya bean. It was technically legal, but showed that the teams and their doctors were still pushing the boundaries of ethics. After all, Intralipid is usually used to feed comatose patients.

Many didn't believe this was the true cause of the fevers – rumours swirled that the PDM team had been using EPO, a naturally occurring hormone synthesised in a lab. It causes bone marrow to produce more red blood cells, improving the body's ability to transport oxygen. It's often referred to as a 'blood booster'. Tarnished by the incident and the rumours, the entire PDM team quit the sport and the franchise was sold to Festina, a Swiss watch brand.

In 1997, the rumours of PDM using drugs back in 1991 were confirmed by their previous manager, Manfred Krikke, who said of the team, 'The one rule imposed from the PDM directors was that there was to be "no drug affairs" rather than "no drug taking".'

The arrival of EPO changed everything in the sport of cycling. Suddenly teams had season-long programs of drug injections for their riders. Every team had an entire team of medical staff supporting them.

In 1993, the Gewiss team's doctor, Michele Ferrari, said in a TV interview that EPO was like orange juice: safe in moderation. He seemed shocked when the team fired him, but he shouldn't have worried too much, you might remember that he got more work, with one of his clients being Lance Armstrong.

But before Armstrong came the biggest scandal the Tour de France had ever seen.

A TRAVELLING PHARMACY

In early July 1998, Willy Voet was driving across Europe on his way to Ireland, where the Tour de France would be starting in a few days.* He was driving an official car of the Festina cycling team – formerly PDM – all decked out in the team's logos. As soigneur of the team, Voet looked after France's biggest cycling star, Richard Virenque, and he was keen to get to Ireland as soon as as possible.

Unfortunately, when he got the Belgian–French border, the customs officials seemed intent on actually doing their job, which was awkward, given that Voet's car was basically a pharmacy on

---

* The Tour has started with stages outside of France numerous times. The first time was in Amsterdam, in 1954. Amsterdam is the perfect place for Tour de France riders.

wheels. Customs officials discovered 235 doses of EPO, 82 doses of the hormone Sauratropine, 160 doses of Pantestone (a derivative of testosterone), and a wonderful assortment of steroids, amphetamines, syringes and other drug paraphernalia.

It seemed like a lot for one person.

Police and customs immediately began an investigation, raiding the Festina offices in Lyon, where they found other drugs and details of the doping program.

But in Ireland, the Tour de France began as if nothing had happened. Rumours of the arrest reached the media travelling with the Tour, but the Festina team downplayed Voet's role in the team and denied all knowledge.

This all changed once the Tour returned to France, with French police quickly arresting Festina's sports director, Bruno Roussel, and physician Eric Rijckaert.

Roussel proved himself to be a poor member of a criminal conspiracy, soon confessing that the team had a systematic doping program in place. Police arrested all nine of the Festina riders.

Tour de France director Jean-Marie Leblanc, reeling from these events, banned the Festina team from the Tour. With police running the investigation, the Tour organisers had little control over what was happening; the police were approaching this not just from a doping point of view, but in terms of importing and distributing illicit substances.

Tour management could only watch as events quickly spun further out of control. The police raided team doctor Eric Rijckaert's office and discovered computer files that detailed much more of Festina's doping program, including that the riders were using EPO.

Under questioning, all the riders except for Richard Virenque and Pascal Hervé admitted to doping. Virenque vigorously protested his innocence to the media.

Festina rider Alex Zülle recalled the frightening experience of being interrogated by police: 'In the beginning, the officials were friendly, but then the horror show began. I was put in an isolation cell and had to strip naked. They inspected every cavity. The next morning, they confronted me with compromising documents they had found. They said they were used to seeing hardened criminals in the chair I was sitting on. I wanted out of that hellhole, so I confessed.'

Any sense that doping was limited to just the Festina team lasted only one day after they were banned from the race. I know, it's unbelievable.

With what became known as the Festina Affair now dominating the news, French police were reminded of an investigation that had been stalled since March that year. An official car of the TVM team from the Netherlands had also been searched while crossing the border on its way back from a race in Spain. Two team mechanics had been caught with 104 vials of EPO in the car, but the case had not advanced much since then.

This changed overnight following the Festina arrests. On a rest day, police swooped on the hotel where TVM was staying, resulting in the arrest of TVM manager Cees Priem and their doctor Andrei Michailov.

In the team's hotel room, various drugs and masking agents were found and, upon examination, traces of EPO were identified in used syringes recovered from their bins. One TVM team member told the media, 'The police were acting like Nazis.' A particularly sensitive comment in France.

Over the next few days, police sent six of the TVM riders to hospital for blood, urine and hair tests. In response, TVM pulled out of the race as well.

The other riders and teams reacted to these raids like they had to the introduction of doping tests thirty years earlier: they protested. First, they went on strike for two hours, but this did little to stop the unfolding disaster. Police were beginning to follow all sorts of leads. A few days later, the riders staged another protest, cycling slowly before stopping completely. The entire field then threatened to pull out of the race. Organisers immediately cancelled the stage.

The problem was that this was now a full-blown police investigation, and the cops didn't care about what the riders and organisers of the Tour thought. On the afternoon after the second protest, police raided the hotels of several more teams: Team ONCE, Team Polti, La Française des Jeux, Lotto and Casino. Arrests were made and teams began pulling out of the Tour at a rapid rate.

ONCE sports director Manolo Saiz announced his team was leaving. They were sick of the dawn raids that had become, by the third week of the 1998 Tour, as common as the mountain climbs. 'I have shoved my finger up the Tour's arse,' Saiz told the media before returning to Spain. All the Spanish teams followed suit and quit the Tour.

With teams dropping out and more arrests being made than the media could keep track of, the Tour itself had become a sideshow. Of the 189 riders that had started the Tour, fewer than 100 were left. Amazingly, the 1998 Tour did actually finish, with Italian Marco Pantani winning.

Naturally Pantini's victory was overshadowed by the Festina Affair, which continued to escalate in the following months.*

In November 1998 the results of the samples taken from the Festina riders became public. They tested positive for human growth hormone, amphetamines, steroids, corticoids and EPO;

---

* Six years later, Pantini died of cocaine poisoning, aged just thirty-four. In 2013, it was revealed that retroactive testing of his urine and blood samples had shown he was also using EPO during the 1998 Tour.

it would have been easier to list what they weren't on. TVM riders returned positive results as well.

The criminal trial of the Festina team began in October 2000. It had been two years and three months since they had been banned from the Tour. But the biggest fish in the net, Richard Virenque, still denied any wrongdoing, which turned the trial into a media storm. Many French cycling fans still saw him as innocent, and the court-room in Lille was surrounded by media when Virenque was called to the stand.

The presiding magistrate began by asking Virenque, 'Do you accept this reality, that you took doping products?'

'Yes,' the French star replied. He then admitted to taking EPO. 'It was a like a train going away from me and, if I didn't get on it, I would be left behind,' he said. 'It was not cheating. I wanted to remain in the family.'

It felt like a betrayal to all the French fans who had defended him. But there was nowhere left to hide from the truth. Virenque had finally faced reality.

Outside of the Tour de France, the Festina Affair helped speed up the development of the World Anti-Doping Agency (WADA), and better testing for EPO use. The whole saga showed how sophis-ticated doping had become, and heightened the need for an equally sophisticated response.

Once again, there were predictions of the end of the Tour. But despite having briefly ripped apart cycling, the whole thing had surprisingly little effect on the event itself. Even in the short term, nothing changed.

Lance Armstrong, recovering from chemotherapy at the time of the 1998 Tour, was reporting on the race for an American TV network. He had a front row for the entire Festina Affair: the arrests, the denials and the very public confession of Richard Virenque.

Armstrong looked at all this and, instead of reading it as a cautionary tale, he interpreted it as a how-to guide. The very next year, in 1999, at the race dubbed the 'Tour of Renewal' by organisers, he won the first of his seven consecutive Tour de France victories.

CHAPTER 12

TEAM EFFORT

What the Tour de France shows, apart from the fact sportspeople do not learn from history, is that when it comes to cheating teams can often be more sophisticated than individuals. But sophisticated isn't always better, as we'll see. Sometimes elaborate cheating just means it ends up being more farcical.

Every team is on a quest to gain advantages over their opposition, so the entire industry around scouting, video reviews and statistical analysis has become more intense than a mission to the moon. And there is a thin line between gathering as much information on an opponent as possible and spying on them.

The problem is that when teams cheat they tend to leave a trail of witnesses, documents and other incriminating evidence. More moving pieces and more people just mean more chances of a plan going awry. And when everything inevitably starts to unravel, teams are left scrambling to cover up what they've done, which can lead to some very bizarre outcomes.

As Benjamin Franklin once observed, three can keep a secret – if two of them are dead.

Franklin is probably a bit more trusting of human nature than I am. I think having one person left seems a bit risky.

SHOCK ME

What's amazing about cheating is how history repeats and repeats and then repeats a little more.

As mentioned earlier, the Houston Astros, winners of the 2017 World Series, were found to have used a sophisticated system to steal their opponent's signs, but that type of cheating dates all the way back to before 1900.

In baseball, stealing the signs is completely legal so long as you don't use technology, and often, when a runner is on second base with a clear view of what the catcher is signalling, teams will change their signals to negate such a tactic.

In 1899, the Philadelphia Phillies had a backup catcher, Morgan Murphy, who rarely played at all. Murphy was coming to the end of his career, so this was no great surprise. But during games he would almost never be on the bench. Instead, he'd be sitting in a suite above deep centre field. From there, he'd use a pair of binoculars to watch the catcher's signals and then relay what kind of pitch was coming by moving some curtains. One side being closed represented a fastball, the other a curveball.

This rather basic system actually seemed to work. At home, the Phillies were 45–23, while on the road they were 30–40. An unnamed Phillies player later said, 'Had it not been for the signal service department we would be in the second division, and in many games where Morgan was not working, we could not hit a balloon.'

Murphy also attempted to use the system on the road, but with less success, since it was more difficult to set up. For games in Brooklyn, for example, he went to the trouble of renting a room across the street from the ballpark and used a newspaper to signal the pitches. Later, Brooklyn figured it out, and they barred him from entering the apartment, resulting in a Brooklyn win.

Many other teams also suspected the Phillies of being up to something – both Louisville and Baltimore would change their signs whenever they played Philadelphia. But Murphy's exploits were revealed to the wider public when a pitcher named Bill Magee, who'd played for the Phillies before moving to Washington, told *The Washington Post* about the scheme. 'Any player in the league will tell you that [the Phillies] were helped to many a hit by a confederate, by means that are perfectly legitimate, because there are no rules in the baseball code to prevent this scheme that was employed to bunco* opposing pitchers out of hits. Morgan Murphy was the villain in this plot.'

He was right. It wouldn't be until 1961 that a rule banning the use of mechanical devices for spying on the opposition was brought in. But even in 1899 it was seen as cheating by the rest of the league, even if it didn't breach the rules.

This is often the case with cheating: there's no rule against the practice because it's so obviously cheating that most teams don't do it. Instead, the cheating is monitored by the other teams and enforced through peer pressure and ridicule. If this wasn't the case, everyone would do it, and openly.

The Washington Post article explained how at Phillies home games Murphy would sit above the Baker Bowl clubhouse 'with a telescope of wonderful magnifying power' and signal the batter 'by certain manipulations of the side curtains of the observatory'. The *Post* also said Morgan had cleared this plot with Phillies co-owner John Rogers.

---

* Swindle or cheat.

But following the article, there were no consequences from the league, just embarrassment and the anger of the other teams. The Phillies put an end to the scheme, but not the spying. They decided they just needed a better, less obvious approach.

In 1900, Murphy decided to include his teammate Pearce Chiles in developing a new scheme for stealing signs.

Chiles was the perfect accomplice. Biographer Ron Schuler described him as 'one of the most slippery, elusive historical characters major-league baseball has ever produced'. Chiles had never been a great player, bouncing around from team to team and league to league, and while he was technically still playing, the Phillies mainly used him as a third base coach.*

Together, Chiles and Murphy came up with a far more sophisticated scheme than the previous season's. Murphy would still sit in the suite above centre field, but he wouldn't use the curtains, as this was now too obvious. Instead, he had a telegraph. Its wires ran all the way from the suite, down under the ground of the outfield, ending under the third base coach's box (which is just lines marked on the ground on the side of the diamond, outside the field of play), where Chiles would stand when the Phillies were batting.

When Murphy pressed the button in the suite, a box under Chiles would buzz. Chiles apparently came up with the idea after he once stepped on a live wire. Murphy would read the catcher's sign, then buzz once for a fastball, twice for a curve ball and three times for a slow ball. Chiles would then signal that information to the batter.

Many observers that season noted that Chiles' leg often twitched while coaching. Many believed this to be a result of Chiles being an alcoholic, an accusation he took umbrage with, arguing he knew how to handle his drink.

---

* A base coach usually stands either near first or third base and assists with sending signals and instructing baserunners.

DIGGING UP A PLOT

On 17 September 1900, towards the end of the season, the Phillies were hosting a double header against the Cincinnati Reds. As usual, Murphy was in his suite, sending the signs to Chiles. But the Reds had been tipped off to the scheme, although they never revealed by whom.

In the second innings, while the Reds were batting, their shortstop, Tommy Corcoran, was acting as the Reds' third base coach for the game. He began scratching vigorously at the ground with his cleats. The crowd began to stir – it appeared he'd lost his mind.

The Phillies, though, quickly realised what he was doing. Philadelphia manager Bill Shettsline and groundskeeper Joseph Schroeder raced onto the field, as did some police officers who were wondering what was going on.

They were all too late. Corcoran had discovered a buried wooden plank and, lifting it up, he exposed the buzzer box. He pulled it out of the ground, with the wires all connected to it.

By this point both teams had gathered around, and no one really knew what to say.

Eventually, Cincinnati coach Arlie Latham broke the silence, remarking with great drama, 'Ha! What's this? An infernal machine to disrupt the noble National League, or is it a dastardly attempt on the life of my dear distinguished friend, [Phillies' owner] John I Rogers?'

Umpire Tim Hurst wasn't that interested. He removed the box, had the hole filled in and then told the players, 'Back to the mines, men.'

The game went on as if nothing had happened.

But the scheme had been exposed, and that was the end of it.

Chiles decided that in the next game against the Reds he would play a prank on them. He buried a wooden plank under the first base coach's box, where he was coaching from that game. He began doing the now familiar leg jerk, and the Reds quickly ran out to dig up the ground, only to find the wooden board and nothing else.

With the story of the Phillies' new cheating system exposed, Phillies owner John Rodgers announced to the media that the wires had been left behind by a travelling carnival group, who had not removed them after using the ballpark years before. 'This was known at first only to our groundskeeper, but the players finally "got on to" it and gave out, as a joke, that it was to give Chiles, our usual coacher, electric shocks through his feet as signals from Murphy . . . it is absolutely too silly to further discuss the subject, and I therefore dismiss it,' Rodgers explained.

The Philadelphia Inquirer responded, 'Neither Artemus Ward nor Mark Twain in his happiest moment ever perpetrated anything so deliciously humorous as that.'

Once again there was no punishment, but the sign stealing was effectively over.

Amazingly, just twelve days after exposing the Phillies' sign stealing, the Reds' Corcoran exposed another scheme when playing in Pittsburgh. This time, he discovered the Pirates had an O on some signage in the stands and would hold an L shaped bit of metal in front of it to make it look like a clock. Noon would signal a fastball, three o'clock an inside curve and nine o'clock an outside curve. Corcoran pointed this out and effectively ended the Pirates using it.

He wasn't the first to notice it, though. The Phillies knew about this scheme too. Instead of reporting it, they had formed a 'no spying' pact with the Pirates, who knew the Phillies cheated too. In games against the Pirates, the Phillies would always seat Murphy on the bench in plain view, as a sign of good faith.

As for Chiles, he was actually arrested after the 1900 season for committing fraud in Texas, and was sentenced to two years of hard labour.

In 1902, with eight months left of his sentence, he managed to escape but was caught again in 1903, when he was arrested for assault. That was the last history ever heard of him; no one knows when or where he died.

I like to think he's buried under a third base coach's box somewhere, tipping off teams as to what the pitcher is about to throw.

STEALING SIGNS

While some spying is comical, there are other times when it becomes a complex endeavour, breaking numerous actual, written-down rules. For that we need to turn to the NFL's New England Patriots.

Mention the Patriots to just about anyone and you will get a reaction. It will rarely be a measured reaction. It will either be an over-the-top explosion of joy – the sort I usually reserve for cheeseburgers – or furious lamentations that they are the most corrupt sporting organisation to ever exist.

There are a few other contenders for title of 'most corrupt', but it would be fair to say the Patriots have always pushed the envelope when it comes to the rules.

Not that they've really needed to. For two decades they had Bill Belichick and Tom Brady, arguably the greatest coach and quarterback in NFL history respectively. In that time the team won six Super Bowls and rose to such heights, it's hardly surprising that many want to tear them down.

The Patriots weren't always like this. For much of the eighties and nineties the team would more accurately be called a joke, except they weren't even funny in their ineptitude. This all changed in 2000, when Belichick and Brady showed up and quickly reversed the team's fortunes in a way that even the most delusional Patriots fan could not have dreamt of.

In 2007, the Patriots were on their way to a perfect 16–0 record, but they were also engulfed in a controversy called 'Spygate'.*

---

* Affixing '-gate' to a scandal may be the laziest journalistic habit. Never does a scandal with that name measure up to the original. In that way, it is a lot like Star Wars trilogies.

It all began during the first game of that season, when they faced the New York Jets, a team that unlike the Patriots of decades past *is* comical in how bad they are. Their coach back then – and it changes almost weekly – was Eric Mangini, who had been a former New England assistant coach under Belichick.

Mangini, from his time at the Patriots, knew they videotaped opponents' signals to learn what plays they were running.

American football is all set plays, both from the offence and the defence. The whole game is about trying to work out what your opponent is about to do and running a play to counter that. So more than in almost any other sport, prior knowledge of your opponent's plays is an immeasurable advantage. If you know, for example, that their defence is going to set up in a dime formation – designed to stop passing plays – you can call a running play for your offence to take advantage.

The same works on defence. If you know what your opponent is going to do, you can adjust accordingly rather than guessing.

To signal plays, teams use everything from hand signals to code-names that they yell out, often making adjustments in the final moments before a play to get an edge.

All teams try to figure out these codes, but there are rules around doing that. For a start, you are not allowed to film during a game; you can study footage from past games all you want, but you can't use film to figure out what's going on within the game you're currently playing.

But in the 2007 season opener against the Jets, the Patriots were filming from their sidelines and trying to decode their signs. Mangini, though, had instructed security to be on the lookout for it, which wasn't that hard – the Patriots' employee doing the filming had stuck a bit of tape over a New England logo and whacked on a red vest with 'NFL PHOTOGRAPHER 138' printed on it. As far as spying goes, sports teams are less James Bond and more Maxwell Smart.

Once alerted, NFL security confiscated the video camera and sent it and some tapes to NFL headquarters.

Mangini later said, 'I didn't think it was any kind of significant advantage, but I wasn't going to give them the convenience of doing it in our stadium, and I wanted to shut it down. But there was no intent to get the league involved. There was no intent to have the landslide that it has become.'

Because a landslide was exactly what it became.

Being really good in a competitive league meant there were plenty of people who were eager to tear down the Patriots. The NFL quickly responded with an investigation. Some would say a little too quickly.

To understand the next bit, you need to know that the NFL is run by the owners of its thirty-two teams. Pretty much every single one of them is a billionaire who is incredibly keen to make more money. Judging by the decisions many of them make while running their teams, winning is definitely secondary to making money.

The NFL commissioner himself works for the owners, and his job is to keep the money flowing to those owners. The state of the game, what the fans think, how happy the players are – these are all secondary to bringing in the money. In fact, they are relevant only in the sense of how they affect the money coming in.

And the money doesn't so much as flow as surge like a raging torrent. For the 2018 season, US$15 billion in revenue poured into the NFL's coffers.

As a successful money-making organisation, the NFL likes to keep things in-house where possible, avoiding punishing owners if it doesn't have to. After all, the NFL commissioner would basically be punishing one of his bosses.

As a result, the NFL's justice system works a bit like a secret society; most things are unknown to anyone outside the organisation, and when the public does get to see behind the curtain, they are baffled by the goings-on.

Most controversies that require an NFL investigation drag on for what seems like an eternity. Then, when a punishment is announced, it's usually shot down by some independent review or panel, and by then the world has moved on.

Which made Spygate one of the stranger scandals the NFL has ever had. Because after the Jets game, it took just four days for NFL Commissioner Roger Goodell to make his decision. This was completely out of character for the NFL; it was as if a sloth had suddenly got up and run the 100 metres in a time that would beat Usain Bolt.

Goodell spoke to Patriots owner Robert Kraft as well as coach Belichick, who said he'd just misunderstood the rules. Goodell then announced the league maximum fine of US$500,000 for Belichick and a US$250,000 fine for the team, as well as docking them a first-round draft pick. He then announced the investigation was over.

This all seemed very odd to the rest of the league, the fans and the media. Not only the speed of the investigation, but the fact that no actual findings were announced at its conclusion. A few phone calls and fines does not an investigation make.

On the one hand it felt a lot like a cover-up – quickly wrapping up an investigation without really doing any investigating – but on the other hand, those fines were extremely harsh. If it was a simple misunderstanding not requiring any further investigation, why the massive fines?

Those around the league were baffled, not least because all the other teams had long believed the Patriots had been cheating in this manner for some time. An unnamed former member of the NFL competition committee told ESPN that the committee spent much of 2001 to 2006 'discussing ways in which the Patriots cheated, even if nothing could be proved'. Another former member of that

competition committee, Bill Polian, said several teams had complained that the Patriots had videotaped their coaches' signals.

Rumours of the ways the Patriots cheated had swirled around
the league for years; some of them were pure conspiracy, but they
were given enough credit that some teams wouldn't talk in the
visitors' locker rooms in New England, assuming they were bugged.

Another rumour was that before games a Patriots employee
would slip into the visitors' locker room and steal the play sheet
detailing the first twenty or so plays. This was so widely believed
that teams left fake play sheets lying around.

Other rumours had some actual truth behind them. For
example, at least two teams caught New England videotaping their
coaches' signals in 2006, the year before the 2007 'investigation'. In
response, the NFL's executive vice-president of football operations,
Ray Anderson, had sent a memo to all teams, including owners and
head coaches, reminding them that 'videotaping of any type, including but not limited to taping of an opponent's offensive or defensive
signals, is prohibited from the sidelines'.

Hence Belichick's claim in 2007 that he had misunderstood the
rules was disingenuous at best. In fact, two months after the memo
from the NFL, the Patriots were again caught filming against the
Green Bay Packers. Again, the league did nothing.

The Jets game the following year was therefore more the final
straw rather than a one-off event, but that just made it stranger that
a wider, thorough investigation wasn't carried out.

A few days later, after Goodall's attempt to draw a line under
the whole incident, it sparked back to life. Fox journalist Jay Glazer
had been leaked one of the tapes that had been sent to NFL headquarters. The public pressure only increased after the footage of the
Jets' signals was shown all across the media.

In response, Goodell sent three of his executives to New
England to do some further investigating. A strange move after

you've already concluded an investigation and handed out the punishments. Sending people to New England seems more like the first step, not an afterthought.

But perhaps most surprising was the ease with which the investigators uncovered a treasure trove of further evidence. The NFL executives quickly discovered a room that only Belichick and a select few had access to, which was filled with an entire library of videotapes of other teams, as well as detailed notes on their signals, going back seven years.

The discovery of such evidence should surely have reopened the investigation. Instead, Goodell arranged for it all to be destroyed. On the spot. The league executives jumped up and down on the videotapes to break them, and the notes were all shredded.

This was either a massive cover-up or the clumsiest investigation ever.

The NFL explained their little act of vandalism by assuring all the other teams in the league that this trove of information could never be used against them again. It's an odd argument, given they could have confiscated everything and the same would still be true, except they'd still have it all as evidence.

Goodell explained, 'I think there are very good explanations for the reason why I destroyed the tapes or had them destroyed by our staff. They were totally consistent with what the team told me. There was no purpose for them. I believe it was helpful in making sure my instructions were followed closely, by not only the Patriots but also by every other team. I think it was the appropriate thing to do. Our discipline sent a loud message.'

Many of the other teams seemed a bit perplexed by what the 'loud message' was saying. Destroying a whole Aladdin's cave of evidence because the team under investigation told you it was all fine doesn't sound like discipline to me. Destroying the evidence is usually something the accused does, not the investigators. The NFL's approach seemed, at best, illogical.

Every team that had ever lost to the Patriots, especially in close, important games – like Super Bowls – began to wonder if New England's cheating had made the difference.

And people did openly question the Patriots. The Pittsburgh Steelers' star wide receiver Hines Ward told reporters that during the 2002 AFC Championship Game, which New England won 24–17, he was sure the Patriots were cheating by filming and reading their signals. 'Oh, they knew. They were calling our stuff out. They knew a lot of our calls. There's no question some of their players were calling out some of our stuff.'

Included in the documents destroyed by the NFL executives were handwritten diagrams of the defensive signals of the Pittsburgh Steelers and notes used in the January 2002 AFC Championship Game. Did they prove Ward's allegation? We will never know.

IF THE CAP DOESN'T FIT

One way for a team to win is to simply pay more money and get the best players. In some sports this is possible, but others have a salary cap, limiting what each team can spend on players in an attempt to equalise the competition. A simple way around this is just to secretly pay more than the salary cap allows.

In the NRL this is a proud tradition. The most famous culprit was Melbourne Storm, who kept two sets of books, one for the NRL to inspect and one with what they actually paid players. Unfortunately for them, the NRL discovered the second set of books, which showed one player who was officially getting $400,000 a year was actually paid $950,000, including a $20,000 gift voucher and a boat.

As punishment, the Storm had their two premierships and three minor premierships stripped from them. Did this stop the practice of salary cap cheating in its tracks? Not at all. It's happened multiple times since and probably always will, because the temptation is just too great.

FAILED INVESTIGATION THE SEQUEL

While the NFL seemed to have even less appetite for uncovering the entire story than I have for hearing about someone's dreams, others were interested.

US senator Arlen Specter of Pennsylvania – home of the Steelers – wanted to get to the bottom of it. He had written two letters to Goodell asking for more information, only to receive no reply.

Being a member of the US Senate, he probably wasn't surprised that something wasn't moving that quickly, but he was annoyed to not even receive a reply. So he did what any politician does to get attention: he gave the list of questions he'd sent to Goodell to the *New York Times* and mentioned Goodell had ignored his letters.

The *Times* helpfully published this on their front page just before the Super Bowl and, in response, Goodell finally responded to Specter. The two met, with Specter threatening a congressional investigation and Goodell stonewalling him.

In fact, not only did Goodell stonewall him, the entire NFL did. They wanted to keep it all in-house; the last thing they needed was the US Congress crawling all over them.

Specter wrote to numerous NFL personnel, both at headquarters and at various teams, requesting interviews. He had no subpoena powers and was met with a wall of silence, eventually giving a furious speech on the floor of congress, blasting the NFL. But he knew by then that there was no support in congress for a wider investigation.

As Specter publicly tore down the NFL in frustration, Goodell, on the very same day as his speech, announced a new edict that all teams had to follow: 'Policy on Integrity of the Game & Enforcement of Competitive Rules'.

In what I'm sure is a coincidence, it seemed to address all the things that the Patriots were rumoured to have done, stating that the 'unauthorized videotaping on game day or of practices, meetings or other organized team activities' was banned, as was 'unauthorized entry into locker rooms, coaches' booths, meeting rooms or other private areas'.

The whole event satisfied no one. A shadow had been cast over the Patriots, who went on to win even more often after Spygate than before it, seeming to confirm their argument that they hadn't done that much spying and didn't really need to.

Yet the whole debacle had the air of a cover-up. The complete lack of an open, thorough investigation meant no one really knew how bad Spygate had been. It allowed any conspiracy that was floated to gain some level of believability.

Which is why in 2014 another scandal involving New England exploded, becoming the biggest story in America for months.

Deflategate, as of course it became known, alleged that quarterback Tom Brady had deliberately made support staff lower the pressure in the footballs to make them easier to throw.

The accusations centred on the 2014 American Football Conference championship game against the Indianapolis Colts. It seemed a strange accusation – the Patriots led 17–7 at halftime and won 45–7. It hardly seemed like the pressure of the balls had made any impact on the game.

But given the Patriots were thought to have gotten away with all sorts of cheating back before Spygate, the media were out for blood. Every sports commentator in America was discussing if Tom Brady had been inappropriately tampering with his balls, leaving them deflated. This was all done with a straight face.

The NFL were keen to avoid the appearance of another rushed investigation, so they hired attorney Ted Wells to get to the bottom of things.

Wells certainly didn't rush this investigation. Instead of four days, this time it took four months. A 243-page document known as the Wells Report was released in full.* It concluded that it was 'more probable than not' that the New England Patriots had broken the rules by deflating balls, and that Brady was 'generally aware' of what was going on.

The NFL suspended Brady for four games and the team was fined $1 million and lost two draft picks.

Brady challenged the decision in federal court, where it was over-turned, and he played all of the 2015 season, only for the Second US Circuit Court of Appeals to overturn *that* decision, reinstating Brady's four-game suspension for the next season.

For many, the harsh punishment for Deflategate was a response to the fact so many people thought the Spygate investigation and punishments were compromised.

The problem is that not only does cheating happen in the shadows, far too often when sporting administrators discover it and try to tackle it, the investigations continue in the shadows too.

Spygate could have been what the Patriots said it was – a mis-understanding of the rules and a normal attempt to get an edge – or it could have been a large, ongoing, sophisticated cheating opera-tion that raises questions over the legitimacy of several Super Bowl wins. We will probably never know the full truth.

On the other hand, we know all too much about Deflategate. An act of cheating that, if true – and it's not a certainty, despite a 243-page report – seemed to have almost no impact on actual games.

What this all shows is that despite cheating being such a wide-spread thing, sporting administrators are terrible at dealing with it. There are no real set procedures to follow when it occurs. An investigation can be thorough, rushed, long, public, secretive – it all varies from case to case.

---

* The entire report is available online. It's well worth a read for anyone wishing to beat insomnia.

It's as if sporting administrators are constantly surprised by cheating, which is odd, given we now know that it's the one thing that happens all the time in sport. When it comes to sporting administrators and cheating, they are like someone who is surprised each morning when the sun comes up.

EYE SPY

A fair bit of 'opposition analysis' is to be expected in sport. Often, cheating in this way is just overstepping the mark, like watching a practice session to get a read on tactics, planned plays and the health of opponents. But sometimes it crosses over the line into outright cheating, often with technology brought to bear.

Before the 2018 soccer World Cup in Russia, the South Korean team was preparing in Austria, where they were holding closed training sessions. One of their opponents in the group stage, Sweden, had sent a scout, Lasse Jacobsson, to see what he could discover about the team.

His first attempt at trying to watch a closed session was hanging around the team's base posing as a tourist. The South Koreans, probably well trained in spotting spies given their geo-political situation, figured this out pretty quickly.

Jacobsson, undeterred, then drove up into the mountains above the training camp, where he convinced a local couple to let him use their house to spy on the team, setting up a telescope and video camera.

The South Koreans heard about this and coach Shin Tae-yong ordered his players to wear different numbers to the ones they wore during games to confuse the spy. Shin told reporters, 'We switched them around because we didn't want to show our opponents everything and to try and confuse them.' He added, 'They might know a few of our players but it is very difficult for Westerners to distinguish between Asians.'

When all this came out, Sweden's coach Janne Andersson apologised to South Korea. 'It's very important that we show respect for opponents, always and in every way. If it has been perceived in another way, we apologise.'

South Korea didn't seem to care that much, with Shin remarking, 'All coaches probably feel their opponents are always spying on them. I think it's perfectly natural that we all try to get as much information on each other as we can.'

Shin even admitted he'd swapped the players' numbers in actual games to try to confuse opponents, claiming that in early warm-up games against Bolivia and Senegal only two players wore their usual numbers, Tottenham forward Son Heung-min and captain Ki Sung-yueng.

BLOODY CLOWNS

Spying is nice and all, but teams can also cheat in incredibly theatrical ways. As in, it would make more sense if it happened in a theatre.

In April 2009, 'The Stoop', home to the Harlequins Rugby Union team,* was hosting the Heineken Cup quarter final against the Irish side Leinster. Late in the second half, Leinster were leading 6–5. Harlequins had been having a torrid time due to injury. Their fly-half and specialist kicker, Nick Evans, had suffered a thigh injury, only for his replacement, Chris Malone, to tear his hamstring clean off the bone twenty minutes later.

With the seconds ticking down, any penalty or drop goal would win the game, but Harlequins were without a specialist kicker. They had to get Nick Evans back on – even with his thigh injury, he was

---

* Harlequins, located in south-west London, was formed in 1867 when the Hampstead Football Club, formed the year before, split after two members fell out. Half the team became Wasps and the other half Harlequins. The name Harlequins was apparently chosen after it was found in a dictionary. That's how you know this is a Rugby Union side – a Rugby League side wouldn't have had a dictionary.

their best bet – but he'd already been subbed off. The only way he could come back on was if someone else got injured.

With five minutes to go, Tom Williams, the Harlequins' winger, was approached by the team's physio, Steph Brennan, who told him, 'Deano says you're coming off for blood.' That was Dean Richards, the Harlequins' director of rugby.

Brennan handed Williams a blood capsule that Richards had instructed him to buy at a joke store in Clapham Junction.

'What the hell do I do with this?' asked Williams.

'Go get into contact, put it in your mouth, and chew it and go down. We'll get you off.'

The plan was simple enough. If Williams went off with a bloody mouth, Nick Evans – one of the best kickers in rugby – could come back on.

It was so crazy, it could almost . . . well, it was just crazy.

Williams went in for a tackle and all of a sudden blood was pouring out of his mouth like a scene in a Tarantino movie; not only was there a lot of blood, it was a very bright colour. He was helped to his feet and, as he was taken off the ground, he winked at the Harlequins bench, in full view of TV cameras.

Leinster's Shane Horgan, who was on the bench, immediately started shouting, 'It's not real blood, it's not real blood!'

The television commentators also noted that it was an incredibly fortuitous injury for Harlequins, and that Williams seemed in remarkably good shape for someone who had a fountain of bright blood gushing from his mouth.

Williams was rushed to the changing rooms, only for Leinster's club doctor to follow him down the tunnel, demanding to see the injury. Wendy Chapman, Harlequins' club doctor, took him into the change room and locked the door. But soon officials from the European Rugby Cup (ERC) joined Leinster's club doctor in banging on the locked door and demanding to examine Williams.

On the field, the match continued. The injured Evans, brought on for his kicking, missed a late drop goal. Leinster had hung on to win the game.

But the pressure of the match was nothing compared to the pressure in that dressing room. Williams was panicking as the banging on the door intensified. If the organisers came in, it would be obvious that he had no cut to explain the blood.

In a panic, he asked the doctor to cut his lip. He needed a wound to show. She hesitated at first and he began begging her, so she took a small scalpel and cut his lip.

The cover-up was underway.

Despite Williams producing a cut, suspicions still lingered over the entire affair. But Dean Richards, who had conceived the idea, was keen to tough out any investigation. In the post-match media conference, Richards swore that Williams had injured himself out on the field, and that his conscience was clean. But the ERC wasn't totally satisfied and began an investigation.

Meanwhile, Richards was moving fast to persuade Williams, Brennan and Chapman to deny everything. The director of rugby presented the player, physio and doctor with written testimonies to sign so their stories were aligned.

Williams felt nervous about going through with the cover-up, but the club told him that even if it went badly, the worst he'd get was a fine, and the club would cover it.

A hearing was convened a few months later and Harlequins presented the story that everything had been above board. Williams had been injured and that was the end of it.

The ERC hearing wasn't completely convinced. There was plenty of TV evidence that something had happened, and that Williams hadn't been injured during the game. Plus there was Williams' wink to the bench.

The hearing decided to ban Williams for twelve months. With

Williams refusing to say anything else, and the others all denying any knowledge, the panel cleared Richards, Brennan and Chapman.

Williams had become the fall guy for the whole affair. He'd trusted the club when they said he'd only get a fine and now he had a year-long suspension.

The player decided it was time to get his own legal counsel. He called the Rugby Union Players' Association, who, according to Williams, said, 'Hold on a minute, you're getting hung out to dry here. They're saying you masterminded the whole thing.'

It would be fair to assume Williams had never masterminded anything. As they say, a person who represents himself at a trial has a fool for a client, but a person who lets a football club represent them needs their head read.

With independent counsel, Williams started to realise that staying quiet hadn't done him any favours. The advice the players' association gave him was to appeal the sentence and come clean. Williams needed to make a full disclosure of the facts to an independent ERC appeals tribunal.

Obviously, the club was less than thrilled with this idea. They'd just had all their key people cleared of wrongdoing and, since Williams wasn't a star player, they could cope without him for a year. Reopening proceedings was the last thing they wanted.

So they doubled down on an already fairly poorly thought out cover-up. Williams claimed that Harlequins chairman Charles Jillings and chief executive Mark Evans put pressure on him to not appeal. Evans impressed upon Williams that it would be very difficult for him at the club if he did.

Playing good cop, Jillings tried to ensure Williams stayed quiet, or limited the scope of his appeal, by offering him a significant package of incentives, including financial compensation, a contract extension, a testimonial game and help with his career post-rugby.

Eventually, a summit was called to thrash out the issue in person. Pressure continued to be brought to bear on Williams, with the discussion focusing on how the mounting legal costs were damaging the club, and that innocent people were likely to have to be let go if the case continued.

Williams went outside to get some air and saw his girlfriend, who was waiting outside. He told her the discussion was going nowhere. Outraged, she stormed inside and asked every single person in the room, 'Whose fault is it that we're here?'

This seemed to shame the club into reflecting on their approach. The next morning, four months after the match, Dean Richards resigned from the club* and Harlequins finally threw their support behind Williams and his appeal. The cover-up was over.

Chief executive Mark Evans apologised to the fans and was gone from the club within a few months himself.

Williams lodged his appeal, this time telling the entire story. The ERC appeals panel reviewed the new evidence before handing down a 99-page report that was scathing of the club and Richards. It detailed the fact that Williams had been put under 'immense pressure to tell lies' throughout the process and identified Richards as the mastermind for both the cheating and the cover-up.

Richards was described as having 'central control of everything that happened' and that his 'primary interest' was 'preventing his own role in events being discovered'. In mounting a defence, Richards said that Williams had decided for himself to lie about the event at the first hearing, and that there was no pressure on Williams to cover up what had happened.

But the committee found this to be ridiculous, stating that the only reason Richards had selected Williams as the one to use

---

* It's always hard to know if someone in these circumstances really 'resigned' or if they were forced to jump before they were pushed. In most cases, it's the latter.

the blood capsule in the first place was that he was a young fringe player who 'could be suborned into cheating'.

The report found Richards 'ought to have known that players such as Mr Williams would likely obey his directions whether it meant cheating or not'.

Richards also tried to argue that the cover-up was only attempted in order to defend the club doctor, Wendy Chapman, to protect her medical licence. The committee's response was blunt: 'We did not believe Mr Richards when he said that the prime driving force was the protection of the personal position of Dr Chapman.'

The committee also found that the physio, Steph Brennan, was a willing accomplice to Richards. Brennan admitted this was actually the fifth time the club had faked blood to substitute someone off. Normally they'd used a piece of gauze with red dye on it, but Brennan had wandered into a joke shop one lunchtime and it seems his theatrical ambitions overtook him. He purchased the blood capsules and even got a receipt so he could claim the money from the club as an expense.

Brennan confessed to the committee, 'Yes, I went onto the pitch with the intention of deceiving the referee.'

As for Chapman, the doctor, she confessed to cutting Williams' lip following his request, and admitted to failing to tell the ERC disciplinary hearing that.

The penalties were harsh. Richards was banned from rugby for three years, Chapman received a reprimand from the General Medical Council and Brennan received a two-year ban, although this was later overturned.

As for Williams, his original twelve-month sentence was reduced to four months, but when he returned to Harlequins he was still shunned by some players who sided with Richards, showing that going against the team leaves you with a bill that comes around again and again.

They say the cover-up is worse than the crime, but in this case it was just one delightful ongoing mess from start to finish.

A CHARISMATIC, FILTHY BASTARD

As far as team cheating goes, Harlequins were as amateurish as any theatre production that uses blood capsules purchased at a joke shop. To get a real sense of the sheer breadth of cheating a club can undertake we must travel to the Mediterranean coast, near the mouth of the Rhône, to the French port city of Marseille.

In the early eighties, Olympique de Marseille was a very average soccer club in the French first division. In 1986 this continuing averageness prompted the city's mayor, Gaston Defferre, to approach a businessman named Bernard Tapie and beg him to purchase the club.

Tapie was the son of a Parisian fridge maker who grew up dreaming of being a professional race-car driver and a singer. But, with these dreams unrealised, by 1986 he'd instead become a self-made multi-millionaire through high-profile and high-risk investments. He'd purchase ailing or bankrupt French companies, renegotiate debts, slash jobs and install new management, turning them around and often choosing to sell them for a healthy profit.

This had not only made him rich but had given him a huge profile. Tapie loved the spotlight and flaunted his wealth, buying an enormous Paris home and a 72-metre yacht called *Phocea*. It was an astonishing rise for someone from such a humble background.

Tapie's money and profile certainly interested Defferre, but so did the fact that he had already been successful in sport. One of the companies Tapie had turned around was *La Vie Claire*, a chain of health product stores, and in 1984 he had set up a *La Vie Claire* sponsored cycling team to compete in the Tour de France. Success came quickly – riders from the team won the 1985 and 1986 Tour de France. Tapie showed he was a man willing to spend anything to achieve success.

Tapie certainly liked the idea of owning a football team, but before agreeing to buy the club he made sure the city of Marseille promised him all sorts of financial incentives, such as upgrading the stadium and the practice facilities.

By the end of 1986, he was on board; Marseille had a new owner and president. A man who would do anything to win. A man who writer Franz-Olivier Giesbert later described as a 'charismatic, filthy bastard'.

HERE COMES THE MONEY

Once Tapie had his feet under the desk, he began to make changes. He didn't really know anything about football, he just treated the club like another one of his businesses. He examined the entire organisation, quickly sacking anyone he believed wasn't up to the task or who didn't flatter him enough.

Tapie wasn't afraid to spend money, and he went on a spectacular spending spree, attracting some of the best playing and administrative talent in the world. And ploughing millions into the team produced immediate results. In his first season in charge, Marseille came second to Bordeaux in the league and made the French cup final, only to lose to Bordeaux in that game too.

Of course this was not enough for Tapie, who poured more money into the club, bringing in new players and firing executives who weren't performing. He signed players like Jean-Pierre Papin, Didier Deschamps, Rudi Völler and Eric Cantona, and Franz Beckenbauer was coach for one season. All this money propelled Marseille to the title in 1988/89, their first since 1972. Success continued, with the 1989/90, 1990/91 and 1991/92 seasons all delivering the league title.

But Tapie wasn't happy. One prize remained frustratingly beyond his grasp: being champions of all Europe. The European Cup, the tournament of all the winners of Europe's major leagues, continually eluded Tapie.

The 1990 European Cup was the first time under Tapie that Marseille made a real effort to win the tournament, only for Portuguese team Benfica to turf them out in the semi-final. The following year saw the Yugoslavian team Red Star Belgrade defeat Marseille in the final via a penalty shootout.

After Sparta Prague knocked Marseille out early in 1992, Tapie's resolve to win the cup hardened. He was determined the 1992/93 season would be the year Marseille won everything.

But by this stage he also had a few distractions on his plate. Since purchasing the team, Tapie had continued to buy and turn around ailing companies, the most famous being Adidas. He'd also been elected to parliament; in 1989 he'd won an election no one expected him to win, becoming the member for Marseille.

In the 1992/93 season, as Tapie was becoming increasingly focused on winning in Europe, he was also tapped on the shoulder to become a cabinet minister in the government of president François Mitterrand. Before becoming Minister of Urban Affairs he had to sell off all his holdings, including Adidas. It was against this background that Tapie sought to remove any possible obstacles that could prevent Marseille from becoming champions of Europe.

A DIRTY CAMPAIGN

In 1993, the Union of European Football Associations (UEFA), organisers of the European Cup, decided to make major changes to the tournament, including renaming it the Champions League. Previously, the European Cup had been a knockout tournament open only to the winners of each national league, but UEFA decided that didn't make them enough money, so the Champions League would be for teams that finished in the top few places of their league and they would compete in a group stage before moving on to the knockouts.

For Marseille, it meant they first had to win Group A, which they shared with Glasgow Rangers, CSKA Moscow and Club Brugge. That first Champions League had no semi-finals, so whoever won Group A would play the winner of Group B in the final.

Marseille started their campaign on a cold night in Glasgow against Rangers, managing to take away a 2–2 draw. Rangers went down by two goals early on, only to rally, with English forward Mark Hateley scoring the equaliser.

The second game was at home against CSKA Moscow. It was at this point that Tapie's strategy to ensure victory became clear: cheating.

The game was a complete whitewash, with Marseille winning 6–0. This was certainly surprising – to qualify for the group stage, CSKA Moscow had eliminated Barcelona, including a come-from-behind 3–2 win at the Camp Nou. To go down 6–0 seemed odd for a team of their calibre

In time, numerous claims of cheating by Marseille came to light. The first was that they had bribed some of the Russian players to not perform. CSKA manager Gennady Kostylev later said, 'I received a telephone call at our team hotel in Marseille, from a person claiming to be a Marseille director, offering money to lose the match.'

The murky affair didn't end there. In his 2006 autobiography, Marseille defender Jean-Jacques Eydelie claimed that the Russian players had been poisoned: 'Our leaders had recovered the water packs of the Muscovite players. In front of us, with a broad smile, they used a syringe with a very fine needle to inject I-don't-know-what through the cap.'

At the time, though, these were just rumours, nothing more.

The next important game in the group saw Rangers take on Club Brugge, with Rangers by now Marseille's key challengers to win the group. Having scored the equaliser in their match, the influence of Rangers' Mark Hateley was obviously a worry for Marseille.

Hateley claimed that before playing Club Brugge he was sounded out about sitting out the next time Rangers took on Marseille.

'It was a friend of a friend, who had got in touch via certain routes, basically asking me not to play. It would be financially rewarding for me, he said, should I not play in the Marseille game. He was not an agent I knew, but another agent had given him the number. It was a French-speaking person, offering me large sums of money not to play against Marseille. It points the finger at a person, or persons, working within that club not wanting me to play.'

According to Hateley, he refused this offer. Yet during the Club Brugge game he got into a minor bit of push and shove only to be shown a red card by the referee, a decision that even at the time seemed an overreaction. It meant he would be suspended for the Marseille game.

Hateley was sure this was no accident. He stormed off the ground and started kicking things in the change room. 'I knew that something had gone off there. It was a bitter pill to swallow.'

When Rangers travelled to Marseille they still managed to eke out a 1–1 draw, keeping them alive in the group, but not having Hateley up forward had certainly blunted their attack.

The group came down to two final games, Rangers against CSKA and Marseille against Club Brugge. The first game turned out to be a bit of an anti-climax, ending in a draw, meaning Marseille just had to beat Club Brugge, who had no skin in the game – it was a dead rubber for them.

Still, it was easier than expected. Two minutes into the game a lazy bit of passing at the back gave Marseille an early 1–0 lead that was never challenged. If anything, Club Brugge's players seemed deeply disinterested, raising even more eyebrows.

The result saw Marseille through to the final, where they would take on AC Milan. But six days before that there was a league game against Valenciennes, which Marseille needed to win to secure a fifth league title in a row. Valenciennes were battling relegation, so they would be highly motivated themselves.

It was a challenging couple of matches for the team with not a lot of time in between them to recover.

A BIG FAT ENVELOPE

The game against Valenciennes was causing Tapie some sleepless nights. Not only did they have to win to secure the league title, fatigue or injuries would make the Champions League final so much harder. Back in 1991, when they'd lost on penalties to Red Star Belgrade, two of Marseille's best players had been out through injury. Tapie was desperate to avoid a repeat of that scenario.

Four days before the Valenciennes fixture, a plan was hatched on Tapie's yacht.* Tapie and general manager Jean-Pierre Bernès discussed bribing Valenciennes to play dead against Marseille. They asked Marseille's Jean-Jacques Eydelie to approach three players at Valenciennes – captain Christophe Robert, Jorge Burruchaga and Jacques Glassman – who he had played with at FC Nantes.

Eydelie later ecalled that Tapie said to him, 'It is imperative that you get in touch with your former Nantes teammates at Valenciennes. We don't want them acting like idiots and breaking us before the final with Milan.'

The plan was put into action, with Christophe Robert and Jorge Burruchaga both being open to taking the money. Of the three, only Jacques Glassmann refused the bribe.

On the night before the match, Robert's wife met Eydelie in the carpark of the hotel where the Marseille players were staying, and he handed her an envelope containing F250,000 (A$66,062 in 1993). It was all set; Robert would make sure his team didn't play too hard against Marseille.

---

* All evil plots are hatched either on a yacht or in an underground lair. I'm unaware of Tapie owning an underground lair, but I wouldn't put it past him.

The next morning, Marseille made their way from the hotel to Valenciennes' ground, Stade Nungesser. In the twenty-first minute Marseille's Alen Bokšić scored what proved to be the only goal in a lacklustre match. In the twenty-third minute, Christophe Robert was substituted off, claiming an injury.

The referee Jean-Marie Véniel knew something was up even in the first half. Valenciennes' Jorge Burruchaga wasn't disputing any of his decisions, the equivalent of gravity ceasing to work. But that wasn't the only strange occurrence. While his teammates were playing like they were sleepwalking, Glassmann, who had refused the bribe, was playing like he was trying to singlehandedly win the game.

In fact, Glassman was furious with his teammates. At half-time he told his manager Boro Primorac of the bribe and that he'd been asked to 'lift his foot' by Eydelie and Marseille director Jean-Pierre Bernès.

As the game resumed, Glassman, still fuming, approached referee Véniel. Without naming anyone, he told him of the bribe. Véniel spoke to his assistant referees and Marseille captain Didier Deschamps, and made a note in his match report.

The game finished 1–0. Marseille had secured their fifth league title in a row.* But in the locker room afterwards, French police entered and interviewed some of the players.

Tapie wasn't particularly concerned, though. There was no evidence, just Glassmann's word. Besides, there was a Champions League final to focus on.

CHAMPIONS OF EUROPE

The final was held at the Olympiastadion in Munich, with 64,400 fans in attendance. The match pitted glamour club Marseille – full of attacking flair – against arguably the greatest defence of all time in the AC Milan side, led by Paolo Maldini.

---

* Valenciennes were relegated, missing out on safety by one point.

AC Milan controlled a lot of the game, playing their defensive style, but in the forty-second minute Marseille earned a corner after a brilliant run from Abedi Pele. Pele took the corner himself and his in-swinging cross found the head of Marseille defender Basile Boli. The ball flew into the corner of the net, with AC Milan's goalkeeper Sebastiano Rossi not even moving.

Boli later said, 'It was a header for eternity.'

The second half saw Marseille defend for their lives as AC Milan searched for an equaliser, but it eluded them. Marseille had done it – they'd become champions of Europe. They are still the only French side to win the European Cup/Champions League.

At the final whistle, Tapie ran onto the pitch in celebration, saying to reporters, 'We were absolutely sure of winning, none of us had any doubt. Two years ago, on paper, we had maybe a better team, but in 1993 I had eleven players who were ready to die for each other.'

But even this victory wasn't without the taint of scandal. Eydelie later testified that the Marseille players had received injections on the morning of the match. 'The only time I agreed to take a doping product was the 1993 Champions League final,' he said. 'In all the clubs I played in, I saw some doping going on . . . but this was the only time I accepted. We all took a series of injections and I felt different during the game, as my physique responded differently under strain. The only player who refused to take part was Rudi Völler.'

Tony Cascarino, who joined Marseille after the final, confirmed in a later interview that Marseille players took drugs. 'It was always before the match. We received an injection in the lower back. I was not quite sure what it was but as everybody told me it was good and as I felt great after every injection, I accepted what was being done to me.'

But none of that was known at the time. It looked like Tapie had accomplished his dream.

BURIED TREASURE

A fortnight after the Champions League final, French police launched a criminal investigation into Marseille's match against Valenciennes. Apart from Jacques Glassmann's complaint to the referee, police had received further information when Robert, burdened by guilt, approached a magistrate and confessed to his role in the affair.

He spoke to detectives and led them to his aunt's backyard, where the police dug up the envelope containing the F250,000. Robert said, 'That cash stunk so much I had to bury it.' Robert's wife then admitted to collecting the bribe from Eydelie and was charged with conspiracy.

Tapie, when questioned, claimed that the money was a loan for Robert to start a restaurant.

The police also raided Marseille's headquarters and questioned twelve members of the team. They found an envelope that matched the one Robert's money had been buried in.

Under questioning, Eydelie confessed to his role in the bribery and implicated both general manger Bernès and Tapie. Eydelie and Bernès were arrested and charged with 'active corruption'.

But Tapie, being a member of the French parliament, was immune from prosecution. Yet as the investigation swirled around him, he was also fighting on numerous other fronts, including campaigning for re-election.

Tapie had a meeting with Valenciennes coach Boro Primorac, who alleged that in this meeting Tapie attempted to pay him to confess to orchestrating the whole thing to make Marseille look bad. Since bribing people had got him into this position, it seemed he was determined he could bribe his way out of it. This didn't work out well. Primorac went straight to the police and told them of Tapie's approach.

The noose was tightening, and public pressure grew for French MPs to vote away Tapie's immunity. They eventually did this, but in relation to another non-football legal matter that Tapie was embroiled in.

In February 1994, Tapie, recently voted out of office, was arrested and charged with both corruption and attempted witness tampering.

GO DIRECTLY TO JAIL

The trial began in 1995 and revealed that the Marseille regime was more corrupt than originally thought. Facing the court were Marseille's Tapie, Jean-Pierre Bernès, Jean-Jacques Eydelie and Valenciennes players Christophe Robert and Jorge Burruchaga.

Bernès, who had been Tapie's right-hand man for years, confessed at the trial, 'We used to buy around five or six games a season.' Bernès said the club would bribe players and referees, both within the French league and in Europe. Apparently, this would cost the club up to £750,000 a year.

The court was quick to find all the men guilty of corruption. Bernès, Burruchaga and Robert all received suspended sentences. Tapie received a two-year jail sentence, including eight months non-suspended. Eydelie was given a one-year suspended sentence and served seventeen days behind bars.

The footballing punishments came immediately after the trial. Tapie was ordered to resign as president of Olympique de Marseille and was banned from football for life, as was Bernès, although his ban was later overturned on appeal. The players all received eighteen-month bans from football, with Eydelie's suspension reduced for having testified against Tapie.

Marseille were also stripped of the 1992/93 title. It was offered to runners-up Paris Saint-Germain, as was Marseille's spot in the following year's Champions League, but they declined both. This was apparently because their sponsor, pay TV provider Canal+, feared the reaction of their subscribers in Marseille.

Third-placed AS Monaco took the Champions League spot but not the title. Which meant that, officially, no one won the 1992/93 season.

Marseille's problems didn't stop there. As part of their punishment they were also relegated to the second division, and quickly fell into financial difficulties. It was revealed that, under Tapie, Marseille's debts had nearly tripled. The club was forced to file for bankruptcy.

In 1997, Tapie faced another trial, which alleged he embezzled money from the club and influenced European games, with three particular games being the focus of the prosecution: a 1989 game against AEK Athens, a 1991 Spartak Moscow match and the Club Brugge game that saw Marseille qualify for the final against AC Milan. Unlike the first trial, there wasn't enough evidence to convict Tapie.

Despite this, UEFA determined that on the strength of the first corruption conviction, Marseille would not be allowed to defend their Champions League title. However, the trophy wasn't stripped from them and their win stands to this day, although with a giant asterisk next to it that you can see from space.

Glassmann was awarded the FIFA Fair Play Award in 1995 for refusing the bribe and informing the referee of the scheme. Eydelie served out his sentence but never regained his form. He moved to Lisbon to play for Benfica but didn't make an impact and finished off his career playing for FC Sion in Switzerland and in the English lower leagues for Walsall.

As the years passed, more and more stories emerged of Marseille's underhanded dealings. Arsène Wenger, who went on to find fame at Arsenal, was Monaco's manager during the Tapie era. He described it as the 'most difficult period' of his life. Monaco were twice runners-up to Marseille in that time.

'We are talking about the worst period French football has been through. It was gangrenous from the inside because of the influence and the methods of Tapie at Marseille. There were little incidents added one to the other, in the end there is no coincidence. But it's very difficult to prove,' he said in 2013.

Wenger has always maintained that he had credible evidence from his players of offers of bribes to underperform. 'I wanted to warn people, make it public, but I couldn't prove anything definitively. At that time corruption and doping were big things and there was nothing worse than knowing the cards were stacked against us from the beginning.'

This wasn't all with hindsight, either. Wenger once had to be restrained during a match in the tunnel as he confronted Tapie.

After the whole affair Wenger headed to Japan, wanting to get as far away from French football as possible. When he finally ended up at Arsenal, he hired as his assistant the former Valenciennes' coach Boro Primorac, the man who had refused Tapie's bribe. Primorac was a key architect of Arsenal's success, helping sign a raft of great players including Patrick Vieira and seeing the team go undefeated in the 2003/04 season.

YOU CAN'T KEEP A CHARISMATIC, FILTHY BASTARD DOWN

Tapie's life after jail was no less colourful. He tried to reinvent himself as an actor, starring in a stage production of *One Flew Over the Cuckoo's Nest*, in the Jack Nicholson role. He hosted TV shows, tried to launch a music career and wrote books. He also managed to purchase a suite of newspapers as part of the La Provence media group.

Tapie sued the state-owned French bank Credit Lyonnais over their purchase of Adidas, claiming they had fraudulently undervalued the sportswear brand when he sold it to them back in 1993. This 13-year court case dramatically came to a head in 2008 when a government arbitration panel intervened and awarded him €404 million.

The decision was seen as politically motivated after Tapie, through his newspapers, swung his support behind presidential candidate Nicolas Sarkozy. After Sarkozy was elected, his finance minister Christine Lagarde (who went on to be chair of the International Monetary Fund), stepped in and sent the case to a government arbitration panel. The finding meant Tapie could settle his outstanding debts, and once again he purchased a new yacht, naming it *Reborn*.

But the huge payout and the suspicion of undue political involvement saw a fraud case brought against Tapie, mainly due to his relationship with one of the arbitrators. In 2015, a court ruled the decision had been fraudulent and Tapie had to pay back the money. Lagarde, who had decided not to appeal the initial ruling, was found guilty of negligence by a court that rules on ministerial misconduct but was spared any penalty.

Tapie appealed that decision, but eventually he had to come up with a plan to repay the money. In 2020 he had all of his assets frozen when a court rejected his repayment plan, freezing his stake in the media group La Provence and taking away control of his upmarket Parisian mansion, the Hôtel de Cavoye.

Tapie's entire life has been one of ups and downs, huge reversals in fortune, all with a dramatic flair that reveals the frustrated entertainer within. Journalist Christophe Bouchet, who wrote a book on Tapie called *L'aventure Tapie* said of him, 'He's convincing because his stories always contain a grain of truth – just enough to make them plausible. I think he also comes to believe them himself.'

CHAPTER 13

FOR THE GLORY OF YOUR COUNTRY

While a team can run a more complicated cheating operation than an individual, if you want to do some really crazy stuff you need an entire nation running the program.

National pride is the greatest motivator for cheating there is – greater even than money, which is saying something. In the modern world, where going to war tends to be frowned upon, sport is one of the few ways countries compete directly. I'm sure underpinning it all, if somewhat unspoken, is humanity's rather unhelpful determination to 'prove' that certain nationalities are superior to others. It's just an evolution on the Special Olympics of the 1904 St Louis games, except it's countries not ethnic groups pitted against each other. After all, nothing underlines your global supremacy like dominating the world in synchronised swimming.

Adding to that dynamic are the different political systems that exist around the world. The Cold War saw the peak of patriotic fervour in sports, but Russia and China in recent years have been just as keen to flex their political muscle on the sporting stage.

The higher the stakes, the more extreme the lengths sportspeople will go to for a win. Whether it's weightlifting or rhythmic gymnastics, when your nation's pride is on the line and that's desperately important to you, you can rationalise all kinds of questionable ways to gain a competitive advantage.

WAR GAMES

In 2019, the Military World Games were held in the Chinese city of Wuhan. They brought together 10,000 military personnel from around the world to compete in various sports. On home turf, China was obviously keen to make a good showing. Winning would show not only that the Chinese athlete was superior, but the Chinese soldier was too.

But in the orienteering, where competitors have to navigate terrain that they are meant to be unfamiliar with, using only a map and compass, it turned out the Chinese had some help. The mixed team, all of whom were serving members of the People's Liberation Army, came under suspicion after the Russians, Swiss, French, Belgians, Poles and Austrians all raised protests with the organisers.

The investigation that followed said 'it was soon discovered and proven that the runners had received illegal assistance both by spectators in the terrain, markings and small paths prepared for them and which only they were aware of'.

Sure, it wasn't the worst thing to ever happen in Wuhan, but the resulting publicity was incredibly embarrassing for the hosts. The *South China Morning Post* criticised the team for 'losing its moral compass'.

While the Military World Games have cachet only in a narrow field, when it comes to bringing sporting glory to the motherland there is no greater event than the Olympic Games. Cheating for power and glory at the games is part of the Olympics origin myth.

The formation of the ancient Olympics was in part in commemoration of the ancient Greek king Oenomaus. He was something of an overbearing father – he believed in a prophecy that he would be killed by his son-in-law, so his solution was to ensure his daughter, Hippodamia, never got married. I guess there's a logic to that.

He decreed that anyone who wanted to marry his daughter had to beat him in a chariot race. Given Oenomaus had the fastest horses in the world, this was a pretty good system.

Still, men took the challenge. After beating them, Oenomaus would behead them and nail their heads to a post in his house.* Despite this, eighteen men raced Oenomaus and met this fate, which proves that men often have inflated optimism when they evaluate their chances with women.

Eventually a man named Pelops came along and Hippodamia fell for him head over heels. She was probably starting to take it personally that anyone interested in her ended up getting beheaded, so together they came up with a plan. They would replace the bronze lynchpins on Oenomaus's chariot with ones made of wax.

Once the race was underway, the wax lynchpins melted, as planned. Oenomaus's chariot flew apart and he was dragged behind his horses to his death.

Thereafter, Pelops and Hippodamia were free to marry, and Oenomaus's death was commemorated with the Olympics Games. It's a beautiful story.

Since then, many countries have taken the moral of this foundation myth to be 'good things happen to those who cheat'.

---

* This, I'm almost certain, is not good feng shui, and probably caused some trauma to his daughter.

And that cheating knows no boundaries. While helping out some orienteers with some markings is cute, it's not enough to win at the top level. For that you need doping. Lots of it.

We know that the Nazis played around with doping at the 1936 Olympic Games, and the largest doping program ever attempted evolved out of that.

IT TAKES A VILLAGE

In 1949, following World War II, the Soviet army occupied parts of Germany that they then converted into a satellite state, the German Democratic Republic (GDR), more commonly known as East Germany. They famously cut themselves off from West Germany when, in 1961 the Berlin Wall was erected, although the East Germans called it an 'Antifaschistischer Schutzwall', meaning 'Anti-Fascist Rampart', which I think is catchier.

As a satellite state of the Soviet Union and a country dominated by the Iron Curtain, the GDR found that sport was a great way for a nation of just 17 million to gain international recognition. On top of that, they could demonstrate the superiority of their communist system by beating the West Germans and the West more generally.

In reality, the GDR was dirt poor and lacked the vast resources of their Western counterparts – all things being equal, they had no chance of beating powerful and rich nations like the United States. Yet, despite all this, they became an international powerhouse.

At the 1968 Mexico City Olympics the GDR won twenty-five medals, an impressive result. But at the 1972 Munich Games they won sixty-six, which was astounding. For context, the Soviet Union won ninety-nine, the United States ninety-four and West Germany, with over 61 million people, only won forty.

This level of success lasted right through until the 1988 Calgary Winter Games. It was an unbelievable record and, while it certainly made East Germany a sporting powerhouse, the cloud of doping always hung over them, although nothing was ever proved at the time.

In 1989, however, it all came to an end. The Anti-Fascist Rampart came down and West and East Germany reunified.

Many thought that, with the wall down, the world would finally discover what the East Germans had been up to all those years. But unfortunately, when the Rampart came down, the first order given out in East Germany was to shred everything. It appeared the secrets of the East German Olympic team might never be known.

In 1990, Werner Franke, the president of the European Cell Biology Organization and a West German, was one of the people sent behind the former Iron Curtain to examine the scientific experiments those naughty East Germans had been doing while cut off from the West.

During one such trip, Franke struck gold. At the Academy of Military Medicine he discovered a huge number of documents outlining the state-run doping program that had powered the GDR to Olympic glory. These had not been shredded, as no one there had received the order. Franke explained, 'In the army, nothing is destroyed without an order.'

The files described a doping program with the full power of the state behind it. It differed from anything seen before. 'Doping was clandestine in the West,' said Franke. 'It existed in small circles, so it didn't have the thoroughness of the East. But doping in the GDR was different from the rest of the East. It was German. It was orderly. It was bureaucratic. It was written up.'

Even the Stasi, the dreaded East German secret police, kept detailed notes on their enforcement of the program and their efforts to ensure it remained a state secret.

What these documents revealed was that, from the sixties until 1989, East Germany's doping program had over 10,000 athletes pass through it, all pumped full of anabolic steroids.

GUINEA PIGS

The first thing the GDR did was set up a sports bureaucracy that funnelled anyone with talent into a very rigid system. Potential athletes were removed from their families, often as teenagers, and sent to special facilities where they were put on gruelling training regimes.

Being an authoritarian state, with secret police watching everyone, saying no to participation wasn't easy. Athletes and their families were relatively well looked after, but anyone who decided they didn't want to go along with it anymore could have all of that taken away from them.

It was in 1966 that the GDR started using steroids on their athletes, starting with shot-put and other throwing events.

Oral-Turinabol was East Germany's favourite drug of choice to use on its athletes. It's an anabolic steroid containing testosterone and some synthetic steroids that act in a similar manner, which help to build muscle. The state-owned company VEB Jenapharm produced the pills and athletes were told they were vitamins.

The German precision was there straight away. Doctors recorded the results and determined the best dosages and the periods to stay on and off the pills.

The sporting results were very impressive. Within four years, male shot-putters increased how far they could throw by between 2.5 to 4 metres, and the women by 4.5 to 5 metres. Other throwing sports had similar outcomes.

You'll have noticed that the women improved significantly more than the men. The scientists and doctors running the program determined that injecting testosterone and synthetic versions of it had a much bigger impact on women due to their normally much lower testosterone levels. This finding led to the doctors pumping women full of even more Oral-Turinabol, often at much higher levels than the men.

While the positive effects were noticed, so were the adverse short-term effects: acne, hair growth, aggressiveness and increased libido. And because the drugs had the biggest impact on women, they also experienced bigger side effects, resulting in virilisation, the development of male characteristics – they developed broader shoulders, deeper voices and more hair on their bodies.

Despite having full knowledge of these problems, the doctors and the government pressed ahead, even though many of the athletes were mere teenagers. In fact, they extended the program from throwing sports to pretty much everything except sailing and gymnastics.

THE MANHATTAN PROJECT OF SPORTS

The 1976 Montreal Olympic Games presented a problem for the GDR: steroid testing was set to became mandatory. Not a great rule for a nation that relied heavily on a sophisticated doping program.

Analyses of urine samples for steroids had started off at the 1974 European Athletic Championships in Rome. In response, East Germany decided that instead of stopping their doping program, they needed to make it more sophisticated. In October 1974 a branch of the Central Committee, the top decision-making body of the Socialist Unity Party, took a step that would deliver the most sophisticated doping program to ever grace the earth.

Known as State Plan 14.25, this government act made doping compulsory across the GDR's sport program.* A central distributor would send drugs to all the Kinder- und Jugendsportschulen,

---

* This nine-page bill, and the papers from the session that approved it, were all destroyed before the Berlin Wall came down. Except for a single copy, which survived in the Stasi files – meaning the body charged with keeping it a secret was the one that allowed us to ultimately know about it. The documents showed that all these decisions were made at the highest level of government.

the schools for young athletes. Doctors and coaches were trained in giving these steroids to young athletes, which was done without their parents' consent. They were not told what they were.

State Plan 14.25 also made it a priority to develop new drugs, and new ways of masking those drugs in doping tests. Strict protocols were developed to make sure athletes were clean when it came to competition time, laying out when athletes should be administered drugs and when to stop.

The organisation of all this was astounding. Through this new act, seven government ministries were integrated in this doping and research program, all working together to dope athletes and cover up the fact that they were doing so. This secrecy was enforced by making State Plan 14.25 and the activities that flowed from it an official state secret.

The Stasi's Central Working Group for the Protection of State Secrets set up a network of more than 1000 informants and spies to monitor the program and enforce both the doping and the secrecy. Every doctor, scientist, athlete and their family was watched. The documents show that any reluctance to participate was noted and these people were watched more closely. In East Germany, where people could just go missing, this made it almost impossible for people not to participate in the program. Even flagging the negative side effects of the drugs brought that person greater scrutiny.

Never before had the whole apparatus of a state been brought to bear on cheating. Brigitte Berendonk, a former athlete and the wife of Werner Franke, and an expert on East German doping in her own right, called State Plan 14.25 the 'Manhattan Project of sports'. It standardised doping, with scientists, doctors and coaches recording everything and then using that information to refine and improve the program, both from a performance perspective and to beat the drug tests.

This constant evaluation developed a standard process for

building athletes. For weightlifters, they usually started receiving steroids at age sixteen. For female swimmers, they started at fourteen or younger. Even Winter Olympic events and canoeing, kayaking and rowing had athletes start on steroids at fourteen.

The children were made to take the oral steroid tablets in front of doctors – they weren't allowed to take them home in case they didn't take them. No one was trusted. Injections of steroids also became more common because it sped up the process of the body clearing itself of traces of the doping.

This highly efficient system, as morally repugnant as it was, got results. At the 1976 Montreal Olympics, East Germany won forty gold medals, six more than the United States. Women's swimming was where the doping really improved performances. East Germany won gold in eleven of thirteen events. Other nations' swimmers complained, noting the broad shoulders, muscular physiques and deep voices of the East German swimmers, only for a GDR official to say that they 'came to swim, not to sing'.

The system wasn't perfect, however. Embarrassingly, in 1977 shot-putter Ilona Slupianek tested positive for steroids. The response of the GDR was, again, not to stop doping but to build a new laboratory where all their athletes would be tested before being sent out to compete, to ensure they would pass as clean.

Only when the wall crumbled and East Germany ceased to exist did State Plan 14.25 come to an end. The destruction of the East German doping program, coupled with more accurate doping tests, meant performances actually went backwards worldwide. It seems the Germans weren't the only ones doping, they were just the best at it because they had an entire bureaucracy driving the effort.

In the women's shot-put at the 1996 Atlanta Olympics, the gold medal winner – Astrid Kumbernuss, who was born in East Germany and competed for Germany at these games – would have finished only in sixth place at the 1980 Moscow Olympics. Her best throw was almost 2 metres shorter than that of the 1980 winner, the GDR's Ilona Slupianek, who had tested positive in 1977.

But while the East German doping program ended in 1989, the damage it caused stays with us to this day.

THE SINS OF THE FATHERLAND

In 1997, Marie Katrin Kanitz received a letter that sent her world spinning. Kanitz had been an athlete in East Germany, and the letter informed her that some of the documents uncovered from State Plan 14.25 revealed she had been given Oral-Turinabol at the age of seventeen. She was twenty-seven when the letter arrived. She had been a figure skater in the program and, like many of the young athletes, had been told the pills were vitamins.

The police interviewed her. They were building a case against those who had run the East German doping program. They showed her the picture of the distinctive blue pills that were Oral-Turinabol and everything fell apart for her right there. Had her success all been a lie? Were her health issues a result of the doping? It was certainly possible.

In July 2016, Germany's Doping Victim Help Society, which had been formed to assist and support the GDR's doping victims, revealed that in a survey of 140 of its female members, 9 per cent of those surveyed had breast cancer, 55 per cent had suffered from gynaecological illnesses and 14 per cent had experienced miscarriages.

The various East German government papers revealed that they knew of many of these problems, often ordering abortions for athletes because they knew the steroids caused enormous pregnancy problems.

Hammer thrower Detlef Gerstenberg was hospitalised because of extensive liver damage and died in 1993, aged thirty-five. A 2008 qualitative study of fifty-two East German athletes found that those who were able to have children reported a higher rate of disability and chronic disease in their children.

As for Kanitz, after receiving her letter and being interviewed by police, she was asked if she'd like to press charges against her former coach, which she agreed to. A two-year trial followed, known as the Berliner Dopingprozess, where numerous athletes told their stories.

Unfortunately, only two convictions came out of it: GDR chief doctor Manfred Hoeppner and Minister of Sport Manfred Ewald both received suspended sentences. Many of the coaches, including Kanitz's, were found not guilty on the basis that they didn't know what was in the pills they were giving to the children.

In the end, it was the athletes who received a life sentence. Thousands of them still suffer myriad health issues, and the German government provides several compensation funds to support them.

Former East German relay runner Ines Geipel was given Oral-Turinabol by her trainer from the age of seventeen and has since had enormous problems with her internal organs. Kidneys are particularly susceptible to damage from steroids.

From 2013 to 2018, Geipel was the chair of the German Doping Victims' Association. She has spent her post-athletics life watching her fellow athletes die in middle age from the long-term effects of the doping program.

'I think I am now one of the oldest ones,' she said.

Geipel says the biggest loser in sports doping is always the individual. 'But if you take a closer look at it, the game is dead, so basically everyone loses.'

They say it takes a village to raise a child, but it takes a nation state to run a sophisticated program to dope them.

RUSSIA

As we've seen time and again when it comes to cheating, people don't seem to consider the events of the past as a cautionary tale but rather as proof that taking shortcuts works. It's almost like they read three-quarters of the story and then stopped before the bit where the whole thing fell apart. Lance Armstrong was like this, copying everything that had happened in the Festina Affair, apparently suffering amnesia on how that all wrapped up.

But it's not that they forget the bad part, it's that they're so arrogant they think they won't get caught. They labour under the false belief that they are smarter than those that came before them, that they will not make any mistakes.

Where Lance Armstrong followed the Festina Affair, Russia followed East Germany.

In some ways, the Russians were smarter picking East Germany as a model, since they only got caught because they ceased to exist politically.

Russia's arrogance was that, as an authoritarian government, they thought they could control every person involved in a sophisticated scheme. They should have listened to Benjamin Franklin's advice about keeping secrets.

WHISTLING INTO THE ABYSS

Four months after the 2012 London Olympics, WADA received an email from the Russian discus thrower Darya Pishchalnikova, who had just won silver at the games. She begged WADA to investigate the Russian Olympic program, writing, 'I want to cooperate with WADA.' As a show of good faith, Pishchalnikova even admitted she herself had taken performance enhancing drugs.

WADA did what most of us do when we get an email that contains a problem that will take heaps of work to fix: they forwarded it to someone else. But in this case, they sent it to the Russian authorities. Which was an odd thing to do. Usually, when someone offers to be a whistleblower, you don't pass the case on to the people they're blowing the whistle on.

In response, Russia banned Pishchalnikova for ten years.

It might seem hard to understand the logic of WADA, the global regulator of anti-doping rules and practices in sports. They didn't just decide against an inquiry, they threw Pishchalnikova to the wolves. But WADA are funded by governments as well as sporting bodies, and angering people who pay your salary is something few people are interested in doing.

It wasn't even that WADA didn't believe Pishchalnikova. Back before the 2008 Beijing Games, seven female Russian track and field athletes had been caught manipulating their urine samples, and Pishchalnikova had been one of them. And in 2011 a scientific paper titled *Prevalence of Blood Doping in Samples Collected From Elite Track and Field Athletes* identified one country as being a serious problem when it came to doping: Russia.

Not that this was news to WADA. Vitaly Stepanov, an employee of Russia's national anti-doping agency and husband of middle-distance runner Yuliya Stepanova, had met with WADA officials at the 2010 Winter Olympics and begun informing on his country. In the years that followed he sent over 200 emails to WADA, detailing all he knew about Russian athletes doping. WADA did nothing; when they weren't forwarding emails, they were ignoring them.

WADA's problem, apart from being funded by the very countries they were supposed to police, was that there are limits to their investigative capabilities and their testing regime. In fact, most of the testing was done by individual countries' own labs, which is like getting drivers to breathalyse themselves.

A TROPICAL WINTERLAND

When Gary di Silvestri and Angelica Morrone of the National Ski Association of Dominica attended the Sochi Olympics, they would have felt right at home: for some reason, Russia had decided to host the 2014 Winter Olympics at one of the few places in their country with a subtropical climate. I'm no expert on hosting the Winter Olympics, but I'd always thought somewhere conducive to snow would be the best place to have them.

Sochi is part of the 'Caucasian Riviera' on the Black Sea and was Stalin's favourite place to holiday.* For Vladimir Putin, it was the place to re-establish Russia's dominance on the sporting landscape and, through that, reassert its international power. Since the collapse of the Soviet Union, Russia had struggled to make an impression at the Olympics, but Sochi 2014 was to be the moment to change all that.

To ensure there was no chance of failure, Russia spent $50 billion converting Sochi into a winter wonderland, despite the subtropical weather. In the town itself, five indoor arenas were built for sports such as ice hockey and figure skating. Other events were held in the mountains, an hour's drive away.

To guarantee snow, Russia built two reservoirs that fed 400 snow-making machines. They also stockpiled 710,000 cubic meters of snow over the preceding winters, putting it under insulated covers to make sure it was available for 2014.

With the weather taken care of, the next major concern for Russia was ensuring the team performed. This was perhaps a bigger challenge than bringing snow to the subtropics. The previous Winter Olympics, in Vancouver, had been a disaster for Russia – they'd finished sixth on the medal table with just fifteen medals, and only three of them gold.

This was something that, in the Russian government's eyes, couldn't be repeated. To make sure Sochi was a success, the Russian state went to extraordinary lengths, leaving nothing to chance. And it worked: Russian athletes won thirty-three medals at Sochi, including thirteen gold medals. But the real story behind

---

* I'm not sure if 'Stalin's favourite place to holiday' is the official slogan of Sochi. It certainly has cut-through, but I'm not sure it sends the right message.

this success took years to come out, and it was breathtaking in its audacity.

KICKING AND SCREAMING

In the early 2010s, WADA's lack of investigative muscle was slowly being addressed within the organisation. They recruited Jack Robertson as their chief investigator. A former DEA agent, Robertson had previously investigated Mexican drug cartels and worked on bringing down Lance Armstrong. At WADA, his office had one of Armstrong's yellow jerseys hanging on the wall. Armstrong had signed it, not knowing who it was for – it said 'Jack, Catch me if you can. Best wishes.'

But for Robertson, his time at WADA would be one of frustration. Despite his appointment, he had little power to compel people to talk to him and his efforts were chronically underfunded. Despite a wealth of information suggesting that Russia was systematically doping their athletes, emails at the time showed that his boss, WADA president Sir Craig Reedie, was more concerned with the public's perception of the organisation than launching an investigation into the drug cheats.

Stymied by his own organisation, Robertson turned to the media, leaking a variety of details about Russia's doping to German investigative reporter Hajo Seppelt. In December 2014, almost a year after Sochi, Seppelt's report 'The Secrets of Doping: How Russia Makes its Winners' aired on the German television channel ARD. It told the story of Yuliya Stepanova and Vitaly Stepanov – the man who had emailed WADA 200 hundred times – and detailed how the Russians were doping their track and field athletes and covering up the results at their state-run testing lab.

The story appearing in public meant WADA had to do something beyond their normal scope of ignoring emails. They appointed Dick Pound to lead the investigation. Pound had previously been WADA president, and was also the former IOC vice-president who had been pressed into defending Ben Johnson back in 1988.

His 335-page report, published in November 2015, revealed a 'deeply rooted culture of cheating' and went as far as saying that Russian state security services were involved in covering it up.

Considering WADA had sat on a lot of this information for years, it speaks volumes that it only took about a year for this report to be written. They probably just had to copy and paste.

The response was swift. The International Association of Athletics Federations (IAAF) suspended the Russian Athletics Federation, and WADA were forced to suspend the accreditation of the Moscow laboratory and declare the Russian Anti-Doping Agency (RUSADA) non-compliant.

The IOC, however, saw the whole mess as a massive inconvenience. They reacted by telling the international federations of every Olympic sport to make their own mind up on whether to allow Russian athletes to compete in their discipline at the Rio Olympics in 2016. It was a rather obvious way to pass the buck, and the decision was met with anger by other countries and clean athletes everywhere.

WADA's resistance to properly pursue Russia was further underlined when, in January 2016, they announced Jack Robertson had retired, only for Robertson to deny this, telling media he'd been sacked.

THE SORT-OF-GOOD DOCTOR

If WADA hoped that was the end of it, they were to be sorely disappointed. In May 2016 the *New York Times* ran a long exclusive detailing the scale of cheating by the Russians, this time at the Sochi Olympics.

The *Times* article relied on another whistleblower, Dr Grigory

A CLEVER FIX

Back in the seventies, the modern pentathlon had a major drug problem. The sport faced the widespread problem of competitors taking drugs that act as downers in order to slow their heartbeat for the pistol shooting event, improving their aim.

Instead of an expensive program of drug testing, the organisers made a simple change: they rearranged the order of the events. The shooting would now come right before the cross-country running. After that, pentathletes using downers basically stopped. No one wanted to take them right before running 3200 metres.

Rodchenkov,* who'd been the director of Russia's anti-doping laboratory – the lab that had just had its accreditation withdrawn by WADA.

Where Dick Pound's report had identified systemic cheating by Russia, Rodchenkov had all the juicy details. It went well beyond what anyone else had ever imagined.

Rodchenkov was a man with a long history in the fight against doping in sports. He often travelled the world speaking about Russia's efforts on this front. In 2012 he published a paper about his breakthrough work on 'detecting peptides and long-term steroid metabolites of prohibited substances'. So important was this work that other international labs praised his achievements. He was a man making a significant contribution to stamping out doping.

But Rodchenkov was like a magician, distracting the audience with one hand so they weren't looking at what the other hand was doing. When he wasn't winning people's trust by developing new methods of detecting drugs, Rodchenkov was coming up with ways for Russian athletes to avoid detection.

In the lead-up to the London Olympics in 2012, Rodchenkov had developed a cocktail of drugs he called 'The Duchess'. As far as cocktails go, it packed quite a punch. In it was the East German

---

* Rodchenkov left his family behind in Russia to flee to the United States, where he is enrolled in the witness protection program.

drug of choice, Oral-Turinabol, as well as Oxandrolone and Methasterone.*

Athletes would drink The Duchess after it had been dissolved in alcohol, making it literally a cocktail of drugs. In a nice but somewhat old-fashioned move, Rodchenkov would dissolve the drugs in Chivas for the male athletes and Vermouth for the female athletes.

Taking them in this manner actually made sense. Swishing the cocktail around in your mouth and then spitting it out, while a waste of good Chivas, means you absorb the drugs through the buccal membrane – the inside of your cheeks – which reduces the detection window to just 3 to 5 days.

The *Times* article revealed that dozens of Russian athletes had used this method at the Sochi Olympics, including at least fifteen medal winners.

Rodchenkov said his problem wasn't getting athletes to take his custom cocktail but that many would take other drugs without his approval, putting them at risk of getting caught. 'All athletes are like small children,' he said. 'They'll put anything you give them into their mouths.'

The actual doping was one thing, but it was the Russian efforts to cover up any positive tests at Sochi that showed the full lengths they had gone to. Rodchenkov's claims of a Russian cover-up were given weight when, in response to the *Times* article and a subsequent *60 Minutes* story, WADA announced another inquiry.

Leading this inquiry was Canadian law professor Richard McLaren, who had worked with Dick Pound on the earlier report. In a two-part report, which in sections reads more like a spy thriller than a bureaucratic tome, McLaren confirmed Rodchenkov's claims.

Russia had a government policy known as the 'Disappearing Positives Methodology', which involved the Russian anti-doping

---

* Respectively a synthetic version of testosterone and an active anabolic–androgenic steroid that has never been sold legally in any capacity.

lab covering up positive tests. Whenever a positive test was discovered, it was entered into WADA's Anti-Doping Management System (ADAMS) as a negative test.

It was a simple enough plan, so long as WADA didn't audit its computer system too carefully. Which they didn't.

The Disappearing Positives Methodology had begun after the disastrous Vancouver Winter Olympics, but it faced issues at Sochi. The problem was that for these games the anti-doping lab was to be staffed by almost 100 experts from around the world. Unlike the Russian lab Rodchenkov ran, it wouldn't be possible to falsify positive tests in front of them.

While the Russian government were planning the logistics required to turn a subtropical seaside resort into a venue to host a Winter Olympics, a similar level of preparation was going on to ensure the Disappearing Positives Methodology would still work at Sochi.

Rodchenkov said that, as part of this planning, in early 2013 a man working for the FSB* began showing up at the anti-doping lab. The man's primary interest was the bottles used by testers to collect urine samples. These bottles are designed to be tamper proof – once closed, they cannot be opened again without it being very obvious that they've been opened. This mechanism involves toothed metal rings that lock when the cap is tightened; opening a sample breaks these metal rings, making it impossible to close it again.

The FSB agent took away hundreds of these bottles. Over the next few months, the FSB worked around the clock to develop a method to reseal the bottles in a way where no one would ever know they'd been opened. To this day no one knows how they did this, but they figured it out. Now bottles could be opened, emptied and filled with clean urine, and then placed back as if nothing had ever happened.

* The Russian Federal Security Service, the successor of the KGB.

Knowing this, the Russians began building up a bank of clean samples from all their athletes, ready for substitution in case of any negative tests during the games.

But while they could now swap dirty urine for clean, the Russians faced another problem: the lab at Sochi had a very high level of security. There were surveillance cameras everywhere and a high level of security clearance was required just to be in the lab.

One gap in this security was identified, though. During the day, an independent observer ran the lab, but overnight they wouldn't be there. This presented an opportunity. But it wasn't possible to do the urine swapping in the lab, and taking the bottles out of the lab would be seen on the security cameras.

The solution was, again, ridiculously simple. The Russians, who were building all this infrastructure, just drilled a small hole in the wall of the lab, connecting it to the building next door – which just happened to be the FSB building where all the clean urine samples were being held.

The Russian's system kicked into work every night during the games. Any Russian samples that were suspected of being positive were passed through the small hole, where the FSB used their trick to open the bottles, wash them out, fill them with the stored clean urine from the appropriate athlete, sealed them again and returned them to the official laboratory. The next morning the official testers, none the wiser, would open the samples, test them and find they tested negative.

One hundred dirty urine samples were 'cleaned' in this manner at the Sochi Olympics.

It was a wonderful system for Russia. Having no chance of being caught meant their athletes could dope a lot closer to competition time, and possibly all the way through, unconcerned about being found out.

This system worked so well and the athletes performed so well that after the games Rodchenkov was awarded the prestigious Order of Friendship by no less than President Vladimir Putin.*

The first part of the McLaren Report, clocking in at ninety-seven pages, was released publicly in July 2016. It outlined this process and found that all parts of Russian state were involved, including the Russian sports ministry, the FSB and the Centre of Sports Preparation of National Teams of Russia (CSP).

Under the Russian's system, the deputy minister of sport, Yuri Nagornykh, who was appointed in 2010 by executive order of Vladimir Putin, was advised of every positive finding from the Moscow Laboratory since 2011. The report found that he decided which athletes would benefit from the Disappearing Positives Methodology and who would not be protected.

The report also confirmed that the bottles in question had all been tampered with, as Rodchenkov had claimed. Microscopic analysis showed scratches on the caps and bottles, invisible to the naked eye. McLaren's team had discovered how to identify those bottles that had been tampered with, but they still couldn't figure out how the Russians had done it.

Perhaps most worrying was that McLaren admitted that his report identified only a small part of what the Russians had been up to. 'This is a slice of what is going on, not the total picture. But this included most of the winter and summer sports. And we do know that every single positive was sent up the chain of command and sent back down again.'

WHO GOES TO RIO?

McLaren's report came out just months before the 2016 Rio Olympics, causing the IOC to scramble to figure out what to do with Russia. IOC president Thomas Bach called it 'a shocking and

---

* The Order of Friendship sounds like something they'd normally give out at childcare.

unprecedented attack on the integrity of sports and on the Olympic Games', but that didn't mean he particularly wanted to deal with it.

Again, the IOC pushed the problem on to the sporting federations of individual countries. Athletics upheld their ban on Russian athletes, but other sporting federations let them participate, leading to Russia still finishing fourth on the Rio medal tally.

The IOC's failure to ban Russia from the Rio Olympics was seen as a massive betrayal of clean athletes. By contrast, the International Paralympic Committee voted unanimously to ban the entire Russian team from competing at the Rio Paralympics. In the following years the feeling that the IOC had failed clean athletes only increased.

Four months after the Rio Olympics, McLaren released the second part of his report, which showed Russia's cheating went way beyond the Sochi Games. It found that from 2011 to 2015 more than 1000 Russian competitors across the Olympics and Paralympics had required the covering up of positive tests.

As well as revealing more details around the Sochi cheating, the new report showed the depth of Russian cheating at the London Olympics. The report stated:

> The Russian Olympic team corrupted the London Games 2012 on an unprecedented scale, the extent of which will probably never be fully established. This corruption involved the ongoing use of prohibited substances, manipulation of samples and false reporting into ADAMS.

Given Russian athletes won twenty-four gold, twenty-six silver and thirty-two bronze medals without a single positive test, this is an astounding finding.

The report also showed how the Russian state worked to protect their athletes even outside of competition times. A surprise visit by WADA to the Russian lab in 2014 wasn't a problem, because the WADA officials had requested visas in order to enter the country, allowing the FSB to inform the lab of the visit in advance and giving technicians time to clean up any evidence.

Even after the second part of the McLaren Report was released, the Russians continued to deny many of its accusations, and they refused to cooperate with WADA. One request they denied was to hand over all the data from testing between January 2012 to August 2015.

But in November 2017, this data was leaked to WADA. It confirmed much of what the McLaren report had found. But Russia denied they were legitimate copies of the files, claiming they had been manufactured by Rodchenkov, who had manipulated the results as part of an extortion scheme against the Russian state.

Despite all these protests and counterclaims by Russia, they were banned from the 2018 Pyeongchang Winter Games. However, 168 Russians athletes were allowed to compete as an 'Olympic Athlete from Russia'.

Two of these athletes tested positive for prohibited drugs, one being our old friend Alexander Krushelnytsky, the curler that decided he needed to dope. The other was bobsleigh pilot Nadezhda Sergeeva, another sport I'm unsure needs doping.

ALL IS FORGIVEN

As part of the attempts to get Russia to clean up its act and be allowed back into the fold, WADA released a 'Roadmap to Compliance', which had two key criteria Russia had to meet:

- accept the findings of the McLaren Report, and
- grant access to Moscow's anti-doping laboratory, mainly to allow access to the database of testing from 2011 to 2015, by 31 December 2018.

In a letter to the committee overseeing the 'Roadmap to Compliance', the Russian sports ministry said it had 'sufficiently acknowledged the issues identified in Russia' and that they agreed to accept the two remaining conditions.

This undertaking led WADA to announce, in February 2018, that it would reinstate Russia's Olympic membership with immediate effect. Given two Russian athletes had just tested positive at Pyeongchang, and Russia had still not actually handed over the testing database, this was a controversial announcement. It went against the recommendations of numerous national anti-doping bodies around the world. This was followed by WADA reinstating the Russian Anti-Doping Agency in September 2018, a move seen by many athletes and anti-doping experts as a betrayal.

Unsurprisingly to all but WADA, the deadline of 31 December 2018 passed with no movement. It took until the 10 January 2019 for a WADA team to be allowed into the Russian lab, where they made forensic copies from various servers of over 23 terabytes* of data.

It now appeared all was back on track for Russia. Their ban had already been lifted and their anti-doping body had been re-accredited.

With the database now in hand, WADA began the arduous work of going through all the data. An obvious concern was how accurate the information was, and part of the process was comparing this database to the one leaked to WADA in 2015. The early finding was the two didn't match. Records that were in the 2015 version were gone in the 2019 version, and the 2019 version had records that weren't in the early copy.

Forensic examination revealed the full extent of the changes. The Russians had been making changes not only right up to

---

* How big is a terabyte? It's so big a number that I don't understand it.

the day the WADA team came to Moscow to copy the database but even while the WADA team were already in the lab making the copy.

The alterations included the deletion of files that showed positive test and attempts to make the data appear to have been untouched since 2015. Over 450 database back-up files were deleted with a 'zeroing command' – which, after deleting data, overwrites that space on the disk with all zeroes, making the deleted files impossible to recover.

Even worse, the Russians had planted fabricated evidence into the database to advance their claims that Rodchenkov and two other conspirators had manufactured false evidence to extort money from athletes. The lab had an internal messaging service and the Russians added messages purporting to be from Rodchenkov and his co-conspirators where they discussed this scheme. Analysis showed that these messages had been added in the days leading up to the WADA visit in January 2019, long after Rodchenkov had any access to the system.

In perhaps their boldest move, while WADA were copying the databases, the Russians told them that removing the server's hard drives might make it impossible restart the server later. Instead, they suggested, why not allow them to transfer the contents onto another server first to ensure this wouldn't happen? WADA agreed, but in reality this transfer of data was of course used by the Russians to further delete information and backdate files.

Unfortunately, deleting your history on a computer is hard, as my experience with my browser history has proved. All of this became obvious once WADA and computer security experts began combing through everything. Once again, WADA's trust in Russia had been unfounded.

They had no choice. In December 2019, Russia was banned from the Olympic Games and the FIFA World Cup for four years.

Yet while Russian athletes would be unable to compete under Russia's flag, or hear their anthem at medal ceremonies, they would still be able to compete as independent athletes, provided they could prove they were drug free. This loophole was seen as a cop-out by many countries and athletes.

Russia has challenged the ban, lodging an appeal in the Court of Arbitration for Sport. Whatever the outcome, the saga proves the point that cheating is with us forever, from simplistic, opportunistic cheating by individuals to the state sponsored conspiracies of the East Germans and the Russians.

CONCLUSION

This has been in no way an exhaustive history of cheating – there's just too much of it to cover in one book. It's impossible to include all the weird, wonderful and awful things athletes have done to cheat their way to glory.

What has been enlightening – and sometime alarming – is to see how timeless cheating is in sport. It's widespread, and it's infiltrated so many political agendas.

But what has been entertaining is to witness how fast cheating escalates from the foolish to the sinister. It really goes up a notch very quickly. The type of sport is irrelevant – cycling or curling, sprinting or soccer, it doesn't matter.

Which takes us right back to that basic premise: for cheating to occur, all you need is competition and people.

The path to cheating begins when people want to gain a competitive edge by pushing the limits of the rules. Committing fouls, engaging in gamesmanship, breaking minor rules. And often that's as far as people go – just because someone does some low-level cheating doesn't mean they'll be running a sophisticated doping program a few years later. But some in some cases, that is exactly what happens.

Many forms of cheating are just opportunistic, like sitting out a whole lap of a horse race in the fog. Others are just weird, like licking, kissing and inappropriately touching opponents. These are the acts of cheating that are so bizarre that sports administrators don't even have rules against them, because what sane person would expect these incidents to occur?

Some types of cheating are a bit more premeditated; plans to injure opponents, taking a blood capsule from a joke shop onto the field.

Then there are the practices that start out legal but continue long after they've been banned. Using dangerous glues on table tennis bats started off as legal, but when it was banned, table tennis players didn't stop. When you're wearing a gasmask to glue the rubber to your table tennis paddle, you must know you've crossed the line.*

Then there is the whole world of doping. Many argue that the fight against doping is pointless, that we should just let athletes do it, but we've learned from the East Germans just how dangerous it is to athletes' health. We know that cheating is inevitable, but that doesn't mean it's something to stop caring about. Even under proper supervision, how can you tell what a cutting-edge drug is going to do to the human body decades from now? Russia should, if anything, be punished harder. They knew full well the long-term health effects of what they were doing.

Perhaps the most surprising thing about cheating is our ability to constantly forget what has gone before. The world was shocked by Lance Armstrong's cheating, but it came right after the Festina Affair. The fact that he knew all about it but still threw caution to the wind says a lot about the mindset of those are driven to do whatever it takes to win. But it also says something about the

---

* Although, since learning about paddle doping, I've been using it to defeat my six-year-old nephew. He's in a world of pain now, and it's not just the fumes.

organisers of the Tour, who learned nothing from the Festina Affair either, letting Armstrong rattle off seven consecutive victories without catching him. That's like having your house robbed and then not even locking the doors afterwards.

The authorities and organisations that oversee sport seem to be constantly ill prepared for dealing with cheating, even though, based on history, it should always be assumed cheating is going on. Yet anti-doping bodies remain underfunded, and they're set up with conflicts of interest that make their task impossible. Then, when they do find cases, it's as if they're annoyed by it because it makes their jobs harder.

Fundamentally, cheating should be cracked down on harder when it's discovered, and the efforts to uncover it should be pursued with far more vigour than is usually the case.

As East German relay runner Ines Geipel said, while it's true individuals lose, 'if you take a closer look at it, the game is dead, so basically everyone loses'.

In May 2018, the IOC approved a new process called the Olympic Medal Reallocation Principles for when an athlete is discovered to have won a medal by cheating. As testing of old samples with new techniques increases, more 'winners' are being exposed, and medals are being stripped and reallocated to those who should have received them. Retested samples from the Beijing and London Olympics have led to hundreds of athletes being sanctioned, with the medals then going to the real winners.

At the London Olympics, Spanish weightlifter Lidia Valentín finished fourth and left the event in tears. Years of hard work hadn't paid off; she had missed out on her dream. Valentín lived with this feeling of failure for six-and-a half years. Then, in February 2019, the IOC announced that the top three – Svetlana Podobedova of Kazakhstan, Natalya Zabolotnaya of Russia and Iryna Kulesha of Belarus – had all been found to have used banned substances.

All were stripped of their medals and, suddenly, Valentín was a gold medallist.

Valentín received her gold medal in a ceremony organised by the Spanish Olympic Committee in Madrid. It's a wonderful thing that justice was finally served, but there was Valentín, receiving her medal almost seven years later, in a small ceremony, instead of at the games with a huge international audience watching on. She missed out on hearing her national anthem in a full stadium, missed out on walking out in the closing ceremony with all her dreams having come true. She didn't get to return home a hero. All this was stolen from her.

Cheating is constant and common. But that doesn't mean we should accept it. It means we should double down on our efforts to stop it.

However, given sporting administrators are about as good at tackling cheating as athletes are at doing it without getting caught, I expect in the future we'll only have more harebrained schemes to delight us.

ACKNOWLEDGEMENTS

I wrote this book during the first few months of the COVID pandemic, which as I write this is still raging on around us. This book provided a nice distraction, reminding me that there once existed a somewhat normal world. I hope that by the time you read this something like that world has returned, or at least is well on the way to returning.

My editor Andrea McNamara was again a wonderful support, and I withdraw my accusations that she was a super spreader and patient zero for COVID in Australia. Those remarks were made in a time of high stress and are probably incorrect.

I want to thank Antigone and Cillian for all their support; there's no one I would prefer to spend lockdown with. Rachael Frawley also deserves special mention for keeping me almost sane during the writing of this book. She even told me at one stage that it could 'actually be good'.

As always, I must thank the Twomey family. Not being able to see you guys during the lockdown certainly added to 2020 being a year to forget.

A big thanks to the team at Tinker, who let me write there when we weren't all in lockdown, and big thanks to Ben and Bec for even occasionally feigning interest in what I was saying.

The one thing the lockdown has taught me is that what I missed most was the Commercial Club Hotel, and Paddy and Lucy at that fine establishment. Until I started drinking at the Commercial Club Hotel, I didn't know what true love was. It's totally normal to love a pub. Every other kind of love is weird.

The team at Penguin Random House have again been a delight to work with and were incredibly patient as I laboured away. Justin Ractliffe, Ali Urquhart, Louise Ryan, Johannes Jakob, Emily Hindle, Maddie Garratt, Adam Laszczuk and Radhiah Chowdhury all pretended everything was fine despite the entire world collapsing around us.

Lastly, I'd like to thank you for reading this. Writing is a lonely process and it's always nice when someone actually decides to read what you wrote. Occasionally they even like it, which is as satisfying as it is surprising. So thank you.

Titus
August 2020

REFERENCES

Norman Ferguson, *Sports Scandals: True stories of cheating, corruption and greed*, Summersdale, 2016.

Scott Ostler, *How to Cheat in Sports: Professional tricks exposed!*, Chronicle Books, 2008.

John Perry, *Rogues, Rotters, Rascals and Cheats*, John Blake Publishing, September 2007.

Fran Zimniuch, *Crooked: A history of cheating in sports*, Taylor Trade Publishing, 2009.

INTRODUCTION: THE CONDITIONS FOR CHEATING

Edward Champlin, *Nero*, Harvard University Press, 2003.

Tim Daniels, 'Gary, Angelica Di Silvestri's Timeline as Controversial Dominica Olympic Skiers', *Bleacher Report*, 26 February 2014.

CHAPTER 1: THE WONDERFUL EQUALITY OF CHEATING

Giles Tremlett, 'The Cheats', *The Guardian*, 16 September 2004.

Nina Lakhani, 'Learning disabilities: Paralympic "cheats" no more', *The Independent*, 25 August 2012.

Simon Tomlinson, 'Man that led shameful Spanish basketball team who pretended to be disabled to win Paralympic gold found guilty of fraud', *Daily Mail*, 15 October 2013.

Alex Dunham, 'Stop playing well, they'll know you're not disabled', *The Local*, 11 October 2013.

Duncan Mackay, 'Spaniard behind Sydney 2000 Paralympic basketball scandal finally brought to justice', *Inside the Games*, 7 October 2013.

Matt Blitz, 'Stolen Gold', *The Smartset*, 6 August 2014.

Guy Hedgecoe, 'Case against paralympian fraudsters dropped as man behind scam is fined', *Irish Times*, 8 October 2013.

'Former Spanish sports boss fined for fielding athletes with no disabilities at Sydney Paralympics', *ABC News*, 8 October 2013.

Dave Reynolds, '"Intellectually Disabled" Athletes Banned From 2004 Paralympic Games', *Inclusion Daily Express*, 5 February 2003.

Robert Sanchez, 'Dirty Pool at the Paralympics: Will Cheating Ruin the Games?', *Sports Illustrated*, 3 March 2020.

CHAPTER 2: AN INDIVIDUAL PURSUIT

David Goldblatt, *The Games: A global history of the Olympics*, W. W. Norton & Company, 2017.

Sandra Bailey, 'Chinese Woman First to Test Positive at Games', *New York Times*, 5 August 1992.

CHAPTER 3: GAMESMANSHIP

Brian Dick, 'Fry urinated on the Birmingham City pitch', *Birmingham Live*, 2 March 2018.

'Ericson admits to adjusting ventilation system', *ESPN*, 27 July 2003.

Daniel Edwards, '"I cut myself with a razor . . . I cut my own dignity" – the goalkeeper banned for life for faking an injury', *Goal*, 4 August 2019.

Rob Hunt, 'The Chilean Plot to Steal a Place at the 1990 World Cup', *The Set Pieces*, 9 October 2017.

Stephen Moss, 'Rugby's Cup of Shame', *The Guardian*, 27 May 2002.

Paul Stephens, 'I did what I had to do to win the game', *The Telegraph*, 25 May 2002.

'The infamous Hand of Back incident of 2002', *Rugbydump.com*, 27 January 2009.

CHAPTER 4: SENSIBLE AND OPPORTUNISTIC CHEATING

Kerrie Ritchie, 'NZ lawn bowlers guilty of match fixing', ABC Radio, 12 January 2010.

Mike Rowbottom, *Foul Play: The dark arts of cheating in sport*, Bloomsbury, 2015.

Simon Gardiner, *Sports Law*, Routledge, 2005.

'Jockey Convicted of Hiding in the Fog', Associated Press, 15 March 1991.

CHAPTER 5: MORALLY CHALLENGED

MaryAnn Spoto, 'Denver Nuggets guard J.R. Smith is sentenced to 30 days in jail for car-crash death', *NJ.com*, 1 July 2009.

Kelly Dwyer, 'J.R. Smith says he'd still be untying opponent's shoelaces if the NBA hadn't started fining him', *Yahoo! Sports*, 11 September 2014.

Nick Schwartz, 'A strange history of Brad Marchand kissing and licking NHL players', *For the Win*, 5 May 2018.

Andrea O'Neil, 'Sean Fitzpatrick's ear bitten in Springbok attack', *Stuff.co.nz*, 9 June 2015.

'Aussie rules player banned for testicle bite', *The Guardian*, 1 May 2002.

Ian Steadman. 'You are more likely to be bitten by Luis Suarez (1 in 2,000) than a shark (1 in 3,700,000)', *New Statesman*, 25 June 2014.

Shive Prema, '"I'm proud of my finger antics": Notorious footy bad boy John Hopoate says he has no regrets about sticking his digit up opponents' backsides', *Daily Mail Australia*, 19 June 2019.

CHAPTER 6: INTIMIDATION

Donald Hall, '11 Pitches, Three Hit Batters: The Day Dock Ellis Went To War', *Deadspin*, 4 June 2015.

Jon Tayler, 'Today is the 47th anniversary of Dock Ellis' acid-fueled no-hitter', *Sports Illustrated*, 12 June 2017.

Will Sharp, 'Andoni Goikoetxea: The Butcher of Bilbao', *These Football Times*, 14 December 2017.

Todd Brock, '"Bounty Bowl" 30th anniversary and Cowboys–Eagles still at it', *Cowboys Wire*, 22 November 2019.

Brian Fonseca, 'NFL Rumors: Ex-Eagles LB claims Buddy Ryan's "Bounty Bowl" vs. Cowboys was real, far more expensive than the story goes', *NJ.com*, 23 December 2019.

Kevin Skiver, 'Eagles fans are the absolute worst, and here are 9 times they proved it', *CBS Sports*, 2018.

Peter King, 'Way Out of Bounds', *Sports Illustrated*, 12 March 2012.

'Gregg Williams apologizes for role in bounties', *NFL.com*, 2 March 2012.

'Shane Stant, Who Clubbed Nancy Kerrigan, Apologizes and Says He's Now a "Different Person"', *NBC*, 19 January 2018.

E.M. Swift, 'Anatomy of a Plot', *Sports Illustrated*, 14 February 1994.

Jordan Crucchiola, 'A Fact-checked Guide to *I, Tonya*', *Vulture*, 11 December 2017.

Lauren Efferon, 'Tonya Harding says she was scared after infamous 1994 baton attack on Nancy Kerrigan', *ABC News*, 20 January 2018.

CHAPTER 7: DODGY EQUIPMENT

Buster Olney, 'Yankee Ends Real Corker Of a Mystery', *New York Times*, 11 April 1999.

Buster Olney, *The last night of the Yankee dynasty: the game, the team, and the cost of greatness*, Ecco, 2005.

Jens Felke, 'Table Tennis is Going Green', *USA Table Tennis Magazine*, March/April 2009.

'China's Ma brushes off "bat doping" claim', *Bangkok Post*, 14 April 2016.

Keith Wheatley, 'Great British Olympians: Jim Fox', *The Times*, 7 November 2002.

CHAPTER 8: BALL TAMPERING

Derek Zumsteg, 'Perry greased batters with his stuff', *ESPN*.

'Biggest cheaters in baseball,' *ESPN*.

Sam McManis, 'A Different Tack: Honeycutt Can Talk About Cutting Baseballs; Experience Left Him Bloodied', *LA Times,* 6 August 1987.

Glenn Moore, 'Imran admits cheating', *The Independent*, 9 May 1994.

'Steve Smith, David Warner banned from playing for Australia for 12 months, Bancroft for nine', *ABC News*, 29 March 2018.

CHAPTER 9: SCHEMING

'Madrazo DQ'd from Berlin Marathon for taking shortcut', *ESPN*, 10 October 2007.

Ramatsiyi Moholoa, 'Sergio faces long drugs ban', *Sowetan Live*,
	22 July 2010.

'Marathon Imposter Foiled by a Mustache', *New York Times*,
	17 September 1991.

CHAPTER 10: DOPING

'I never blamed mum for drugs scandal: Shane Warne', *The
	Australian*, 18 October 2015.

Neil Katz, 'ExtenZe Doesn't Enhance "Maleness" or LaShawn
	Merritt's Dreams of Olympic Gold', *CBS News*,
	19 October 2010.

'Japan Takes Positive Action', *Irish Times*, 12 November
	1998.

'Gasquet cleared to resume playing', *ESPN*, 16 July 2009.

Duncan Mackay, 'Lovemaking marathon cause of drug test
	failure – athlete', *Irish Times*, 22 January 1999.

Adrian Ballantyne, 'Cyclist Jonathan Tiernan-Locke says his
	doping results were the result of 33 alcoholic drinks',
	news.com.au, 19 August 2014.

Richard Bath, 'A Drugs Cheat? Not Me!', *Sunday Herald*,
	12 December 1999.

William Fotheringham, 'Banned cyclist blames "twin" after dope
	test', *The Guardian*, 5 June 2005.

Duncan Mackay, 'Cuban faces second drug ban', *The Guardian*,
	26 November 2001.

Adam Kilgore, 'Doping charge angers Olympic curlers, but
	they admit there could be benefits', *Washington Post*,
	19 February 2018.

'What is meldonium and why did Maria Sharapova take it?',
	The Guardian, 9 June 2016.

Trip Gabriel, 'The Runner Stumbles', *New York Times*, 19 July
	1992.

Mary Ormsby, 'Ben Johnson was fast, justice was faster',
    Toronto.com, 25 September 2016.

Vivek Chaudhary and Duncan Mackay, 'Christie fails steroid test',
    The Guardian, 5 August 1999.

Sarah Crompton, 'Forgotten heroes who rose above the scandal of
    drugs,' *The Telegraph*, 17 October 2012.

Duncan Mackay, 'Lewis: "Who cares I failed a drug test?"',
    The Guardian, 24 April 2003.

'The drug runners', *Sydney Morning Herald*, 18 April 2003.

John Mehaffey, 'Smith true winner of "dirtiest race" in history',
    Reuters, 24 September 2013.

James Montague, 'Hero or villain? Ben Johnson and the dirtiest
    race in history', *CNN*, 23 July 2012.

Sarah Bridges, 'Athlete Jones stripped of Olympic medals',
    The Guardian, 23 December 2007.

'Gamze Bulut becomes fifth from 1,500 final in 2012 to face
    allegations', *ESPN*, 7 March 2016.

CHAPTER 11: A MASTERCLASS IN CHEATING

Chriss Abbiss, 'Suffer score: how demanding is Le Tour de
    France?', *The Conversation*, 3 July 2012.

William Fotheringham, 'Lance Armstrong: I would probably cheat
    again in similar circumstances', *The Guardian*, 27 January
    2015.

Marina Zemovich (director), *30 for 30: Lance*, ESPN, May 2020.

Matt Seaton, 'Lance Armstrong team "ran most sophisticated
    doping scheme in sport"', *The Guardian*, 11 October 2012.

'How Lance Armstrong beat the drug testers for more than a
    decade', *Herald Sun*, 12 October 2012.

Tony Manfred, 'The USADA Explains How Lance Armstrong
    Never Tested Positive For Doping', *Business Insider*,
    11 October 2012.

Tim Carmody, 'Hacking your body: Lance Armstrong and the science of doping', *The Verge*, 17 January 2013.

Martin Ziegler, 'Lance Armstrong failed four drugs tests in 1999, UCI admits', *The Independent*, 17 April 2013.

Richard Sandomir, 'Armstrong is suing accuser', *New York Times*, 16 June 2004.

'Commentary: We should still ask Lance Armstrong hard questions', *VeloNews*, 21 February 2018.

Stephen Farrand, 'Dr. Ferrari found guilty of doping by Italian court', *VeloNews*, 4 April 2017.

'Whistleblower reveals Armstrong threats', *Sydney Morning Herald*, 16 October 2012.

'Drug Scandal in the Netherlands', *Cyclingnews*, 28 November 1997.

John Lichfield, 'Allez le Tour', *The Independent*, 3 July 1999.

'Festina Chief Queried in Drug Scandal', *New York Times*, 16 July 1998.

'Police detain riders', *Irish Times*, 29 July 1998.

Jeremy Whittle, 'Twenty years on the Festina affair casts shadow over the Tour de France', *The Guardian*, 4 July 2018.

'And now TVM', *Cyclingnews*, 19 July 1998.

'Police Question Dutch Cyclists', *Washington Post*, 3 August 1998.

'Drugs scandal widens', *BBC News*, 30 July 1998.

Olivier Hamoir, 'Virenque: "I took drugs, I had no choice"', *The Independent*, 25 October 2000.

Geoffery Wheatcroft, *Le Tour: A history of the Tour de France*, Simon & Schuster, 2013.

Chris Sidwells, *A Race for Madmen: The history of the Tour de France*, Sports Publishing, 2012.

CHAPTER 12: TEAM EFFORT

Bob LeMoine, 'Phillies' Pearce Chiles caught using technology to steal signs', Society for American Baseball Research.

Don van Natta Jr and Seth Wickersham, 'Spygate to Deflategate: Inside what split the NFL and Patriots apart', *ESPN*, 8 September 2015.

Will Brinson, 'Report: Patriots coaches admit team stole play sheets during Spygate era', 8 September 2015.

Terrance Moore, 'SpyGate II Allegations Are The Latest Example Of The Patriots' Complicated Relationship With NFL's Rules', *Forbes*, 10 December 2019.

Bill Price, Gary Myers and Teri Thompson, 'DeflateGate report finds Tom Brady probably "generally aware" Patriots balls were being deflated', *NY Daily News*, 7 May 2015.

'Brady's NFL ban reinstated by US court', *SBS News*, 26 April 2016.

'Bloodgate 10 years on: Tom Williams on rugby's biggest scandal', *BBC Sport*, 11 April 2019.

Helen Carter, 'Bloodgate doctor Wendy Chapman avoids being struck off', *The Guardian*, 1 September 2010.

Paul Rees, 'Is it fair to label Dean Richards "a bully"? Bloodgate's remaining questions', *The Guardian*, 29 August 2009.

'Richards blamed for "Bloodgate"', *ESPN*, 2 September 2009.

Gavin Mairs, 'Bloodgate physio Steph Brennan wins High Court appeal against striking off', *The Telegraph*, 21 January 2011.

Christopher Weir, 'The Glory and the Corruption of Marseille's Kings of 1993, the Team that Conquered Europe', *These Football Times*, 30 October 2018.

Barry James, 'Tapie Directly Implicated As Marseille Trial Opens', *New York Times*, 14 March 1995.

'Mark Hateley's Revelations that he was offered money to miss a game against the French champions add weight to claims the club should be stripped of their title', *Irish Independent*, 23 February 2011.

'French tycoon Bernard Tapie's assets frozen in fraud case', *The Local*, 1 May 2020.

CHAPTER 13: FOR THE GLORY OF YOUR COUNTRY

Brian Blickenstaff, 'The Rise and Fall of Gerd Bonk, the World Champion of Doping', *Vice*, 11 August 2016.

'Apology over East German Doping', *BBC News*, 5 May 2000.

Sarah Dingle, 'Former East German athletes with doping history warn Russians "it's not worth it"', *ABC News*, 16 August 2016.

Werner W Franke and Brigitte Berendonk, 'Hormonal doping and androgenization of athletes: a secret program of the German Democratic Republic government', *Clinical Chemistry* 43:7, July 1997.

'WADA mishandled doping confession, Dick Pound says', *CBC Sports*, 15 June 2016.

Rebecca R Ruiz and Michael Schwirtz, 'Russian Insider Says State-Run Doping Fueled Olympic Gold', *New York Times*, 12 May 2016.

Juliet Macur, 'The Whistle-Blowers Next Door', *New York Times*, 26 December 2019.

Mark Daly, 'Russia doping crisis: Wada president Craig Reedie faces more pressure', *BBC News*, 21 June 2016.

David Epstein, 'On Eve of Olympics, Top Investigator Details Secret Efforts to Undermine Russian Doping Probe', *ProPublica*, 4 August 2016.

Grigory Rodchenkov, '"I masterminded the greatest cheating scandal in sporting history": Moscow lab boss turned whistleblower Grigory Rodchenkov reveals how he falsified Russian Olympic athletes' drug tests aided by Putin's FSB', *Daily Mail*, 26 July 2020.

'Russia doping in Sochi was state-dictated with secret service backing, WADA report finds', *ABC News*, 19 July 2016.

Martin Belam, 'Russian athlete filmed in "I don't do doping" shirt fails Olympic drug test', *The Guardian*, 24 February 2018.

CONCLUSION

'Weightlifting: Valentin eyes London gold after rivals fail retests', *Reuters*, 28 July 2016.

Discover a
new favourite